The Lots
of Fortune and Spirit

An Exploratory Study

by

Charles Obert

Almuten Press

2019

Published and printed in the United States of America

By Almuten Press

Minneapolis, Minnesota 55418

https://studentofastrology.com

©2019 by Charles Obert

All rights reserved. No part of this publication may be reproduced, stored in or introduced into a retrieval system, or transmitted, in any form or by any means (electronic, mechanical, photocopying, recording or otherwise), without the prior written permission of both the copyright owner and the above publisher of this book.

The scanning, uploading, and distribution of this book via the Internet or via any other means without the permission of the publisher is illegal and punishable by law. Please purchase only authorized electronic editions and do not participate in or encourage electronic piracy of copyrighted materials. Your support of the author's rights is appreciated.

ISBN-13: 978-0-9864187-3-0

A PDF version of this book is available for purchase at the author's website,

https://studentofastrology.com

Dedication

This book is dedicated to my deceased wife, **Cynthia Sue Kissee**. It is being published on her birthday this year, May 21, 2019.

Cindy's natal Sun is at 0 Gemini. This is conjunct my natal Lot of Spirit, and conjunct the Ascendant of my Solar Return chart this year.

If the Lots have to do with fortune, then my time with Cindy is the greatest fortune I could ever have been blessed with. I am deeply grateful for our time together.

Acknowledgements

I want to thank all the people who helped out with this book. This includes all of the people who consented to be interviewed and to talk about how the Lots worked in their charts and lives. A special thank you goes to those who consented to have their charts used as examples in this book, and to those who read and critiqued early versions of the book.

Special thanks to the following people, in alphabetical order: Rebecca Bihr, Betty Edwards, Liat Guy, Susana McClune, Zohar Muskat-Arndt, Raquel Spring, Madeleine Youngstrom, Darleen Yuna.

Also by Charles Obert

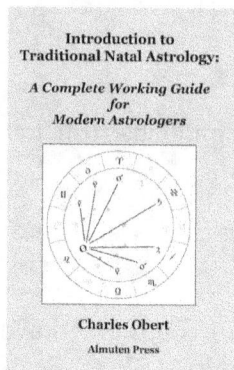

Introduction to Traditional Natal Astrology: A Guide for Modern Astrologers

A user-friendly introduction to the basic concepts and techniques of traditional astrology. This includes number and geometry symbolism, basic concepts of traditional astrology, differences from modern astrology.

Instructions are given for evaluating planetary strength and conditions, and a full outline of traditional chart interpretation.

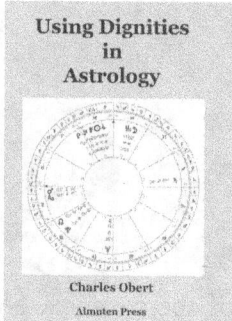

Using Dignities In Astrology

An in-depth study of the traditional system of dignities and debilities for weighing up the condition of planets and points in a chart. Major and minor dignities, debilities, accidental dignities, how to weigh and combine all of the different factors.

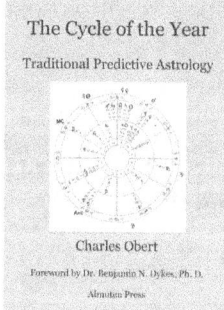

The Cycle of the Year: Traditional Predictive Astrology

This books covers the full traditional suite of techniques used annually in traditional predictive astrology. This includes distributions or primary directions through the bounds, profections and solar returns.

Foreword by Benjamin N. Dykes, Ph. D.

All of these books are used as textbooks for classes at Kepler College.

These books are all available through the usual retail outlets.

A PDF version of each of these books is available for purchase at the author's website,

https://studentofastrology.com

Table of Contents

Introduction...8
SECTION ONE: THEORY..10
   Definition of the Lots..10
   The Geometry of the Lots...20
   What the Lots Mean...26
   What Is Covered in this Study..30
   Evaluating the Lots..33
   Reading Symbols in the Chart..41
   Evaluating Dignity and Debility..42
   Technical Notes...46
SECTION TWO: EXAMPLES..47
Natal Charts - General Introduction..47
   Garry Kasparov..48
   Camille Paglia..51
   Albert Einstein...55
   Leonard Bernstein...57
   Clint Eastwood..59
Fortune and Wealth..62
   Bill Gates...63
   Steve Jobs...67
   Warren Buffett..71
   Donald Trump...76
Transits to the Lots..78
   Angela Davis...79
   Adolf Hitler...83
   Margaret Thatcher..91
Personal Chart Examples...96
   Michael...97
   Selene...101
   Rachel..104
   Deborah..108
   Natal Chart with Lot of Fortune - Charles Obert......................................112
   Natal Chart with Lot of Spirit - Charles Obert...116
   Solar Returns - Charles Obert..119
   Client Session Example - Eric...124
Event Charts..130
   Jimi Hendrix..131
   Pope Francis...138
Synastry..142
   Synastry - Charlie and Cindy..143
   Lennon, McCartney & Company...146
Final Notes..161
   Using the Lots in Client Work...161
   Summing Up..164
   Sources...167

Introduction

In this book I am studying the Lot of Fortune, and its partner point, the Lot of Spirit.

This book is my attempt to figure out what the Lots mean by watching how they act in live charts and actual life histories.

The Questions

I started this project to answer some questions I have about the Lots.

First, how did the early astrologers come up with the Lots in the first place? How did they figure out that those points were important?

They are mathematically calculated points, so it seems to me that the meaning of the Lots should come out of how they are constructed.

Second, what do the Lots mean, and how are they supposed to be used? The early books give some definitions, but precious few examples.

Third, what is the difference in meaning between the two related Lots, Fortune and Spirit? Is one more important than the other? Do they have distinctly different meanings?

And fourth, why do traditional and modern astrologers calculate the Lots differently, and which way is correct? This relates to the difference in meaning between Fortune and Spirit, since traditional and modern astrologers don't agree on which is which in night charts.

My Sources

These are the main influences on how this book took shape.

The first, and most important, is Lind Weber's 1997 book, *The Arabian Parts Decoded*. He suggests that the Lots were used to predict periods of good and bad fortune from the transits of Jupiter and Saturn to these points. He also suggests they were used for elections, for good times to act. I think he is on to something there, and I use his ideas as the starting point for this study.

I was also very inspired by the harmonic astrologer David Cochrane. He points out the importance of the geometric shape of the Lots, and how that connects with the modern use of midpoints. I reference some of Cochrane's material in the bibliography at the end of this book.

Within the traditional framework, Ben Dykes has done some very useful work on how to calculate and interpret the most important Lots. Some of the interpretive meaning of the Lots is influenced by his material. I view my work here as building on and extending the traditional meanings.

These three influences are the starting points for this study.

My Goal

What I am trying to do in this book is to re-think what the two basic Lots mean, and how they work, starting with their geometry.

I want to rethink the Lots from the ground up. Along with that I also want to see how the Lots actually work, in the same way as I like to test anything else in astrology - by studying many test cases and watching what they do.

Traditional and Modern Techniques

Along with traditional astrology techniques, I am also using concepts and techniques from Uranian astrology, cosmobiology and harmonic astrology. Thanks to David Cochrane's work I was inspired to look into these modern branches of astrology, and I discovered that much of the geometry underlying those systems is exactly the same as the geometry underlying the traditional Lots - not similar, not related, but identical. I think that the useful concepts in those areas can be derived or developed from concepts in the tradition about the Lots.

One of my purposes is to establish a conceptual bridge between traditional astrology and the modern use of midpoints and planetary pictures.

Basic Framework

What I hope to establish here is a useful basic framework for how the Lots work, how to use them, and how to interpret them. I do not intend this study to be either definitive or comprehensive, but suggestive. I view it as a useful basic starting point for further work and exploration.

I offer this framework as a way to start to really explore the use the Lots in a strong and systematic way in chart interpretation and prediction. It is a complex area, and I feel like I am only making a start here.

I went into this study with some things I wanted to test, and some hypotheses I was making, things I assumed I would find. Some of my discoveries did match my hypotheses, and some of them led me in new directions I did not expect.

SECTION ONE: THEORY

Definition of the Lots

Lots and Arabic Parts

The Lots are often referred to as Arabic Parts, or just as parts. They were referred to as Arabic largely because of the influence of Ptolemy. For a very long time Ptolemy was widely considered to be the main authority on traditional astrology, and in his *Tetrabiblos* he makes very little use of them. Many of the texts that refer to large numbers of Lots have come down to us from Arabic originals, so for a long time it was thought that they were an innovation of the Arabic astrologers - hence, Arabic parts. Arabic Astrologer Al-Biruni compiled a listing of all of the Lots or Parts in *The Elements of Astrology*, which dates from 1029 AD, and that listing served as one of the main sources for information about the parts in the West.

We now know that the Lots go back much further in history than the Arabic period. In recent translations of old material we have learned that the use of multiple Lots goes back to the earliest material we have - multiple Lots are in Dorotheus and in Vettius Valens. They are not Arabic innovations at all. Rather, it was Ptolemy who was likely outside of the main tradition of Hellenistic usage in his not referring to them.

Returning to the earlier term, Lot, also helps recover the original meaning and connotations of the word.

The term Lot has to do with random casting of Lots, what we would call the luck of the draw, or the roll of the dice. It has to do with fortune in the sense of what kind of luck the Gods dealt to you, what kind of Lot did you draw. We still have the phrase "your Lot in life", meaning the situation you are in through no doing of your own, including where were you born, your parents, your gender, the kind of body were you given, and so on.

The two main Lots are the ones that involve the Ascendant, Sun and Moon. We know them as the Lot of Fortune and its partner the Lot of Spirit. I am going to start with the definitions of the two Lots in daytime charts.

The Traditional Definition

This is how the Lots are described in the earliest texts.

In the traditional texts you take the distance between 2 points and cast or measure that same difference from a third point.

For the Lot of Fortune in a day chart, you would take the distance between the two lights, from the Sun to the Moon, and cast or measure that same distance from the Ascendant. The point you arrive at is the Lot of Fortune.

Here is what it looks like in a chart diagram.

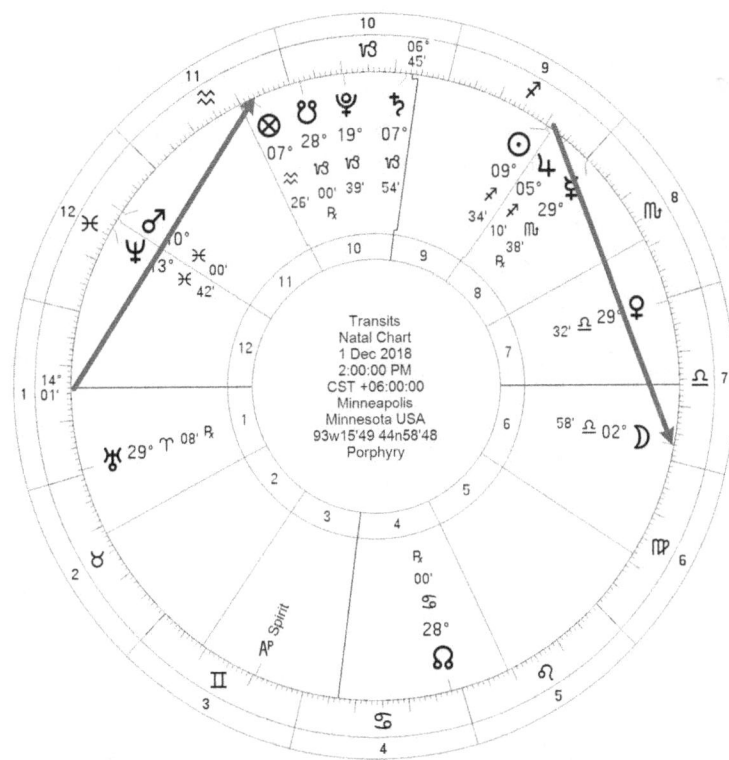

In this chart, the distance in degrees from the Sun (at 9 Sag) to the Moon (at 3 Libra) is roughly 66 degrees, or 2 signs plus 6 degrees. Measure exactly the same 66 degree distance from the Ascendant (at 14 Aries) in the same direction, and you get the Lot of Fortune (at 7 Aquarius). That is the mathematical definition of the Lot. This is shown by the two arrow lines being the same length in the diagram.

Another way of phrasing that, is that the distance from the Sun to the Moon is the same as the distance from the Ascendant to the Lot of Fortune.

Or, The Sun and Moon have the same relation as the Ascendant and the Lot of Fortune.

I'm going to draw that as a formula this way:

Sun -> Moon = Ascendant -> Lot of Fortune

Here the arrow means *the distance from*. The above formula reads, The distance from the Sun to the Moon is the same as the distance from the Ascendant to the Lot of Fortune.

In a day chart, the Lot of Fortune is at the same relative location that the Moon would be if the Sun were sitting right on the Ascendant. That is illustrated in the following diagram of a chart with Ascendant to Fortune on the left, and Sun on Ascendant to Moon on the right.

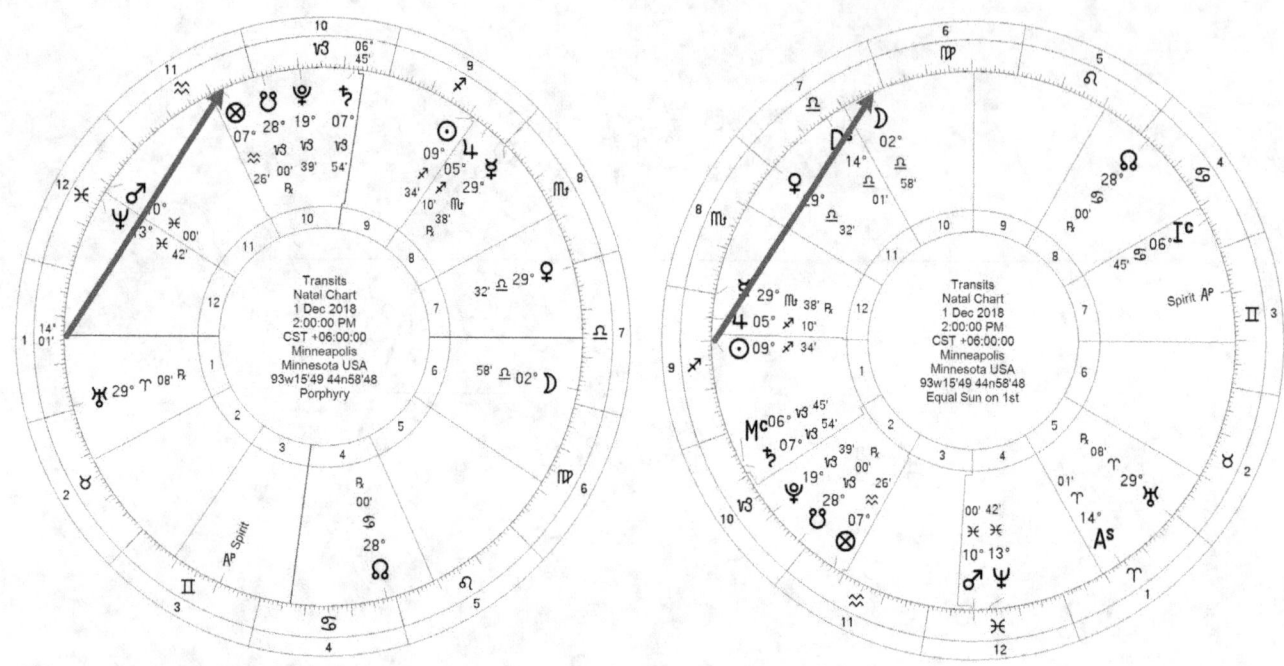

It is a statement of equal relation, and that will become very important when we consider the meaning of the Lots.

The Other Lot, Spirit

What happens when you switch the direction between the two lights, and cast from the Moon to the Sun in a day chart? What you get is referred to as the Lot of Spirit, as in the following diagram.

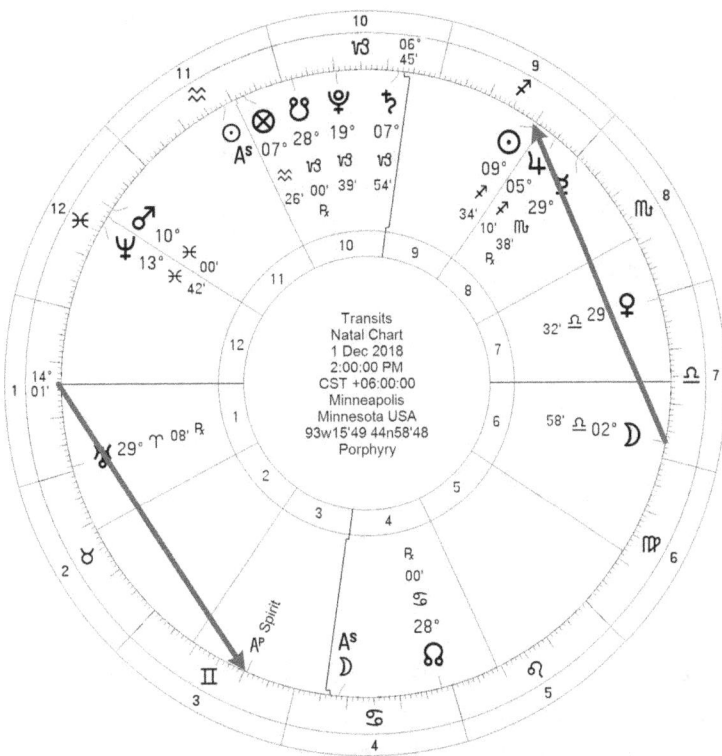

Take the distance from the Moon to the Sun, and cast that distance off the Ascendant.

In terms of our formula,

$$\text{Moon} \rightarrow \text{Sun} = \text{Ascendant} \rightarrow \text{Spirit}$$

Reciprocal Lots

The two main Lots involving both lights, the Lots of Fortune and Spirit, are mirror images of each other. I will use the term *reciprocals*, which was coined by Lind Weber is his book.

The two Lots, Fortune and Spirit, are always the same distance from the Ascendant, but on opposite sides. One of the Lots will be above that axis, and one below. The two Lots are like mirror images of each other above and below the Ascendant/Descendant axis.

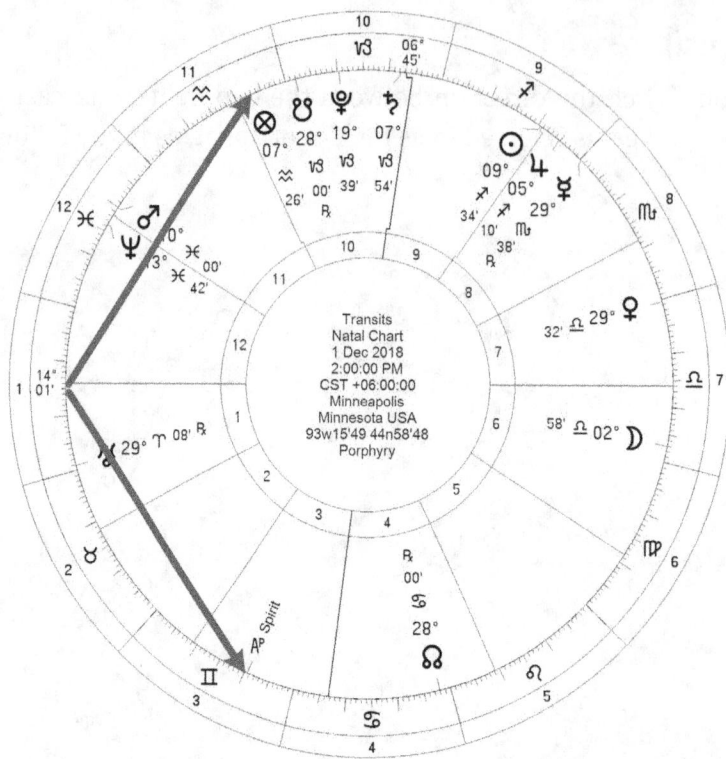

In this chart the Ascendant at 14 Aries, is 66 degrees in one direction to the Lot of Fortune at 7 Aquarius, and 66 degrees in the other direction to the Lot of Spirit at 21 Gemini. The two arrows in the diagram are exactly the same length, and point in opposite directions.

The reciprocal Lot Spirit is cast in the opposite direction from Fortune.

Note that either Lot can be at any location in the chart, either above or below the horizon. Once you have one of the Lots, it is easy to spot the other one, on the other side of the horizon at the same distance from the Ascendant.

Going forward I will sometimes refer to Fortune as LOF and Spirit as LOS, or sometimes just as Fortune and Spirit.

The Lots of Fortune and Spirit: Reciprocal Lots

The two basic Lots, Fortune and Spirit, define the relationship between the Sun and Moon, and their relation to the Ascendant, as primary to the individual. Sun and Moon represent the 2 great lights, the 2 sects, the 2 halves of the day and so on. The Lot is a relation point and an integration point. Important things happen where the opposites meet; events come from opposites or balanced pairs or groups interacting.

Lots and the Phase of the Moon

Since the Lots are both calculated using the distance between the Sun and Moon, it follows that the location of the Lots in the chartwheel will be related to the lunar phase. When you are near a new

Moon, where the Sun and Moon are very close together, the two Lots will be very close to the Ascendant. Near a full Moon, where Sun and Moon are nearly opposite each other, the two Lots will both be very nearly opposite the Ascendant, over on the right side of the chart on either side of the Descendant. When the Moon is at either waxing or waning quarter Moon, roughly 90 degrees from the Sun, the two Lots will be roughly opposite each other, making a square aspect to the Ascendant/Descendant axis.

Fortune in Traditional and Modern Usage: Day and Night Charts

Lots, Sect and the Lights

The formulas we have looked at so far are for the two Lots for a day chart. To deal with night charts, we need to come back and examine the situation further.

The earliest astrology placed a strong emphasis on Sect, which is division of the chart, and the planets of the chart, into two groups, day and night, diurnal and nocturnal.

The rulers or defining planets of the two sects are the two Lights, the Sun and the Moon. In a day chart, the Sun is the light of day. In a night chart, when the Sun is below the horizon, the Moon is the light of the night.

"God made the greater light to rule the day, and the lesser light to rule the night." - Genesis

You can think of the Sun and Moon as the lords of the day and night.

This next point is important:

> **In traditional astrology the calculation of the two main Lots changes depending on whether you have a day or night chart, and which of the two lights is lord of the chart.**

To find the Lot of Fortune, take the distance from the light of the chart to the other light, and cast that same distance off of the Ascendant. ***The casting of the Lot is directional, and always moves FROM the light of the chart TO the other light.***

In casting terms:

> **Sect Light -> other Light = Ascendant -> Fortune**

In a day chart we get the formula we have already seen.

> **Traditional, Day Chart: Sun -> Moon = Ascendant -> Fortune**

In traditional usage, in a night chart you flip the positions of the Sun and Moon since the Moon is now the light of the chart. In a night chart you cast the distance from the Moon to the Sun, and cast that off the Ascendant. The formula looks like this.

> **Traditional, Night Chart: Moon -> Sun = Ascendant-> Fortune**

The main Lot, Fortune, always moves from the light of the sect to the out of sect light. The other Lot, Spirit, moves in the opposite direction.

> **Traditional, Day Chart: Moon -> Sun = Ascendant-> Spirit**

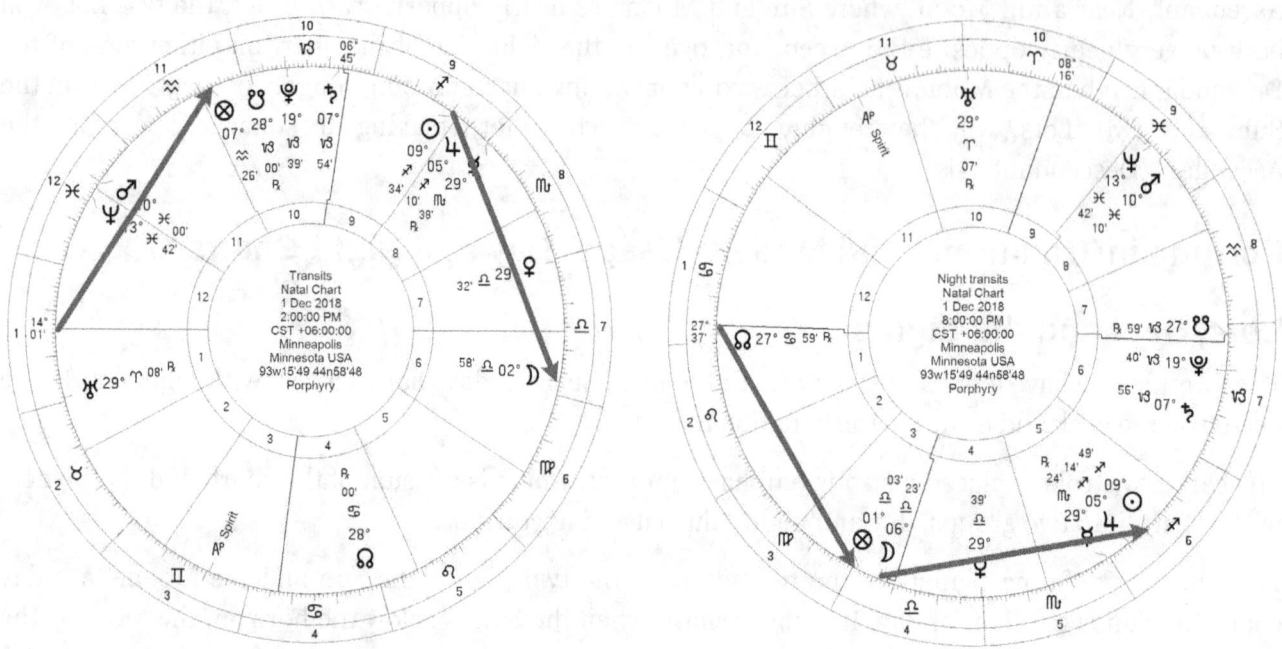

The left is a day chart (Sun -> Moon), the right a night chart (Moon -> Sun). Note that the Lot itself can end up either above or below the horizon in either a day or night chart.

Modern Astrology Usage

Modern astrology has pretty much lost the notion of sect. Even when it is recognized it usually not regarded as particularly important. Without the notion of sect, switching the directions of the Lot of Fortune makes no sense. Consequently, it is common in modern usage to drop switching the direction of the Lot in day and night charts.

Modern, Any Chart: Sun -> Moon = Ascendant -> Fortune

Modern, Any Chart: Moon -> Sun = Ascendant-> Spirit

This means that traditional and modern astrology differ in how they calculate the Lots of Fortune and Spirit in night charts.

Which Formula is Correct?

This difference between traditional and modern usage in calculation of the Lots in night charts raises some very important questions.

- Should the direction of the Lots be switched in day to night charts?

- Are the two Lots of equal importance, or is Fortune always more important than Spirit? Or, are they each important, but in consistently different ways?

- If Fortune does turn out to be more important, which formula for Fortune is most consistent, switching day and night or keeping them the same in both?

- Do the two Lots have consistently different meanings? Does Fortune always mean one kind of thing and Spirit something else? And if so, which way of calculating the Lots works best?

For the purpose of this study I am starting by suspending judgment. I am looking at BOTH of the Lots, the two reciprocals, Fortune and Spirit, and considering whether they are of equal importance. I am looking at both Lots, Fortune and Spirit, to study how they actually work.

The Lot Formulas in Algebraic Format

Most modern books on the Lots define them in terms of an algebraic formula. This is the form it is usually presented.

$$A + B - C = D.$$

For the Lot of Fortune for a day chart the formula looks like this:

Ascendant + Moon - Sun = Lot of Fortune.

The addition and subtraction is in terms of zodiac degrees.

That formula is mathematically correct, but it obscures the geometric structure of the Lots, and it is very different from how the Lots were described in much of the earlier traditional material.

In algebraic terms,

Traditional: Ascendant + out of sect Light - Light of chart = Lot of Fortune

Traditional: Ascendant + Light of chart - out of sect Light = Lot of Spirit

When you understand how the Lots are created the traditional language of casting a distance is much more descriptive than the algebraic formula. Looking at just the formula has led to some common misunderstandings.

$$A + B - C = D$$

In the algebra it looks like you are ADDING the influence of B or the out of sect light, and SUBTRACTING C or the Sect light. B looks like the more important of the two planets.

In traditional terms, C or the Sect light is the defining planet. Measuring the Lot starts there.

Modern astrology does not take into account the switch of the formula based on the Sect of the chart. The two Lots are calculated in the same way in all charts.

The modern formulas of the two Lots look like this for both day and night charts, without switching.

Modern: Ascendant + Moon - Sun = Lot of Fortune.

Modern: Ascendant + Sun - Moon = Lot of Spirit.

Traditional and Algebraic Formulas are Equivalent

Before we go any further I want to demonstrate that the two formulas for calculating the Lots, the traditional and the algebraic, are mathematically identical.

Start with the algebraic formula.

$$A + B - C = D$$

Now subtract A from both sides.

$$B - C = D - A$$

You find the distance between two points by taking their location in zodiac degrees, and subtracting one from the other. Stated differently, saying B - C is exactly the same as saying B -> C.

Therefore,

$$B - C = D - A$$

Is exactly the same as,

$$B \rightarrow C = D \rightarrow A$$

Switching directions, it is equally true that

$$C \rightarrow B = A \rightarrow D$$

And substituting the points for fortune in a day chart, we get

$$\text{Sun} \rightarrow \text{Moon} = \text{Ascendant} \rightarrow \text{Fortune}$$

and that is the traditional method for calculating the Lots.

The Geometry of the Lots

To understand the relationships between the points in a Lot, it helps to see pictures illustrating the geometry. I am going to build this in stages to show the relations being formed.

It is worth taking your time to get these points very clear in your mind. This geometry is the basis of the interpretive meaning of the Lots.

These are the 4 points in the Lot of Fortune in a day chart, labeled and connected.

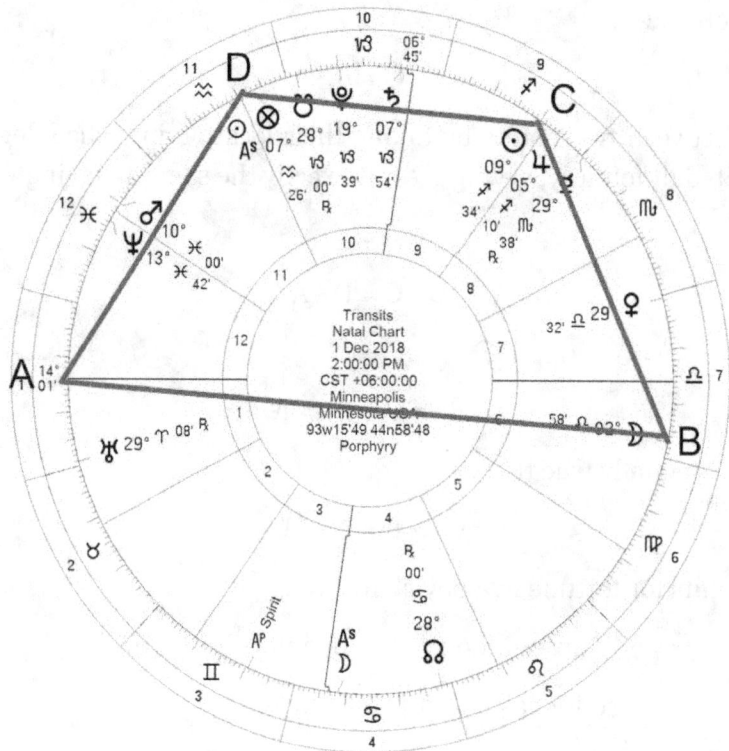

I have the 4 points labeled as they would be in the usual formula for Lot of Fortune day chart. A = Ascendant, B = Moon, C = Sun, D = Fortune.

In terms of lengths of arc, C -> B equals A -> D. Sun -> Moon = Ascendant -> Fortune.

Connect the 4 points and they form what is called an isosceles trapezoid, where two of the sides are parallel, and the other two are the same length. You can picture it as an isosceles triangle with the top lopped off.

The four points of ANY Lot always form an isosceles trapezoid.

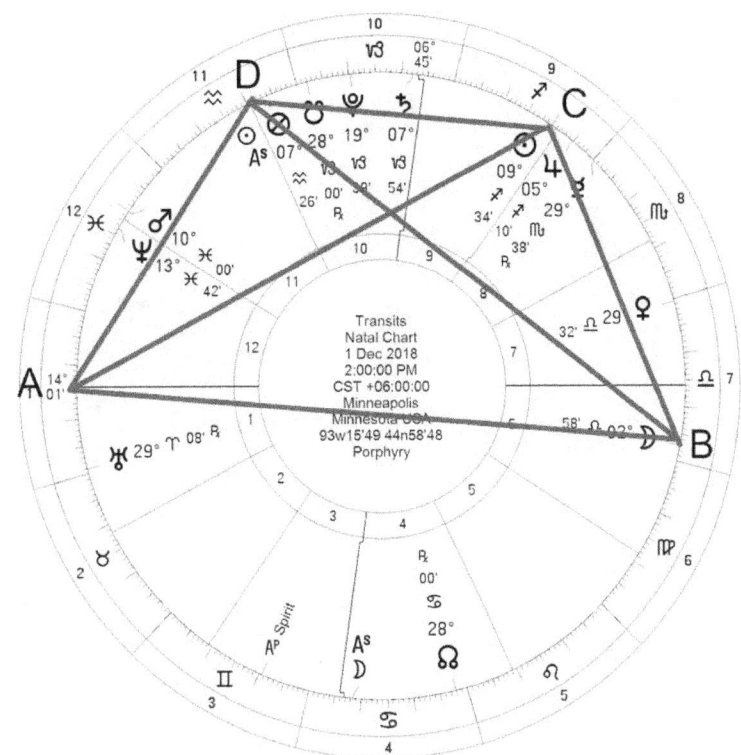

So far we have looked at only one pair of equal relations in the figure. There is another pair, as shown in this figure. Here I added lines connecting the corner points. We have another pair of equal relations.

A -> C equals D -> B.   In planet terms here, Ascendant -> Sun equals Fortune -> Moon.

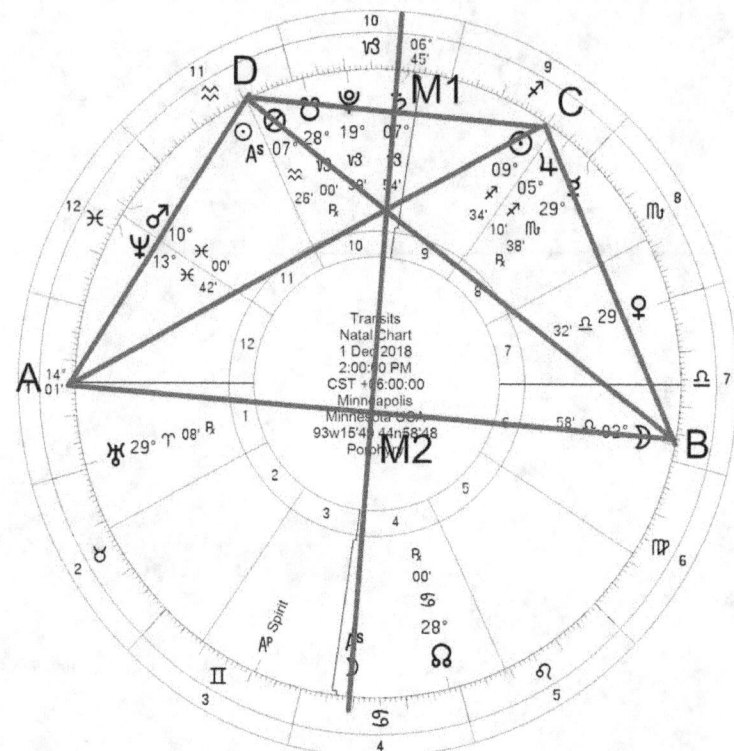

There is one more important set of relations in this figure, as shown in the third diagram. Here I drew another line right up the middle of the trapezoid, cutting lines AB and DC in half. You can see that line AB and line DC share the same midpoint: M1 equals M2 in the diagram.

In midpoint astrology, the midpoint of A and B is written, A/B.

Midpoint of line A B equals midpoint line D C.

$$A/B = C/D$$

Midpoint of Ascendant and Moon equals Midpoint of Fortune and Sun.

Ascendant/Moon = Fortune/Sun

Lots and Midpoints

Here I want to make the case that the traditional geometry and symbolism of the Lots is related to the symbolism of midpoints.

Midpoints are points of equal relations, and so are the Lot structures. Let's unpack that.

Midpoint theory says that when a point has exactly the same distance or relation to another two points then those points are specially combined there. Modern Uranian astrology, which works with similar concepts, says that when two pairs of points share the same midpoint, then those pairs of points are strongly integrated together.

The formula for two pairs of points sharing the same midpoints is,

$$(A + B) / 2 = (C + D) / 2$$

Multiply both sides by 2 and this is algebraically the same as

$$A + B = C + D$$

Now subtract C from both sides, and that is equal to

$$A + B - C = D$$

As we already know, this is the usual algebraic formula for the Lots.

The traditional definition of the Lots says that when there is an equal distance between two sets of points, they are tied together. Another way of defining them, which is mathematically equivalent, is that a Lot structure is formed whenever two pairs of points share a common midpoint.

Lots, Midpoints and Planetary Pictures

This same Lot formula. algebraically, A + B - C = D, shows up again in an important and radical branch of modern astrology - Uranian astrology, invented in Germany in approximately the 1920's. The landmark document of this school is Alfred Witte's *Rules for Planetary Pictures*. Somewhat later the brilliant German astrologer Reinhold Ebertin streamlined Uranian astrology in the system he named Cosmobiology. The main textbook by Ebertin is the midpoint dictionary called *Combinations of Stellar Influences*. I think that these two books, by Witte and Ebertin, are two of the greatest and most suggestive astrology books ever written.

The formula for the Uranian planetary pictures is A + B - C = D, exactly the same formula as for the traditional Lots.

Witte had the genius to rediscover the basic geometry of the Lots and to apply it more broadly, examining cases where any four points in the chart form that pattern.

Any two pairs of points that share a common midpoint create a planetary picture.

Modern Planetary Picture = Traditional Lot. The two definitions are not just similar, they are mathematically identical.

Lots as Relations

Here is where we can start considering the meaning of the Lots. The geometric pattern of the Lots gives two pairs of equal distances or arcs, and one pair of shared midpoints. It is a tightly knit group of multiple relations. The Lot point describes where, and how, the three other points in the Lot work together and relate to each other.

Midpoints and Equal Arcs

For traditional astrologers, the use of equal arcs is the bridge to understanding midpoints.

The Lots are built by definition on equal relations. The most basic definition of the two main Lots, Fortune and Spirit, is that the relation between the two lights is the same as the relation between the Ascendant and the Lots.

Equal relations tie pairs of points together.

Midpoint theory says that when two pairs of points share a common midpoint, those two pairs of points work together. They are integrated.

The midpoint between two points is that spot that has equal relations to each of the points. A midpoint is a statement of equal relation of two points to a third point. ***Midpoints and equal arc relations are sister concepts, two ways of thinking about the same thing.***

The special shape of the Lots, which is the same shape as Uranian planetary pictures, has two pairs of equal relations and one pair of shared midpoints. The four points are tightly knit together by this combination.

That is why the Lots are important and sensitive points in the chart. They integrate, they close a circuit, they activate, they stimulate.

Midpoints in Astrology Tradition

In modern astrology texts you will sometimes see the claim that midpoints are used in traditional astrology. Specifically, you will often see a reference to use of midpoints in Guido Bonatti's *The Book of Astronomy* from the late 13th century. You will even see a reference to midpoints on the Wikipedia page about Bonatti, so this is a widely believed assertion.

I checked with Ben Dykes, who translated Bonatti's complete text, and he says that there is no such reference. Strictly speaking there is no validity to the claim that midpoints show up in traditional astrology.

I think that I have found the reference where that claim about midpoints began, and it ties right into our connecting midpoints with the Lots.

Reinhold Ebertin is one of the most influential astrologers in the field of using midpoints, and his foundational text, *The Combination of Stellar Influences*, is arguably the main reference book of midpoint meanings.

In one of Ebertin's books, *Man in the Universe*, published in English translation in 1973, we find the following passage.

> *A certain kind of midpoint was already used by the most famous astrologer of the 13th Century, Guido Bonatti... his most famous treatise is 'Liber Astronomicus'...The German edition appeared in Basel in 1572." (English translation p.40)*

Note here that Ebertin is using a German edition of Bonatti, not the Latin original.

Back to the passage from Ebertin.

> *As far as I can tell, Bonatti ascertained that birth did not occur at random, but that in fact either there is some important heavenly body located at the Ascendant, or the Ascendant is to be found in the middle between two bodies. Even so long ago, the attempt was made to rectify the time of birth.*

*The midpoints also have their origins in the **sensitive points**. Here, the distances of two heavenly bodies are added to the Ascendant.* (The phrase 'sensitive points' is highlighted in the original text.)

The phrase 'sensitive points' is Ebertin's term for what we know as the Lots or Arabic parts. **In our exploration of the geometry of the Lots, we have seen that, by definition, the Ascendant is always at the exact midpoint of the two main Lots, Fortune and Spirit.**

In other words, it is likely that Ebertin interpreted a reference to the Lots as being a reference to the use of midpoints.

In terms of our exploration of the Lots, we have established that the geometry of midpoints and the geometry of the Lots are the same. Lots and midpoints are two different ways of getting at the same geometrical structure. You can view the Lots as being a traditional astrology analog or parallel to the use of midpoints.

Strictly speaking, are midpoints referred to in traditional astrology texts? No, not in those terms. However, the geometry of the Lots serves as a conceptual bridge from traditional astrology to the modern use of midpoints. Ebertin was on to something valid when he made the connection of Lots and midpoints.

Now that we have the geometric framework in place we can move on and consider their meaning.

What the Lots Mean

In this section I want to think through the meaning of the Lots. We are going to take the geometric structure of the Lots as the key to their interpretive meaning.

The key concepts that sum up the meaning of the Lots are:

relation, integration, stimulus, action, and balance.

And, Luck.

The traditional description of a Lot arises from a relation. You take the arc distance or relation between the two lights, the Sun and the Moon, and cast that same arc distance from the Ascendant or other point. In the traditional formulation the most basic of the Lots, that of Fortune, moves from the light that matches the sect of the chart, and casts the distance to the other light.

The Lot has the same relation to the Ascendant as the lights do to each other.

We can think of the lights here as polar balancing opposites, so the Lot location shows a relationship between the lights, an integrating point. The location of the Lot is a point where the relationship between the two lights is related to the Ascendant, in a pattern that includes all four points.

The symbolism of the geometric pattern gives a similar meaning.

This very special structural shape, with two pairs of equal arcs and a pair of shared midpoints, very tightly integrates the four points involved. I think of it as an energy field or structure where the point of the Lot lights up and integrates the other three points.

The critical thing to consider, as Lind Weber points out, is that the two main Lots are the points in the chart that simultaneously stimulate and integrate the Sun, Moon and Ascendant, which are the three most important points in the chart. **The two main Lots tie the Sun, Moon and Ascendant together.**

This means that any planet which occupies the position of the Lot should have a powerful and important effect.

The Lots have an effect when the point is occupied, because that completes the energy pattern. That is one of the main assertions that Weber makes, and it is one of the main points I am testing in this study.

What Does Fortune Mean?

I think there is a reason why the main Lot is referred to as Fortune, and I want to meditate on that here.

Naming the Lot Fortune does not mean it is fortunate in the sense of good luck. I think that is a common and superficial misunderstanding. I do not think you can say the Lot of Fortune is where you are lucky, or where your good fortune comes from.

In ordinary language we also use the word fortune in a broader and more basic sense. We talk of good fortune and bad fortune, of the luck of fortune, and the term has to do with what is fated, what just happens to us. The word fortune in that sense does not imply either good or bad.

Here the word Lot is also meaningful, even in our contemporary language. We refer to your Lot in life, the characteristic kinds of things that the world throws at you. This relates to the concept of casting or drawing Lots, something that is given to you by the luck of the draw.

If we are correct, that the Lots are special points of integration and balance, tying the chart and the person together, then the sorts of things that happen when the Lots are triggered should be characteristic of the defining themes of a person's life.

The Lots have to do with general fortune in that things happen when they are triggered, and the nature of the Lot shows how that works out.

This is the critical point: when the Lots are stimulated Things Happen. For any given chart, there is a theme or pattern that runs through the events that happen when the Lots are activated.

This is the single most important point I discovered in talking with people about the periods when the Lots were triggered. In any given chart you will find a characteristic theme to the kinds of things that happen when the Lot is stimulated, This theme is often a definitive subject or theme in the person's life. The kinds of Lot events are what makes that person who they are.

To use a musical or harmonic metaphor, if the Lots are an energy pattern or a harmonic pattern, then activating the Lots sounds the characteristic tone or keynote of the person's life. When the Lots are triggered that chart sings its characteristic song.

The Lots, Fortune and Luck

For much of our lives nothing much important happens, and life just sort of goes on, day by day. For most people that is the majority of their experience. The Lots are where Things Happen. There is an element of luck, and often events related to the Lots are out of control. That is not all of the meaning of the Lots, but it is a big part.

The Lots tell us about the characteristic sort of luck that people have - sometimes good, sometimes bad, sometimes mixed.

Some people are just lucky; they seem to get the breaks. Some people are just unlucky, and things just don't roll their way. It is like when we think, that is just the sort of thing which happens to that person, it is so very like them for things to turn out that way.

How good or bad fortune plays out is not just a passive experience. In more than a few of the examples that I studied, a great deal of hard work and initiative is involved. In those cases the person has been working consistently hard and preparing, so that when good fortune arrived they were ready to seize it, take advantage and make the best of it. They rise to the occasion. With others, a lucky break can come along... and not much happens. It comes, it passes, and life goes on.

There are also many cases in the examples I studied where initiative or control are just not involved.

Illnesses. Accidents. Jobs ending, or beginning, or changing in a big way. Relationships falling apart. Deaths of relatives, friends, colleagues, or their own death. For more than a few of the examples there were a combination of events. When fortune hits everything happens at once. When it rains, it pours.

Some people are destroyed by misfortune, others rise to the occasion, deal with it and come out stronger, or wiser, or more compassionate than before. What seemed like bad fortune at the time can end up seeming the best thing that ever happened to them.

It is often when the dice roll, when good or bad fortune hits, that the true measure of a person is revealed.

Sometimes misfortune can be severe enough to destroy good and strong people, so there is no element of blame involved. Sometimes good fortune can be big enough to raise people to wealth or fame, so credit or worthiness is not always involved.

Is this fair? Fairness isn't always a factor. That is why we talk of fortune. The luck of the draw. The roll of the dice.

It is when the Lots are activated, when good or bad fortune hits, that we figure out what sort of hand the Universe has dealt us. We also learn a great deal about ourselves by how we deal with the strokes of fortune.

When the Lots are activated, heads up - things are about to happen.

The Lots and Prediction

Since the geometric structure of a Lot shows a strong interrelation between the points, then things should happen when the Lot is completed by a planet. Lind Weber's theory is that this is why the Lots were developed in the first place, and why they continue to be used. I think that Lind Weber is on to something when he says they were primarily used for predictive and elective purposes for that reason. The purpose of this study is to figure out just how they work.

Astrology does not predict specific events, it predicts periods of enhanced activity or stress where significant things are likely to occur, and also the sorts of themes that are likely to surface during those enhanced periods. Periods when the Lots are stimulated are enhanced periods.

If you have an old inflexible tree, you can't predict exactly when a branch will break, but you can say that it is more likely to happen during high winds. You can also learn a Lot about a tree by watching how it behaves during a strong windstorm.

Transits to the Lots are weather forecasts, predicting the periods of high winds.

Watching How the Lots Actually Work

I can't tell, from looking at a chart with no context, how the Lots will work out, or anything else in the chart, for that matter. I can see likely themes, likely strengths and weaknesses, but in order to really interpret a chart in any meaningful way I need to see it in a life context.

This is why I am approaching my study of the Lots in this fashion. This is why I did the studies of famous people, and that is how I structured the studies with individuals. I want to see how the Lots work, I want to see them in action.

To study the health of a tree and its branches I want to see how it behaves during windy storms, when the pressure is turned up.

Given that the three points Sun, Moon and Ascendant are the most important for defining a person, the periods when all three of those points are stimulated and integrated by the Lots should be most characteristic of who that person is.

This means that the major transits to the Lots should reveal the characteristic themes of a person's life, the most characteristic sorts of events that happen to them. The pattern of their lives is most vivid when the Lots are turned on.

So, going through a series of Lot activation periods, there should be a common thread, a characteristic theme, running through all of them, and that theme should describe their characteristic fortune, the Lot that the universe has cast them in this lifetime.

That is what most of this book is all about, watching the Lots in action. The interpretive principles I cover were derived after the studies. I use the astrology interpretation to make sense of why they acted the way they did.

Not surprisingly, the usual sorts of interpretive principles from traditional astrology apply.

Also not surprisingly, some of the principles from modern midpoint and planetary picture work, in Cosmobiology, Uranian Astrology and Harmonic Astrology, are also useful.

Vocation and Relationships.

In looking at the characteristic events occurring when the Lots are activated, there are two main themes that kept coming up, over and over, the themes of vocation and of major relationships.

That makes sense. Those two areas, vocation and relationships, are the things that tie people's lives together, make them feel like they fit, and give their lives a sense of coherence and meaning. This logically follows from the basic definition of Lot points as connecting, stimulating, integrating, bringing things together.

I consistently found that when I interviewed a person about about their Lot transits I felt like I had a very good sense of what was most important to them, what made them tick, what was their characteristic Lot in life.

What Is Covered in this Study

These are the points I am testing for in the case studies I include here. All of these follow from the basic assumption, that these two main Lots are points in the chart that connect and stimulate the Ascendant, Moon and Sun together.

Here I want to list the main points I am studying. *(I will note the conclusions I arrived at after the study in parentheses and italics, like this note.)*

I will also mention some points I did not include in the study that merit further research.

Given that the Lots are points of integration, then **planets conjunct a Lot in a natal chart take on special importance** for the native, and in many cases are the definitive planet, the one the native identifies with the most.

(I take this point to be definitively proven.)

Planets occupying the Lot point by transit activate the Lot, complete the circuit and turn it on. Given that conjunctions to a Lot can have a several degree orb, this means that transits to the Lot by the slower moving traditional planets, Jupiter and Saturn, should mark significant periods where the Lot is activated for months at a time.

Weber's assertion is that Saturn transits mark times of bad fortune, and Jupiter transits mark times of good fortune.

(I do find conjunctions to the Lots to be consistently meaningful. I do not find Saturn transits to be always bad fortune or Jupiter transits to be always good.)

Along with the conjunctions, which should have the most important and sustained effect, Weber also asserts that hard Saturn aspects to the Lot, squares or oppositions, should be what he calls periods of intermittent bad fortune. During the period Saturn is in orb, the Lot circuit is being repeatedly closed by faster moving bodies. The inner planets all touch the Lot point once a year, the moon touches it once a month.

(I find the squares and oppositions to be important very often, but not as consistently or in as sustained a manner as the conjunctions.)

Weber also looks at trines from Jupiter as times of good fortune. For my study I used only Jupiter conjunctions. I did not want to multiply the number of activated periods too much, to help keep the study focused.

I did not focus on transits from the modern outer planets, Uranus, Neptune and Pluto, nor did I include any of the asteroids. This was partly to keep from multiplying the Lot transit periods to the point that they became meaningless. Also, the modern outer planets move slowly enough that you would have them within traditional orb of a Lot for years at a time, and when the periods get that long they lose focus and meaning. This area, transits from outer planets and/or asteroids to the Lots, is an area for further research.

Since Lots are points that activate, integrate and complete the chart, I assumed that **connections to the Lot points should be very important in synastry**.

(Conclusion - oh, man, is that true in spades!)

There is another thesis that quickly began to develop when I started talking to people about how the Lot transit periods worked out. **For each of the people I talked to there was a common thread or theme running through all of the Lot activation periods**. Further, I found that this thread or theme very often struck what you could call the keynote or characteristic theme of the person's life, that which made them uniquely who they are.

(This may be the single most important thing I learned from this study.)

As I watched how the Lots actually worked out in people's lives, I hoped to be able to develop some useful guidelines on how to interpret a Lot, what its themes were, and how strong or weak was its action likely to be. Some of those guidelines are the same interpretive rules I learned from the tradition, and some are tools I learned from modern Uranian and harmonic astrology.

Since Lots are places that stimulate and integrate, places where Things Happen, I hypothesized that **I should see Lots being activated in significant event charts**. This should include close transits from faster moving planets or from the angles.

(That does indeed seem to be the case, and I include a couple of examples.)

I also wanted to gather some data **to see if there is a consistent difference between the two Lots, Fortune and Spirit - and, if there is, which way of calculating each of those Lots is correct, the traditional or modern formula**.

(My final conclusion is that these are the wrong questions to be asking. I visit this point again in the final chapter.)

Since Lots can be stimulated by transits, it makes sense that they can also be activated by forms of symbolic direction, including primary directions and secondary progressions.

(That does seem to be the case, and I will include a few examples in the case studies.)

What About All the Other Lots?

For this study I decided early on to concentrate only on the two most basic Lots, Fortune and Spirit. This is partly to keep the scope of this study focused.

It is also because **I am now convinced that all of the other Lots are secondary or derivative from these two main Lots.**

Lind Weber refers to the other Lots as proliferations; I think of them as spinoffs or derivatives that are looked at depending on the situation with the main Lots, and depending on the topic or event being investigated.

There are so very many different Lots, with so many different interpretations, that they need to be applied on a case by case basis, since not all Lots meaningfully apply to all charts and situations.

It also seems to me that, to be able to usefully employ any other Lots, you will need a very firm grasp of Lot theory and geometry, to the point that you can pick out the Lots by looking at planet positions in a chart. That is not difficult to do once you understand how they were derived in the first place. I include a brief chapter on learning to scan for the Lots by eye.

Evaluating the Lots

This chapter presents the main principles I find useful to evaluate the strength of a Lot and to interpret its meaning. I learned these from working with the Lots in many, many charts, and seeing what kinds of things I found useful. I am reviewing the principles here to provide a framework for the chart examples throughout the book.

You will see very quickly that Lot interpretation is not a cookbook affair.

General Evaluation in the Natal Chart

Lot Pattern as a Whole Important

This is one of the most important things I learned from this study. ***The Lot is not a point, it is an entire harmonic pattern.*** The Lot point itself is important as the point that closes the circuit, but once the circuit is closed the entire Lot pattern light ups and integrates. We look to the point to see where and how it is activated, and we look to the Lot pattern as a whole to see how it acts and what it means.

That is why I drew so many diagrams in the course of this study, and why there are many diagrams in the chart examples that follow. I learned things from the Lot patterns I could not have seen in any other way.

It is also important to realize that ***the two Lots together are related harmonic patterns***. This follows from the mathematical fact that the two Lot points are exactly the same distance from the Ascendant. ***The Ascendant is the midpoint of the two Lots.*** This means it is worth looking at how the two Lot patterns interact.

Planet on Lot or Lot Pattern

A planet conjunct a Lot in the natal chart is very important since it activates the Lot pattern in the natal by itself; the Lot pattern doesn't need to look to synastry or a transit to be completed and activated. Hence a planet on the Lot point is key to the chart integration, and the characteristic action of this person should be strongly colored by that planet.

Using the metaphor of fortune, a person with a natal planet conjunct the Lot makes their own fortune.

Considering the Lots as a pair like this, when you have a planet natally conjunct a Lot, any time a planet activates the other Lot it forms a direct midpoint hit to the Ascendant, which makes the other Lot more powerful - or in other words, anything that triggers the other Lot immediately triggers the planet on the first Lot. ***The two Lots work together on the Ascendant.***

It is important when a planet is conjunct any of the other main Lot points - Sun, Moon or Ascendant - because when the Lot triggered, all the planets that are part of the Lot pattern get activated with it. These planets are all part of a basic structure that integrates the chart.

Evaluating Strength of the Lot

Here I want to consider the main chart factors that are helpful in evaluating the Lot.

Ruler of Lot

The ruler of the Lot is important, perhaps the most important single factor to consider. Consider its location, its dignity or debility, and what kind of aspect the Lot ruler makes to the Lot itself. This can show how much support the Lot derives from its ruler.

When a single planet rules both of the Lots, that planet takes on increased importance and can be an integrating factor for the entire chart. I found this to be very important in my own chart. It helped me figure out why I identify so very strongly with the weakest planet in my chart, and why it seems to have such an out-sized influence and importance.

House Location of Lot

I find the house location of the Lot to be important but not definitive in its overall meaning. Very often the theme of the house will be a characteristic theme of the Lot, but it is only one of many factors.

Planets in Stakes to the Lot

This is one of the most consistently useful factors to consider, and it is one of the basic principles of traditional astrology.

The stakes are the four signs making 90 degree aspects to each other, the conjunction, square and opposition. These are the four signs that make an equal armed cross. Signs in the stakes to each other all have the same mode, either cardinal, fixed or mutable.

When a Lot point is activated, any points in the stakes to the Lot are also activated. Hence, what planets are in the stakes and their condition strongly influence how the Lot manifests. Charts with strongly supported Lots have multiple strong planets in the stakes. Conversely, the lack of planets in the stakes, or weak or debilitated planets in the stakes, can indicate a weakness of the Lot.

Harmonic 8 Aspects Important

Just as the stakes are important, which are the aspects based on dividing the circle by four, I find it important to notice the aspects based on division by eight. I think of them in terms of their fraction of the circle, since that is what the names mean. The semisquare or half a square is 1/8 of the circle, or 45 degrees, and the sesquiquadrate, a square and a half, is 3/8 of the circle or 135 degrees. The harmonic 8 aspects are associated with tension, friction, action. A tight harmonic 8 aspect to a Lot contributes significant energy.

Aspect Between Lots

When the two Lots are in a square or opposition aspect to each other - when they are part of the same stakes - they will be triggered together. A conjunction to one of the Lots makes a hard aspect to the other at the same time. In cases like this, where the Lots are in square or conjunction, I find it hard to separate the meaning of the two Lots from each other.

Three Main Midpoints

The three main points of the chart, Sun, Moon and Ascendant, have three possible midpoint combinations.

      Sun / Moon   Sun / Ascendant   Moon / Ascendant

If you use midpoints you know that the Sun/Moon midpoint is one of the most important ones to consider. The other two midpoints define the midpoint axes for the Lots, so they are equally important. I now include all three midpoints in all charts I look at.

Lots and Other Midpoints

Given that the Lot points have to do with integration, it is worth scanning on either side of a Lot, or the Lot midpoint axis, to see if there are pairs of planets that have their midpoint right on that Lot or axis. An orb of up to four degrees is worth noting.

Lot Midpoint Axis

Any planets on the midpoint axis of the Lot are important. Considering the Lot as an energy pattern, that axis serves as a focus of expression or output for the Lot. Hence, any planet on that axis is important in how the Lot will be expressed. We will see a good example of this in the chart of composer and conductor Leonard Bernstein.

Overall Coherence

It is important to consider how the Lot ties in with the rest of the chart. This includes planets in the stakes to the Lot, other strong planets, main aspect patterns, and the angles. Strong Lots, and strong charts, form coherent and focused patterns. Weak Lots, and weak charts, have a lack of focus.

Lots Triggered by Transits

This is the single most critical point - *when the Lots are stimulated Things Happen*.

Predict Backward to Predict Forward

The best way to learn what the Lot means is to watch it in action.

The best way to interpret how a Lot transit will likely manifest is to check how previous Lot transits worked out, and what their major themes were.

Time of Increased Pressure or Activity

I quickly learned that it is not very useful to think in terms of good and bad fortune with the Lots, where Saturn is Bad and Jupiter is Good. It doesn't work out that way.

The Lots and their signs are sensitive points, and stimulating those points produces times of enhanced energy. There is increased pressure, increased activity, and often, increased significance of events within that period. This includes transits to the Lot, and hard aspects to the Lot. Those transits are likely to be times when important work is done or important things happen, often events that are out of the person's control.

Transits to the Lots are not necessarily good or bad, just active. Even considering the same planet, one transit can be "good" and another "bad", and much depends on other factors.

Characteristic Theme or Key Note

I often find that the Lot stimulation periods in a person's life share a common thread or theme, a main keynote to the person's life. For this reason I find it extremely meaningful to examine a series of Lot transits to look for those repeating themes. Looking just at major transits to the Lots can give a great deal of focused information about the person's life in general.

The Transiting/Activating Planet

The nature of what happens when a Lot is transited depends on the nature and condition of the transiting planet.

The condition of the planet in the natal makes a difference, as does its dignity in the sign of the Lot itself, and the sign it is transiting. For instance, in Hitler's chart, a Saturn transit period to his Lot of Spirit in Aquarius, where Saturn rules, was a very strong and successful year, while Saturn transiting to Fortune in Cancer where Saturn is in detriment marked the period when Germany fell apart and Hitler took his own life.

Lots and Symbolic Prediction Techniques

If the Lots are indeed integration and activation points, then they should be sensitive to symbolic predictive techniques such as solar returns, directions and progressions. That does indeed seem to be the case.

The following conditions are worth looking at:

Activation of the Lot in a solar return, where a Lot is angular, or has a hard conjunction to the Lot point. Conjunctions are by far the most important.

The progressed Moon entering the sign of the Lot can be significant. In this case the entire period of two-plus years that the progressed Moon is in that sign can take on the cast of the Lot. I found this to be true of my personal experience.

If the progressed Moon is important, then any other progressed planet entering Lot sign, and coming to conjunction to the Lot, could be worth noting also.

Lots also respond to primary directions. There will be a couple of instances of this in the example charts that follow.

Lots and Synastry

Wow, is this important!

This is one of the most consistently meaningful factors I found in looking at the Lots. When you have the charts of two people with a strong relationship - marriage partners, working partners, significant friends, or significant enemies - you will consistently find that the two charts stimulate and complete each other's Lot points.

The two people light up each other's lives. They turn each other on.

This is such a strong factor that I would question how close a relationship is where there is no interaction between the Lot points and the partner's chart.

As with all other interpretive techniques, you need to look at the entire pattern of how the Lots are activated, - activating planet, condition of that planet in both charts, and so on.

How to Scan for the Lots

In practice, if you want to use the entire Lot pattern, it will help to be able to pick out the pattern by eye. That is easy to do with just a little bit of practice. The diagrams here show the procedure.

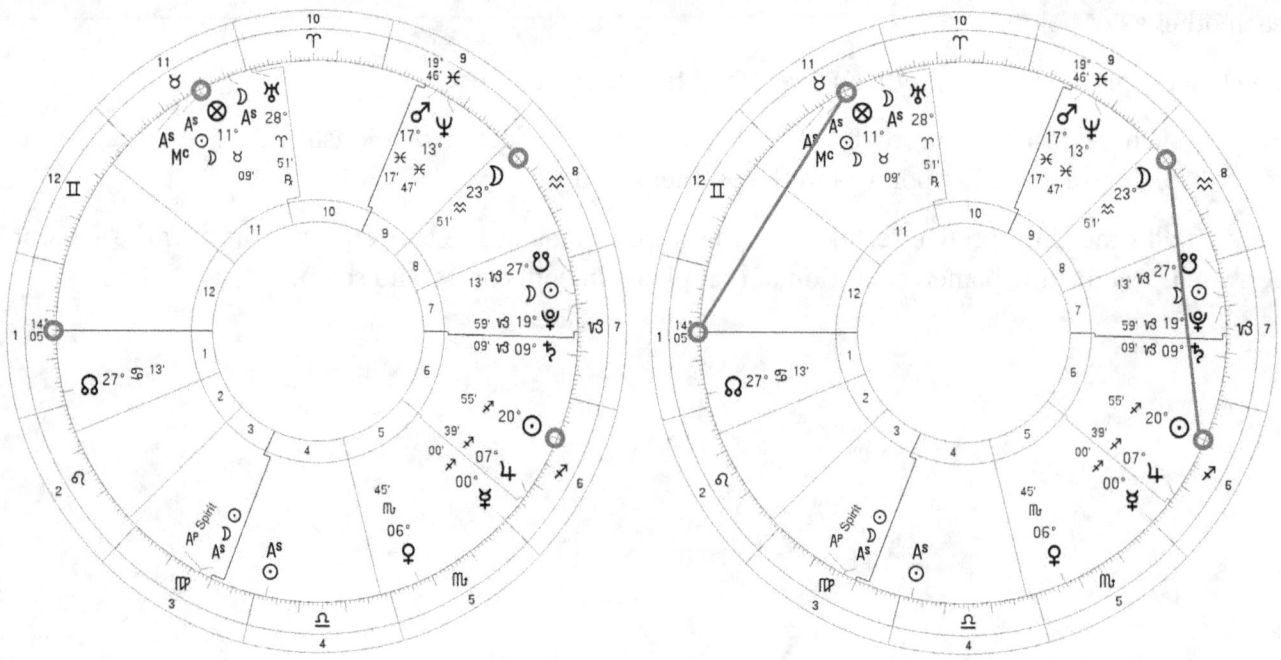

Start by locating the four points, Ascendant, Sun, Moon, and the Lot. Draw a pair of lines - one line from the Sun to the Moon, the other from the Ascendant to the Lot you are looking at. Those two lines will be the same length. You have defined two of the four sides of the isosceles trapezoid Lot shape.

In the example shown above, the two lines drawn do not cross. Depending on the location of Sun and Moon in your chart, those two lines may cross, but the four points still define the same trapezoid shape.

If you don't know the location of Fortune, you can measure the distance in degrees from the appropriate light to the other light, and take that same distance in the same direction to find Fortune.

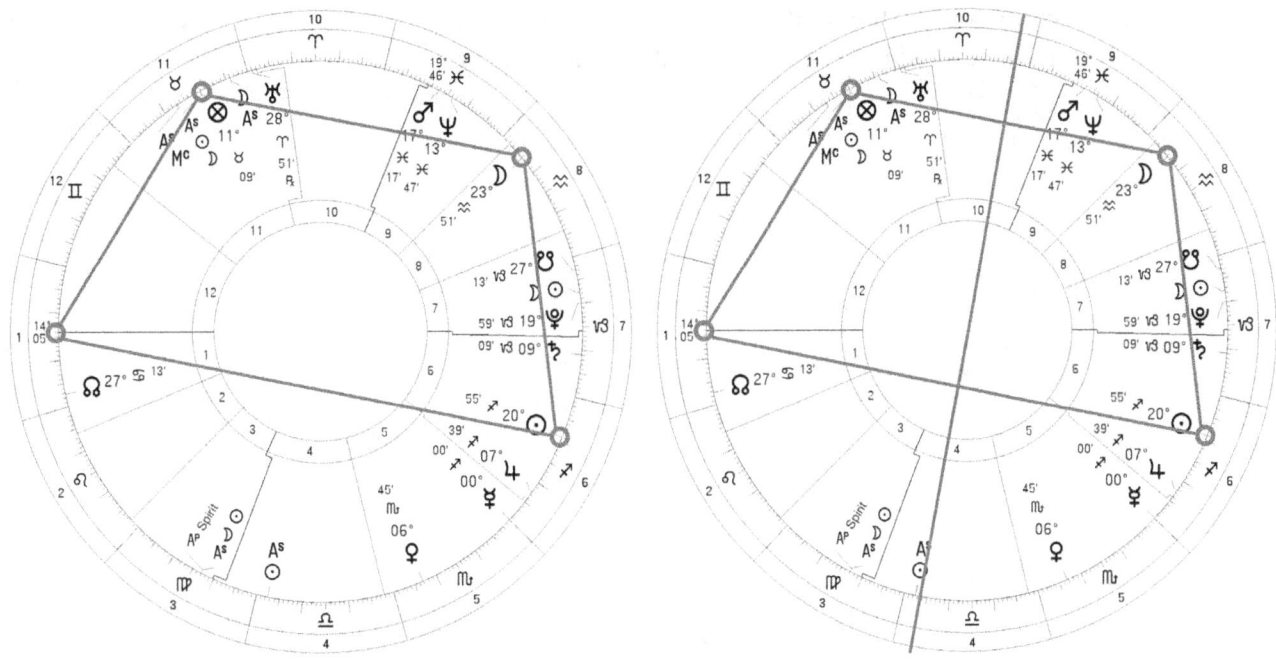

That defines the shape, because the other two sides are always parallel. You can then add the other two sides and complete the figure.

The midpoint axis for the Lot falls right in the middle of the two parallel sides.

You can also picture the first two lines you drew as pointing to the midpoint axis. That would be on a line with where the first two sides would converge if you extended them. If the initial lines you drew crossed each other, they crossed on the midpoint axis.

If you have the location of Fortune and need to find its paired Lot of Spirit, look for the point at the same distance from the Ascendant on the other side of the horizon.

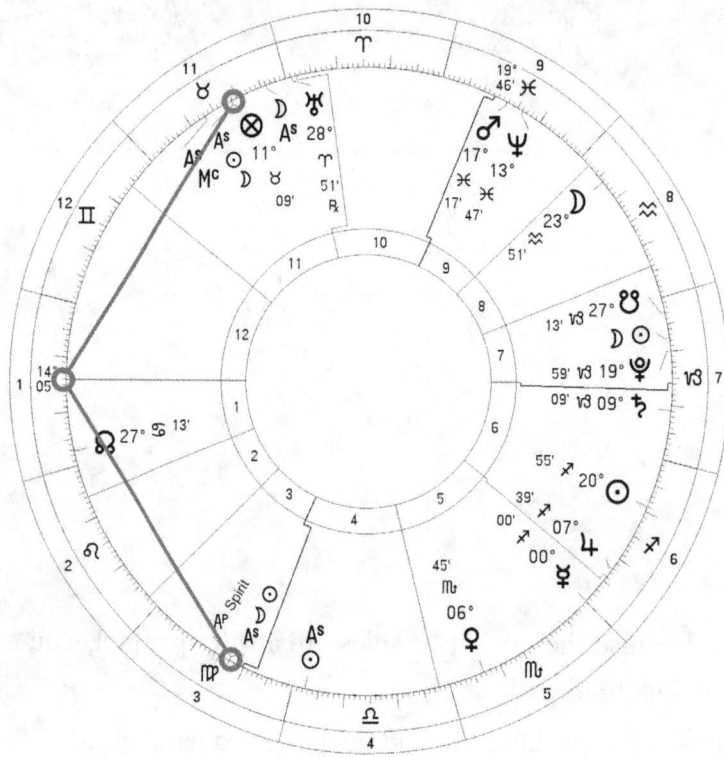

Once you know the location of Spirit, you can use the same procedure as for Fortune to see the isosceles trapezoid for Spirit and its midpoint axis.

Reading Symbols in the Chart

These are the symbols that you will see in the example charts for the various components of the Lots. I am using my chart for these illustrations, and I was born at night.

In all of these symbols you read them starting at the outside rim of the chart and moving in towards the center.

The algebraic formula for Fortune in a night chart is reflected in the symbol. Starting at the Ascendant, in order, it reads,

Ascendant + Sun - Moon.

The usual symbol for Fortune is right next to it.

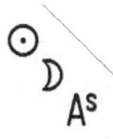
This is the Lot of Spirit in a night chart. The symbol here reflects the algebraic formula in order.

Ascendant + Moon - Sun.

I also have the Lot midpoints marked on some examples. Their symbols are shown here.

This is the symbol for the Sun/Ascendant midpoint. This defines the midpoint axis for the Lot that is measured from Moon to Sun. In my chart that is the Lot of Fortune.

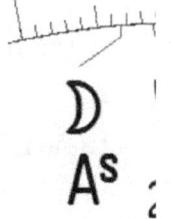
This is the Moon/Ascendant midpoint. This is the midpoint axis for the Lot measured from Sun to Moon, which in my chart is the Lot of Spirit.

Evaluating Dignity and Debility

The heart of traditional astrology is this process of evaluating strength and weakness, dignity and debility. This is a brief summary of the main conditions and vocabulary used. (Please see my book, *Using Dignities In Astrology*, for an extended treatment of these concepts.)

Dignity - A planet having a dignity has an assigned role and responsibility. Dignity strengthens a planet, gives it more influence and makes it more at home.

Debility - The opposite of dignity. A debilitated planet is weakened in some way. It can be off balance, not at home or in an uncongenial environment.

Benefic - Helpful. Jupiter and Venus are called benefic because their action is usually moderate, comfortable and helpful. We usually enjoy benefics, and they feel good.

Malefic - Harmful. Mars and Saturn are called malefic because their action is usually immoderate and extreme. The malefics can limit, injure, oppose or destroy. Malefics are usually not considered to be enjoyable. A Saturn return may end up being a useful and positive time, but not that many people would describe it as fun.

Sect - This divides chart and planets into day and night, or diurnal and nocturnal. A day chart has the Sun above the horizon, and with night it is below. The day planets are Sun, Jupiter and Saturn. The night planets are Moon, Venus and Mars. Mercury varies - when rising before the Sun at an earlier degree he is diurnal, and after the Sun at a later degree is nocturnal. Planets are more at home if the sect of the chart matches their sect. The Sun and Jupiter are happier and more helpful in day charts, while the Moon and Venus are more at home and effective in night charts. Similarly, the day planet Saturn is more crabby and harmful at night, and the night planet Mars is more irritable and hurtful during the day.

Essential Dignities are based on zodiac position, so they are the same for everyone on the planet at a given point in time. There are five essential dignities, two considered major and three considered minor. There is a table of essential dignities at end of book.

Each of the major dignities has a corresponding detriment at the sign opposite.

The Major Dignities are as follows:

Rulership is the strongest dignity. The ruler of a sign is its controller, manager, owner. The ruler is the main planet responsible for the affairs of a sign.

Detriment happens when a planet is in the sign opposite to one it rules. A planet in detriment is out of its home in an unfriendly environment. It is off balanced, uncomfortable and stressed. A planet in detriment can be a loner or an outsider working for change, so detriment can be turned to advantage.

Exaltation is the other major dignity. An exalted planet is valued, honored, listened to and given respect. I could also connote arrogance or a high opinion of oneself.

Fall is the opposite of exaltation. A planet in fall is not valued, not honored, ignored and not given respect. Often planets in fall work extra hard to over-compensate for this lack of respect and attention.

The minor Dignities are as follows:

Triplicity is a group or tribe dignity. There are three planets that have triplicity in each of the four elements. a planet in triplicity is at home in its group and has general support and good fortune from its tribe or extended family.

Term or Bound is featured in the traditional use of primary directions. A planet with dignity by term is competent and functional, and it is in charge of how things are implemented. That is why the technique of directing through the bounds is so important.

Face is a very minor dignity, with very little power and no authority. Face usually concerns appearance, ornament, the image or mask that a planet presents to the world.

In terms of their strength the dignities are additive. A planet with two minor dignities is considered equal in strength to having one major dignity.

Peregrine is the condition of a planet with no essential dignity. The word means homeless or wanderer, someone out on the street with no accepted place. Peregrine planets rely heavily on the condition of their rulers, the planets having dignity over it, for how well they function. A peregrine planet with rulers in good condition is greatly supported, and a peregrine planet with weak or harmful rulers gets no support from its environment.

The remaining concepts have to do with how the planets interact with each other and with their position relative to the angles and houses.

Reception is a very important principle. It concerns how the planets interact and relate to each other in terms of their dignity with each other.

Reception is the relationship of ruler to ruled. Venus in Aries is received by Mars in its rulership - Mars manages or rules Venus, and is also responsible for treating Venus as well as it can given its own condition. Reception also applies to the other dignities. That same Venus in Aries is received by the Sun in its exaltation, and by its three triplicity rulers, Sun, Jupiter and Saturn.

Mutual Reception is the beneficial condition where each of two planets receives the other into one of its dignities. Venus in Aquarius and Saturn in Libra are each in the sign the other rules. Mixed reception, where the planets are received in different dignities, are also valid. For instance Saturn in Aries and the Sun in Capricorn have a mixed mutual reception from exaltation to rulership, and this greatly enhances their relationship.

Reception in a minor dignity is not as strong, but is definitely preferable to no reception. Two planets having mutual reception in two minor dignities is considered equivalent to major mutual reception.

Planets with reception are more inclined to work with each other, and planets without reception lack good will and responsibility towards each other.

Aversion concerns relationship and communication. The main Ptolemaic aspects are the conjunction, sextile, square, trine, opposition, in which planets can see each other and have communication. Aspects are by whole sign in the earliest Western astrology - a planet anywhere in Aries is considered trine to a planet anywhere in Leo. Planets which do not have a whole sign aspect to each other are called averse which means "turned away". Planets in aversion can't see each other. They are out of touch, and there is a lack of control and communication.

Combustion is a debility. Being too close to the Sun is the worst thing that can happen to a planet. Any planet within roughly 8 degrees of the Sun or less is called combust, meaning burnt up. A combust planet loses all its strength. There is a transition condition - planet that is between 8 and 17 degrees from the Sun is under the rays, also called under the beams, which weakens, inhibits and hides its action. Combustion or under the rays is considered much worse when a planet is approaching conjunction than when it is separating. The effect of combustion is strongly influenced by the dignities of the Sun and the other planet, and by any reception between them.

Cazimi is a special case where a planet is within 17 minutes of the Sun, at the heart of the Sun. Instead of being weakened, a planet cazimi is greatly strengthened. It is the king's favorite and sitting right on the king's lap on his throne. (17 minutes is the most commonly used orb for a planet being cazimi, but there are some traditional texts that use an orb as large as one degree.)

Angularity is the measure of the strength of a planet relative to its proximity to one of the four angles. Planets close to an angle are angular and considered very strong and prominent, visible and active in the world. The next house over is called succedent and is not as strong. The weakest condition is called cadent which means "falling away". A cadent planet is furthest from the angle and is very weak. Cadency can also indicate action turned inward.

Retrograde describes a planet moving backwards in the zodiac. Retrograde is moving against the grain and is generally considered a debility. It weakens, delays and impedes action. A retrograde planet can be stubborn or ornery, or it can be rebellious. Like all of the other conditions here, a retrograde condition is greatly influenced by how it combines with the other dignities and debilities. A retrograde planet that is otherwise dignified can be quite strong.

Tables of Essential Dignities

Sign	Ruler	Detriment	Exaltation	Fall	Triplicity Day	Triplicity Night	Triplicity Partner	Face 0-9	Face 10-19	Face 20-29
♈	♂	♀	☉	♄	☉	♃	♄	♂	☉	♀
♉	♀	♂	☽		♀	☽	♂	☿	☽	♄
♊	☿	♃			♄	☿	♃	♃	♂	☉
♋	☽	♄	♃	♂	♀	♂	☽	♀	☿	☽
♌	☉	♄			☉	♃	♄	♄	♃	♂
♍	☿	♃	☿	♀	♀	☽	♂	☉	♀	☿
♎	♀	♂	♄	☉	♄	☿	♃	☽	♄	♃
♏	♂	♀		☽	♀	♂	☽	♂	☉	♀
♐	♃	☿			☉	♃	♄	☿	☽	♄
♑	♄	☽	♂	♃	♀	☽	♂	♃	♂	☉
♒	♄	☉			♄	☿	♃	♀	☿	☽
♓	♃	☿	♀	☿	♀	♂	☽	♄	♃	♂

Bounds or Terms

Sign										
♈	0	♃	6	♀	12	☿	20	♂	25	♄
♉	0	♀	8	☿	14	♃	22	♄	27	♂
♊	0	☿	6	♃	12	♀	17	♂	24	♄
♋	0	♂	7	♀	13	☿	18	♃	26	♄
♌	0	♃	6	♀	11	♄	18	☿	24	♂
♍	0	☿	7	♀	17	♃	21	♂	28	♄
♎	0	♄	6	☿	14	♃	21	♀	28	♂
♏	0	♂	7	♀	11	☿	19	♃	24	♄
♐	0	♃	12	♀	17	☿	21	♄	26	♂
♑	0	☿	7	♃	14	♀	22	♄	26	♂
♒	0	☿	7	♀	13	♃	20	♂	25	♄
♓	0	♀	12	♃	16	☿	19	♂	28	♄

The degree in the term table is the degree that bound starts. For instance, Venus term in Aries begins at 6 degrees.

Technical Notes

Rulership and Dignities

I consider myself primarily a traditional astrologer. I use only the traditional planetary rulerships - Mars rules Scorpio, Saturn rules Aquarius, and Jupiter rules Pisces.

I use traditional dignity and debility in evaluating charts. I also refer to the three minor dignities of triplicity, term or bound, and face. If you do not use the minor dignities, you can think of them as adding some strength and balance to how a planet expresses.

You will also see that I place much less emphasis on the modern outer planets - Uranus, Neptune and Pluto - than do most modern astrologers.

Concerning aspects, I use mainly the traditional Ptolemaic aspects - conjunction, opposition, trine, square, sextile. The only non-traditional aspects I use are those that come from dividing the circle by eight - the semisquare (1/8, 45 degrees) and sesquiquadrate (3/8, 135 degrees). I find it significant that the German astrology schools of Uranian astrology and Cosmobiology use the harmonic eight aspects extensively, and it is those same schools that re-discovered and extended the geometric structure of the Lots in what they call planetary pictures.

House Systems

The primary house system I use is whole sign.

Since we are working in this book with Lots that are measured from the Ascendant, the chart examples show the Ascendant/Descendant axis horizontal with the Ascendant at the far left. I use proportional house displays, so the location of the Midheaven on the wheel will vary.

I currently use both whole sign and quadrant house systems at the same time, and I like to compare the house placement in the two.

Quadrant house systems have the Ascendant as the start of the first house and the Midheaven as the start of the tenth house. All house systems have the Ascendant and Midheaven the same, and the different quadrant based systems vary as to placement of the intermediate houses between the main angles.

I currently use the Porphyry quadrant system. It appears to be one of the earliest and may go back to Ptolemy, and the mathematics are very simple and logical. I pay attention to house placement, but I do not give great importance to the exact degree of the intermediate house cusps. The single wheel examples in the book have the numbering of the whole sign houses around the outside rim, and the porphyry houses around the inside rim. In the bibliography I refer to the blog post where I discuss using two house systems.

All Solar Returns are drawn up using birth place as location.

SECTION TWO: EXAMPLES

Natal Charts - General Introduction

Given that the two Lots should be important integration points, I researched several charts that have a planet conjunct one or both of the main Lots. That conjunct planet should then be a main integrating factor that defines who the person is and how they act.

What I found strongly confirmed that is true, as we will see in the following examples.

I also found some charts where there are planets conjunct both Lots. In that case the effect should be exceptionally strong and distinct in defining the person.

For some of the charts in this section I will focus only on the importance of the Lots in the natal configuration. I have added transit periods by Jupiter or Saturn to a few of the examples here, to illustrate how those transits to the Lots can coincide with significant event periods in the person's life. Even where a Lot is already activated in the natal chart by a conjunct planet, the major transits can still mark periods of increased emphasis and activity.

Note that I am not doing a complete chart interpretation in these examples. I am focusing primarily on the aspects of the chart related to the Lots. In all of these examples I think it is clear that the Lots do add an important dimension of meaning.

In the second part of this section I chose the charts of four very successful and wealthy people. My purpose in analyzing those is to look at how we can see strength of support to a Lot. Given their exceptional good fortune, there should be evidence of that in one or both of the Lots.

Garry Kasparov

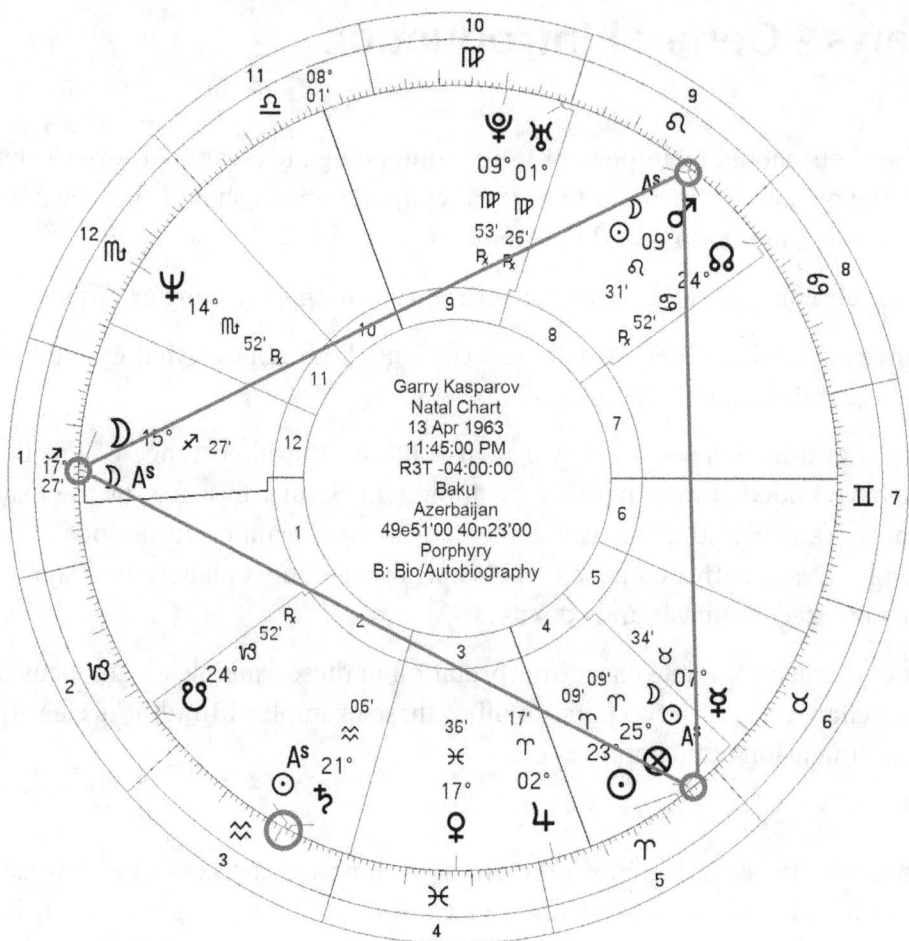

Garry Kasparov, April 13, 1963, 11:45 PM, Baku Azerbajian. Rodden Rating B.

Garry Kasparov was chess champion of the world from 1985 to 2000, and highest rated player in the world until his retirement in 2005. Kasparov was considered by some to be the greatest chess player in history. He was known for being forceful, arrogant, imperious and outspoken, a fierce competitor with a fiery temper.

Kasparov is also known for an event unique in chess history, his widely publicized loss to the IBM computer "Deep Blue" in 1997. After the loss he was furiously angry and accused the IBM programmers of cheating and helping the computer.

Currently, since leaving the world of professional chess, Kasparov is best known for his political activism and his opposition to what he calls the dictatorship of Vladimir Putin.

All of these characteristics are vividly mirrored in his chart, and with the two Lots.

This chart has a planet on each of the Lots. The Sun is conjunct the Lot of Fortune in Aries in the whole sign fifth house, and Mars is conjunct the Lot of Spirit in Leo in the ninth house by whole sign. By definition the two Lots make a direct midpoint to the Ascendant, and Kasparov has his Moon tightly conjunct the Ascendant in Sagittarius.

Planets conjunct the Lots define the person, and Kasparov is defined by the Sun and Mars in mutual reception in fire signs with the Sun in its exaltation, aimed at a Moon and Ascendant in the fire sign Sagittarius - arrogant, imperious, demanding, with a hot temper, fiercely competitive and fiercely independent.

The Ascendant and the two Lots are all in fire signs, which means they make a grand fire trine by sign.

Of the two Lot midpoints, the one for the Lot of Spirit is at 16 Sagittarius, tightly conjunct the Ascendant, which increases the focus there.

The other Lot midpoint, for Fortune, is at 21 Aquarius, and is tightly conjunct his Saturn in rulership in Aquarius. That Saturn makes a comfortable sextile to the Sun and Lot of Fortune on one side, and to the Moon and Ascendant on the other. Saturn is also opposite Mars by whole sign, so it adds another opposition axis to the structure. That strong Saturn adds structure and patience, ability to perform under pressure, and probably a great deal of internal pressure that he places on himself.

Mars in Leo opposite Saturn in Aquarius is also a very strong signature for opposition against any kind of restriction or oppression. This kind of aspect pattern is what modern astrology calls a kite, with the focus being on the Mars in Leo. ***This very powerful pattern has planets on both Lots and on both Lot midpoints.***

Transits to the Lots

In this section I want to look at the three of the most important events in Kasparov's professional life, and consider how they correlate with major transits to the Lots by Jupiter and Saturn.

Because Kasparov already has planets conjunct both Lots in the natal chart, the Lot patterns do not require a transit to be activated. However, from these examples, it does appear that a major transit to a Lot still does intensify its activity.

First World Championship Win

1984 through 1985 was the period when Kasparov engaged in the extended matches that concluded with his winning the title of chess world champion. ***In both 1984 and 1985 Saturn was transiting through Scorpio, square to Mars in Leo and Saturn in Aquarius.*** In traditional terms, Saturn was transiting in the stakes of Mars and Saturn.

In addition to that, ***in 1985, the year he first won the championship, Jupiter was transiting through Aquarius, another fixed sign, and the sign of his natal Saturn and the Lot midpoint.*** He won the championship when both Jupiter and Saturn together were in fixed signs, activating Mars and the Lot of Spirit, and Saturn was at the midpoint of Fortune. That is intense pressure and intense achievement.

This is a good example of how transits in the stakes to a Lot mark a period of intensified activity, and in this case, intensified achievement.

Loss to "Deep Blue" IBM Supercomputer

Transits to the Lots are eventful but not always fortunate. Probably the most famous event in his life was the loss in 1997 to Deep Blue, an IBM supercomputer, in a widely publicized match. This was a very public contest being closely watched by the whole world of chess, and by much of the computer world. (I am a computer professional with only a casual interest in chess and I was paying attention to the match.)

During this period Jupiter was transiting very near his natal Saturn, one of the Lot midpoints, and Saturn was transiting near his Sun and the Lot. ***Transiting Saturn was in Aries, the sign of Saturn's fall.*** Saturn in fall transiting the Sun in its exaltation is appropriate symbolism for this loss. It is also appropriate that Saturn transiting Sun in a Mars ruled sign should result with his being furiously angry about losing the match.

Looking at outer planets, Uranus was very near exactly opposite his natal Saturn and a Lot midpoint, so there is a double stress involving Saturn at this time. Modern astrologers associate Uranus with computers and technology, and that symbolism is apt here.

Linnares Tournament and Retirement from Chess

In 2005 Kasparov won his last major chess tournament in Linnares. It was shortly after the end of the tournament that he announced his retirement from professional chess, and his intention to enter politics in order to oppose Vladimir Putin and his oppressive regime. During this period Jupiter is transiting opposite the Sun from Libra, and Saturn is square the Sun from Cancer. The cardinal signs and his Sun and Lot of Fortune in Aries are triggered.

It is worth noting that this period of major transition, starting a new phase of his public life, coincided with a transit to a Lot in cardinal signs, which are associated with change and starting new activities.

Camille Paglia

This is the opening paragraph of the short biographical sketch of Camille Paglia at the astro.com astrology databank site. It is so much fun I want to quote from it here.

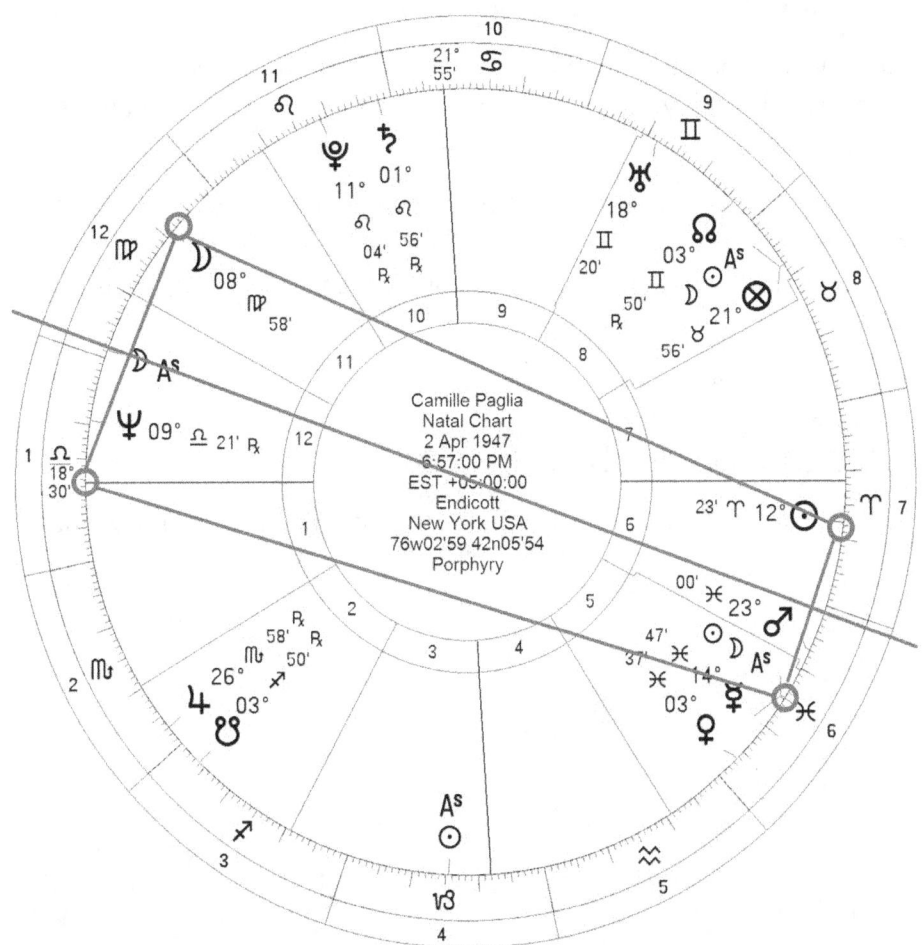

"American writer, scholar, iconoclast, speaker, academic, social critic and neo-pagan, known for-- among other things--her anti-feminist backlash. Said by some to have a Napoleon complex, she is one of the more colorful and controversial writers to come out of the '80s and '90s intelligentsia... She offers her thoughts on everything from pagan sexuality to Hillary Clinton to Gay Stalinism. With a rapier-sharp wit and tongue, she knows who's hip and who's hot on the campuses of America in the '70s to '90s. "Camille Paglia, April 2, 1947, 6:57 PM, Endicott, New York. Rodden Rating A.

I would describe her writing as coming from an alternate and libertarian, sex-positive style of feminism. She is definitely outside of the feminist mainstream and was, shall we say, not fondly regarded by Steinem, Friedan and other feminist leaders.

I want to start looking at Paglia's chart with the Lot of Spirit, shown in the diagram above. There are some interesting and powerful combinations here.

The Lot of Spirit is at 14 Pisces, and Mercury is very tightly conjunct. Paglia is best known as writer, teacher and commentator, so this fits. But what style of teacher and writer?

The midpoint of this Lot is at 28 Virgo/Pisces. Mercury is in Pisces, in the same sign as Venus, its exalted ruler. Paglia's writing does exalt Venus in many ways, and one of her main subject areas is sex in the arts and media.

Also in Pisces is Mars at 23 Pisces, within orb of conjunction of both Mercury and the Lot itself (9 degrees), and within orb of the Lot midpoint (5 degree orb).

Mars takes on additional importance by being in major mutual reception with Jupiter in Scorpio, which makes a close mutually applying trine with Mars. Jupiter also rules the Lot itself, and Mars rules Paglia's Sun in Aries.

Mars is also stronger in dignity than it looks at first glance. Mars has dignity by triplicity, term and face, all 3 of the minor dignities. In traditional astrology having two minor dignities is considered equal to one major dignity, so here Mars is as strong or stronger than being in his own rulership.

So we have Mercury plus Venus plus Mars plus Jupiter. Her writing is about art, and especially art as sexual expression. She is libertarian, pro sex, pro art, pro pornography, pro free expression of sex, and her writing has a sharp belligerent Mars like quality that angers many people. Her writing style and speaking style is sharp, staccato, pointed and edgy.

We mentioned that Mercury is close to its exalted ruler Venus. Venus is also Ascendant ruler.

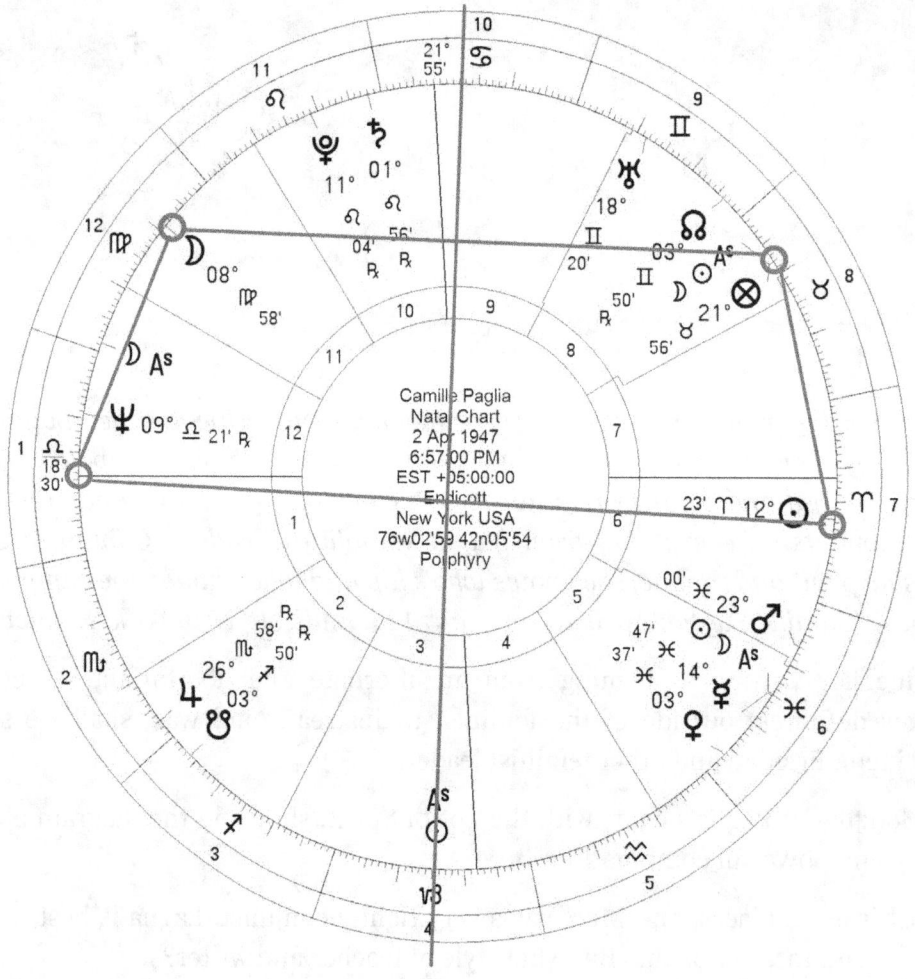

The Lot of Fortune has some interesting points. This Lot has an angular midpoint axis, close to the MC/IC axis. The Lot midpoint is at 15 Capricorn/Cancer, and the Midheaven is at 21 Capricorn 55.

Jupiter is opposite the Lot of Fortune, and Jupiter is also ruler of the other Lot, Spirit, and is also the exalted ruler of the Cancer Midheaven.

The Venus/Jupiter midpoint is 15 Cap 18, very near the Lot midpoint, so these two planets combine on the midpoint axis. Jupiter in Scorpio plus exalted Venus is apt symbolism for writing that exalts female sexuality, and Paglia is noted for pieces about 'hot' women that our culture has forgotten about.

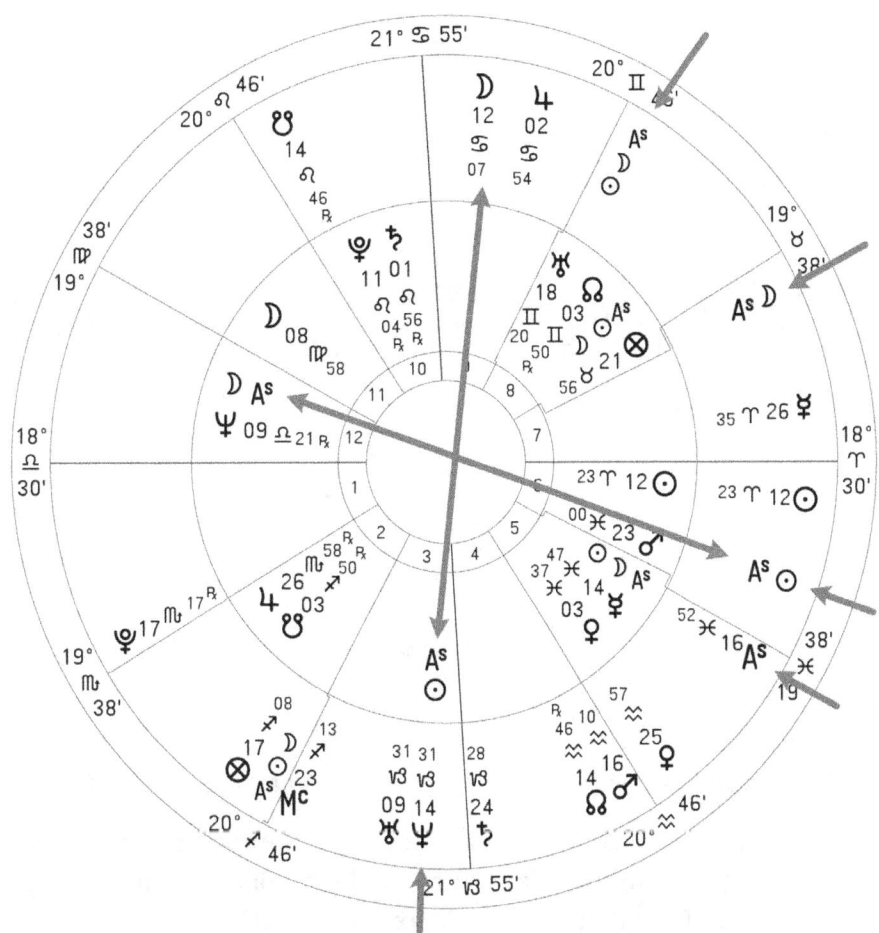

Inner: Camille Paglia natal. Outer: Solar Return 1990.

I want to consider the year that her career took off, and examine the Lots in the solar return. 1990 was the year that Paglia's best-selling first book *Sexual Personae* was published and her career went nova. The cross-connections between the Lots in the two charts are quite striking.

One of the two solar return Lot midpoints, the Moon/Ascendant midpoint, sits on top of Paglia's natal Lot of Fortune. The other solar return Lot midpoint is on the same axis as the natal Lot of Spirit midpoint axis.

The solar return Moon at 12 Cancer is closely opposite the Lot midpoint of Paglia's natal Lot of Fortune.

53

I want to look at another two important connections between the two charts with their frame of reference switched.

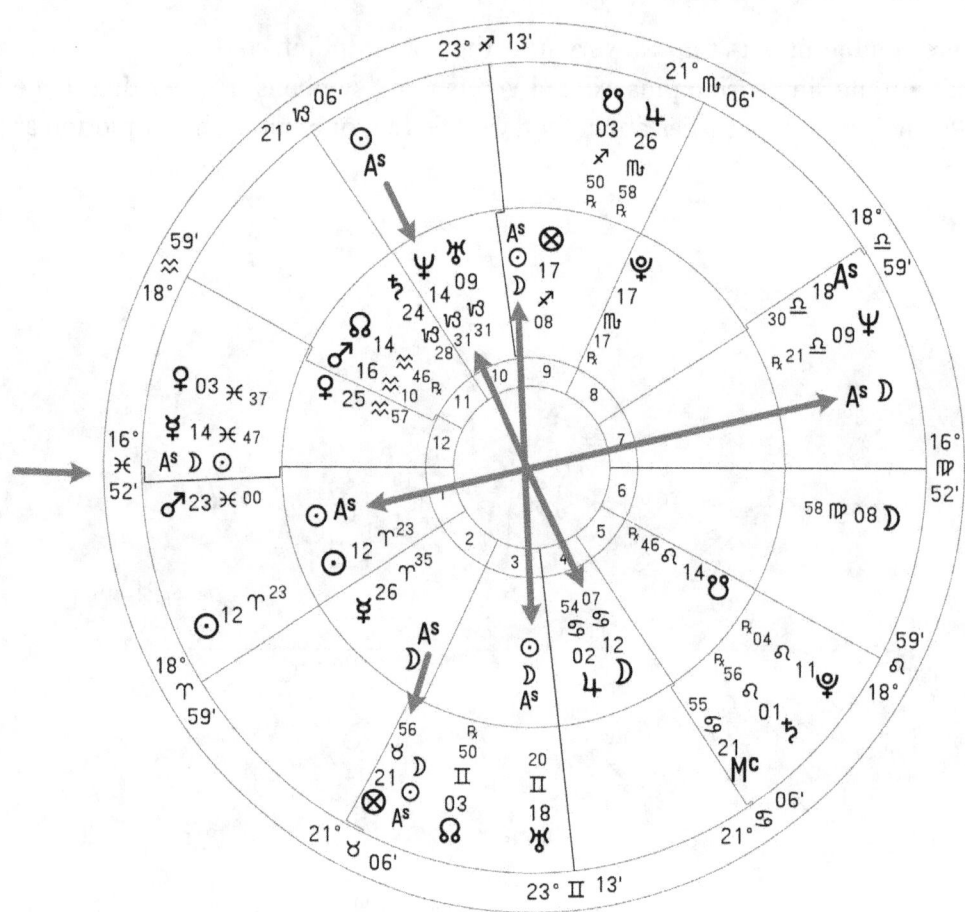

Inner: Camille Paglia Solar Return 1990. Outer: Paglia natal.

In this second chart diagram the two charts are switched, with the 1990 solar return on the inside, and Paglia's natal chart on the outside. In the solar return the Moon phase is an exact first quarter square, and this puts the 2 Lots of the SR right on the MC/IC axis of the SR.

Also note that the very strong Lot of Spirit in Pisces, flanked by Mars and Mercury, are sitting right on the Solar Return ascendant.

The amount of angular activation of Lots is quite striking in the solar return, which is very appropriate for a year that she was very active and publicly visible.

Albert Einstein

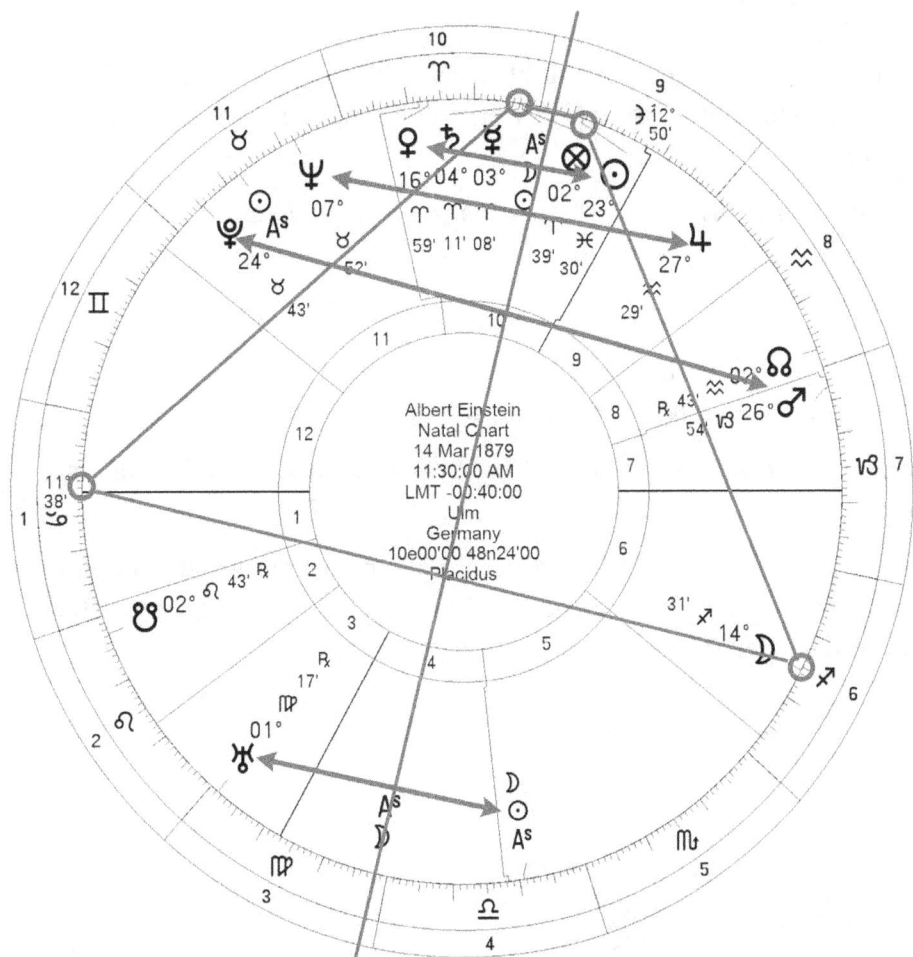

Albert Einstein, March 14, 1879, 11:30 AM, Ulm, Germany. Rodden Rating AA>

Albert Einstein is so well known that he is practically the archetype of the genius scientist, best known for his breakthrough formulations of the general and special theories of relativity.

I want to concentrate just on the natal pattern here. This is an interesting and unique chart because of the tight focus all in a single area. This pattern was not visible to me until I drew the shape of the Lot of Fortune.

Fortune in this chart is 2 Aries conjunct both Mercury and Saturn. The combination of Mercury and Saturn is a good metaphor for focused, detailed intellectual effort.

The Sun is at 23 Pisces, and the midpoint axis of this Lot is at 28 Pisces/Virgo. This means that the Sun and the Lot midpoint are conjunct in a 4 degree orb.

Once I saw that pattern I noticed that there are other pairs of planets, arranged on opposite sides of the Lot midpoint axis.

Going from top to bottom:

The Sun/Venus midpoint is 5 Aries 14, conjunct the Lot. Further, the Sun and Venus are in mutual reception by exaltation. Sun in Pisces is where Venus is exalted, and Venus in Aries where Sun is exalted. Sun and Venus in mutual exaltation is a good metaphor for a sense of harmony, beauty and proportion. The mutual reception works to strengthen both the Sun and Venus, and helps the planets work together well.

The Jupiter/Neptune midpoint is at 2 Aries 40, tightly conjunct the Lot of Fortune and near the Lot midpoint axis.

The Mars/Pluto midpoint is 25 Pisces 49, conjunct the Lot midpoint axis.

Finally, if we include the other Lot, the midpoint of Uranus and the Lot of Spirit is around 25 Virgo/Pisces. Again, this is conjunct the Sun/Ascendant midpoint axis.

All of the significant points in the chart line up in pairs around the Lot of Fortune and its midpoint axis.

Everything in the chart clusters around, and points at, the Mercury/Saturn conjunction. Those two planets in combination are very apt symbolism for the kind of one-pointed, focused and detailed scientific thinking and writing that makes Einstein distinctive.

Leonard Bernstein

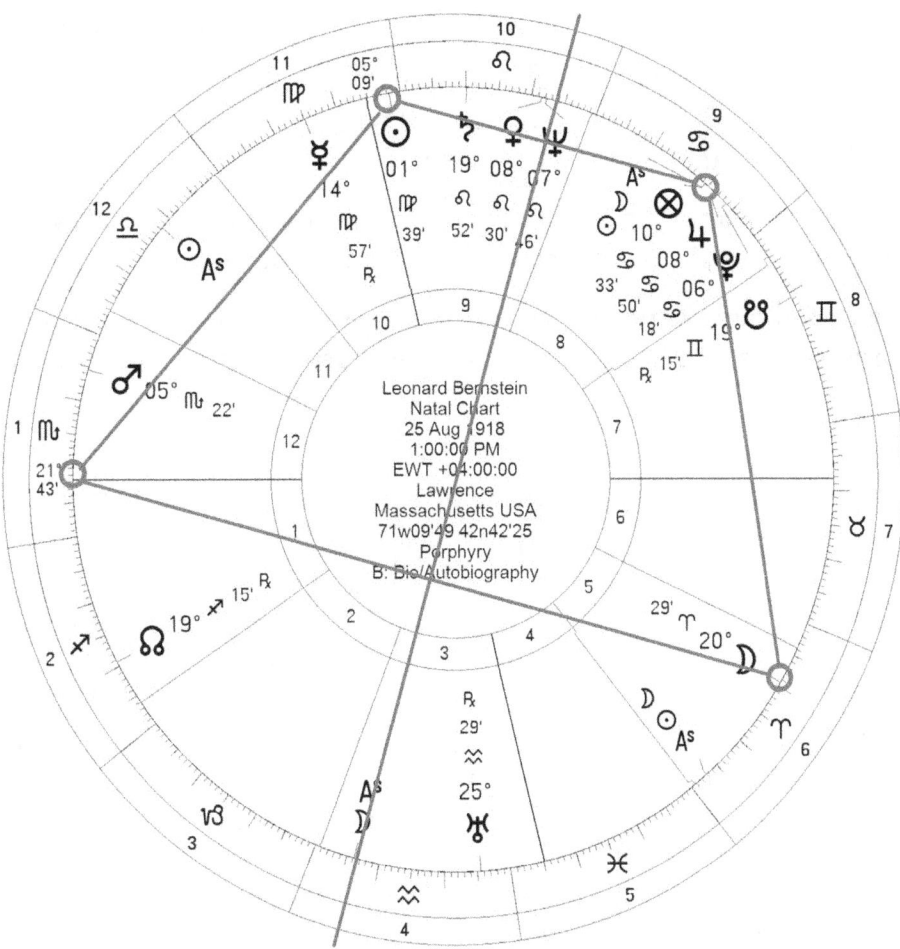

Louis Bernstein, August 25, 1918, Lawrence, MA. Rodden Rating B.

I was in grade school in New York City during the period that Leonard Bernstein was conductor of the New York Philharmonic, and I also remember his television concerts and young people's concerts. Bernstein was well known for being a showman. He was outgoing, flamboyant, romantic, expressive, and passionately dedicated to his art, and also warm and friendly. The music he loved, composers like Gustav Mahler and Beethoven, were larger than life, and so was he.

Looking at the chart as a whole, first note some propitious points, The Sun is conjunct the Midheaven in Virgo, and Mercury its ruler is also in Virgo in the quadrant tenth house. I mentioned that Bernstein was known for his young people's concerts, and his talks before the music to help make it accessible, so there was definitely a Mercury side to his public persona.

The Ascendant is Scorpio, and its ruler Mars is also in Scorpio above the Ascendant.

You would think that these two planets in rulership, Mercury and Mars, would dominate Bernstein and his chart.

Not so. The Lot structure pinpoints that.

57

Fortune is the dominant Lot in this chart, and I want to examine it here.

The Lot is at 10 degrees Cancer, and Jupiter is beautifully conjunct the Lot, in his exaltation. Jupiter in Cancer in exaltation describes the personality of Leonard Bernstein.

Note that Ascendant ruler Mars in Scorpio makes a very strong trine to Jupiter in Cancer. Mars plays a strong supporting role here, but I think we can argue that Jupiter conjunct the Lot is very much the dominant planet, and sets the tone for the whole chart.

The Lot midpoint is at 7 Aquarius / 7 Leo, and **the Lot midpoint forms a close conjunction to Venus and Neptune in Leo**, in the 10th by whole sign, 9th by quadrant.

Exalted Jupiter in Cancer, focused through Venus and Neptune in outgoing expressive Leo. Put those three planets together and you have a vivid description of what Bernstein's conducting style was like.

Jupiter is the defining planet in this chart. Jupiter in his exaltation describes Bernstein's personality very well, and it is the conjunction to the Lot of Fortune that makes Jupiter so important and definitive.

Clint Eastwood

This is another chart where the planet that defines Eastwood's personality is most clearly shown by a Lot. I will add some biographical information about Eastwood after we identify that planet.

We will also see that there is a strong interconnection between the two Lots here.

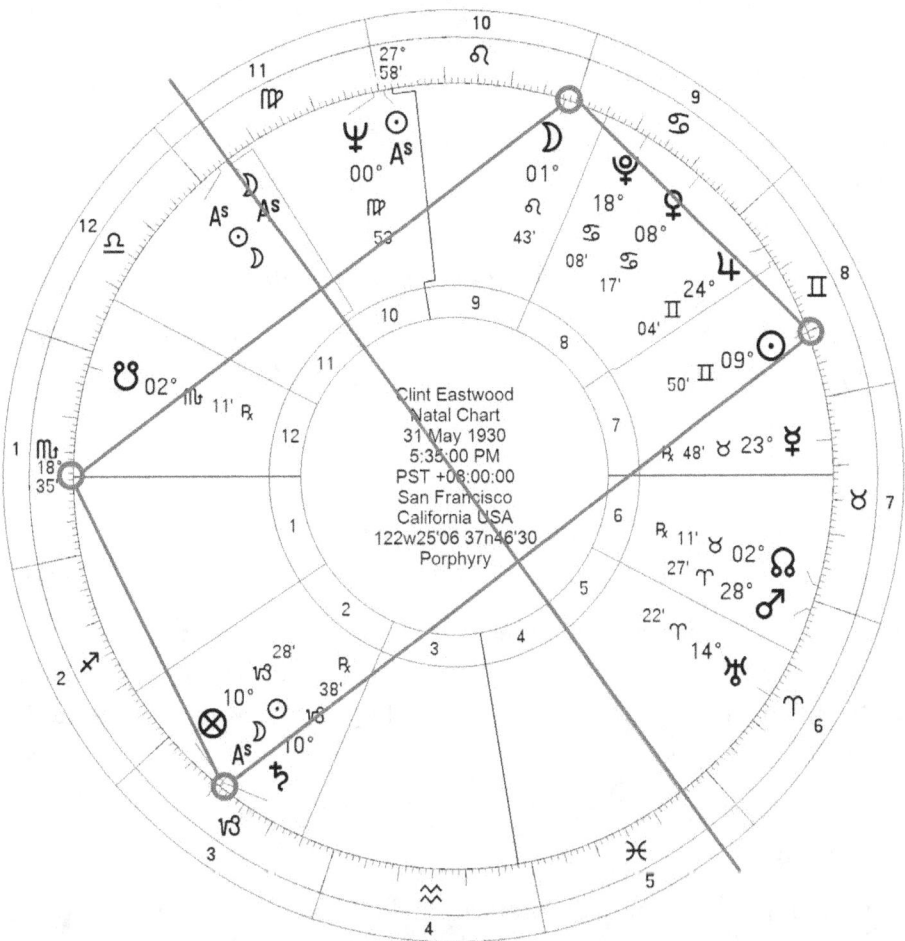

Clint Eastwood, Jr, May 31, 1930, 5:35 PM, San Francisco, CA. Rodden Rating AA.

The Lot of Fortune is tightly conjunct Saturn, within 10 minutes.

Saturn is in rulership in Capricorn and is retrograde. Saturn here is not angular, and it has no dignity at either angle. The tight conjunction to the Lot of Fortune is the main factor that points out the defining importance of this planet.

Before we look at anything further about this Lot, and its relation to the Lot of Spirit, I want to quote a couple of phrases out of the short biographical sketch at the astro.com site. Try to guess which planet dominates these descriptions.

> *"American actor in tough-guy roles, a rugged 6'4" star with a face that has become craggier every year."*
>
> *"A Depression kid, Eastwood's dad was constantly looking for work, and he grew up learning that 'nothing comes from nothing, you've got to work for what you get.' ... He grew up introverted and self-reliant, qualities that have been a repeated theme in his film roles."*
>
> *"He played handsome Rowdy Yates in the popular TV series 'Rawhide' until 1966 and then graduated first to stony-faced macho roles in westerns and then to detective films as his famous character 'Dirty Harry.'"*
>
> *"Eastwood becomes silent when asked about his active private life."*
>
> *"When Leslie Stahl asked him in a February 2005 interview about retirement, he said, 'I'm just never going to say never. Or never say anything. That's the main thing. It's just — just keep my big mouth shut.'"*

Another distinctive feature of this chart that helps to tie it together is the midpoint of Fortune in late Virgo, tightly conjunct the Lot of Spirit. This means that the action of each Lot triggers the other.

Along with the importance of Saturn, the planet Mars is also in its rulership in Aries, and Mars is the Lord of the Scorpio Ascendant from Aries in the sixth house. There is indeed a strong martial component to Eastwood, his personality and his political opinions. Mars is important here, but Saturn dominates.

The chart as a whole does describe Clint Eastwood and his long-lived success, and the defining planet is Saturn conjunct Fortune.

It is worth examining the Lot of Spirit also, since in this chart the two Lot patterns tie together so closely.

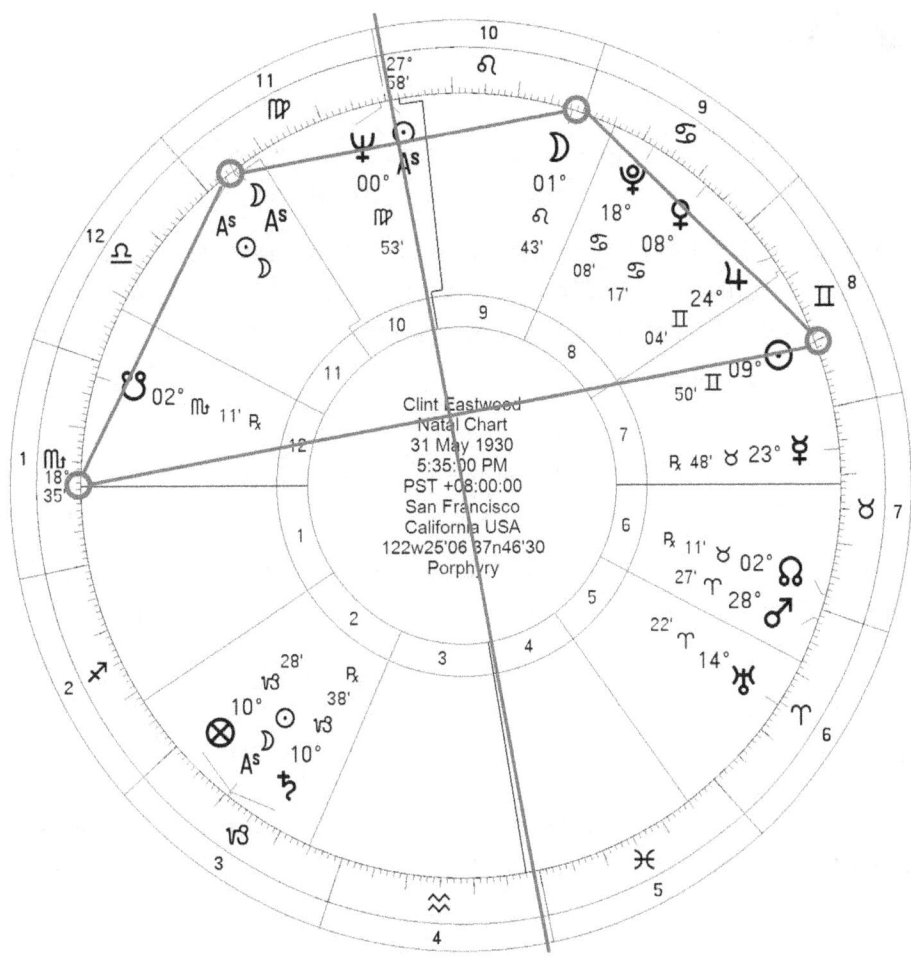

We mentioned that the Lot of Spirit in Virgo is tightly conjunct the midpoint of Fortune. The midpoint of Spirit is dead on Neptune, and also dead on the Midheaven.

We noted that Eastwood has an extreme sense of privacy, which is characteristic of a dominant Saturn. This also makes Neptune on the Midheaven more important. Neptune very near an angle is common in charts of media and entertainment figures, since we see them through the lens of the fictional characters they create. We see Eastwood the man only through the fictional characters he portrays, which increases the hidden-ness and privacy of the strong Saturn.

That is worth emphasizing: ***the midpoint of Fortune points directly to Spirit, and the midpoint of Spirit points directly at the Midheaven.***

This is an interesting and unique interweaving of the two Lots in this chart. We have Fortune conjunct Saturn, with the Fortune midpoint axis aimed at Spirit, and the Spirit midpoint axis aimed at Neptune and the Midheaven.

Fortune and Wealth

In the first part of this natal section I focused on charts that have one or more planets on the Lots, to show how very important that is to understanding a person's character.

In this next group of charts I am looking at four of the most wealthy, famous and successful business people in our recent era - Bill Gates, Steve Jobs, Warren Buffet, and Donald Trump. None of these people have a planet conjunct a Lot, yet all are extremely fortunate in one of the ways we normally think of fortune - monetary wealth.

I picked out these charts as subjects for the book before I did any analysis of them. If the Lots are related to general good or bad fortune, then we should see evidence of that in these charts. The Lots should show strong placement and support.

In order to make sense of the Lots in these charts, I needed to examine the overall chart pattern, and where the Lots fit within that, and take the analysis to the point that the pattern is strong and conclusive.

Let's see what shows up.

Note: Unfortunately there do not seem to be reliable birth times available for Mark Zuckerberg and Jeff Bezos, or I would have added them to this section.

Bill Gates

By any measure Bill Gates is extremely blessed by fortune. He is one of the wealthiest and most influential men in the world, co-founder of Microsoft which revolutionized the computer world, founder of the Bill and Melinda Gates foundation with his long time partner. We should be able to see support or strong configuration to one or both of the Lots here. In this chart we will see that the strength of the configuration includes how the Lots interact with the overall aspect pattern of the chart.

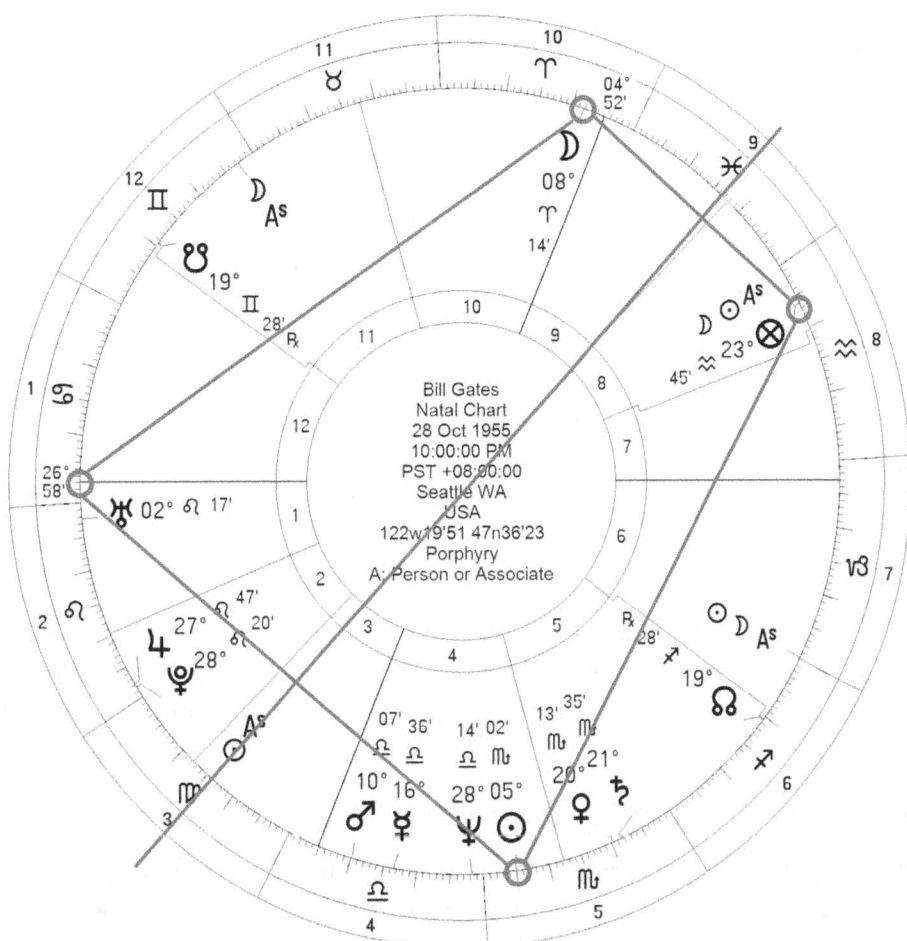

William Henry Gates III, October 28, 1955, 10 PM, Seattle, WA. Rodden Rating A.

First note that both Lots are ruled by Saturn. The Lot of Spirit is at 0 Capricorn, and Fortune is at 23 Aquarius. Saturn does not look particularly strong. It is peregrine at 21 Scorpio and is loosely conjunct Venus which is in detriment.

Both planets, Saturn and Venus, are ruled by a tightly angular Mars, in detriment in Libra very near the IC, and ruling the Midheaven. Mars is very important in this chart, as it is one of three angular planets, along with the Moon on the MC and Uranus on the Ascendant. Saturn is much stronger and more important than it looks at first glance here. We will see that in the aspect pattern shown in the next diagram.

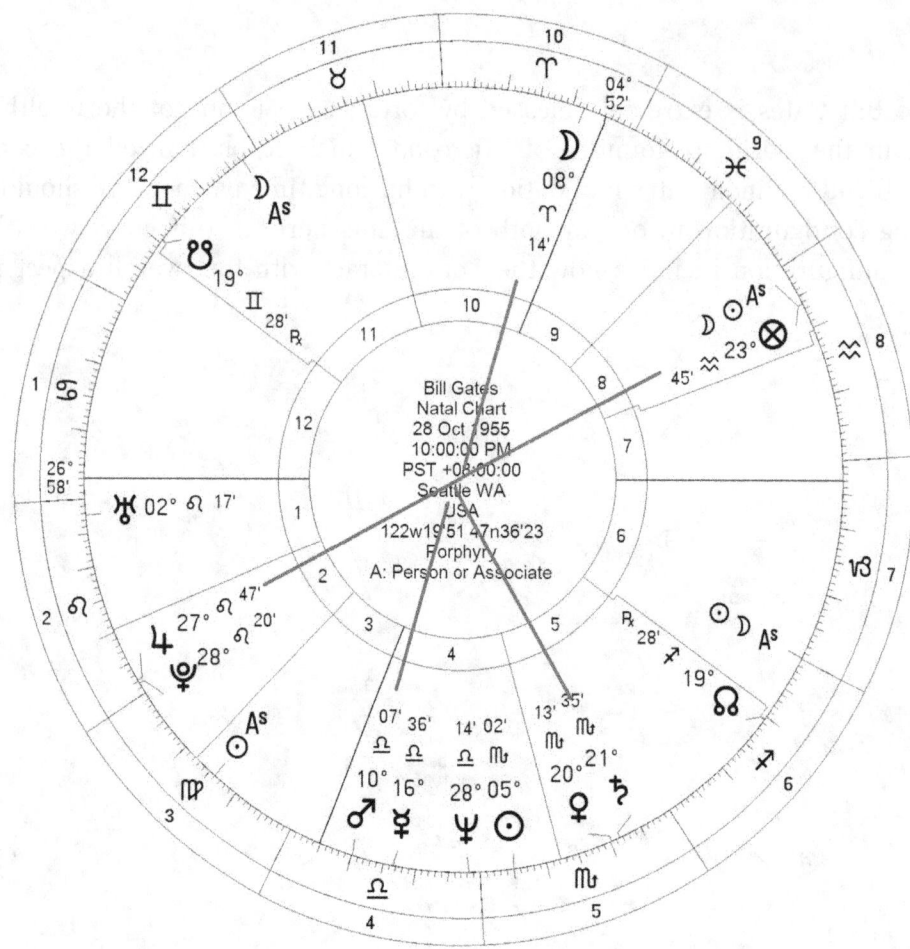

We mentioned that traditionally planets in square and opposition to the Lots have a strong affect on the Lots. Saturn and Venus are tightly square, and are also square Jupiter and Pluto in the second house. These four planets which are in the stakes with the Lot of Fortune are part of the support for that Lot.

There is an important connection here between these four planets and the Mars/Moon opposition.

Mars is the dominant planet in this chart. It is tightly angular and rules both the Midheaven and the Moon on the Midheaven, while the Moon in turn rules the Ascendant. And, very important, **Mars has a strong major mutual reception with both Saturn and Venus** which are conjunct in Scorpio. Mars connects by mutual reception with the planets in the stakes to the Lot.

Looking more closely, we find that Mars makes a tight 3/8 or sesquiquadrate aspect, within a 2 degree orb, to the Lot of Fortune itself. This tight harmonic 8 aspect ties Mars to the support for that Lot. Also note that, by dignity, the Lot of Fortune is in the minor dignity of the terms of Mars. The dignity of terms affects how things are actually implemented, so Mars affects how the Lot of Fortune works out. Mars is connected to Fortune by aspect and by dignity.

Mars is also important to consider with the Lot of Spirit, which is pictured in the next diagram.

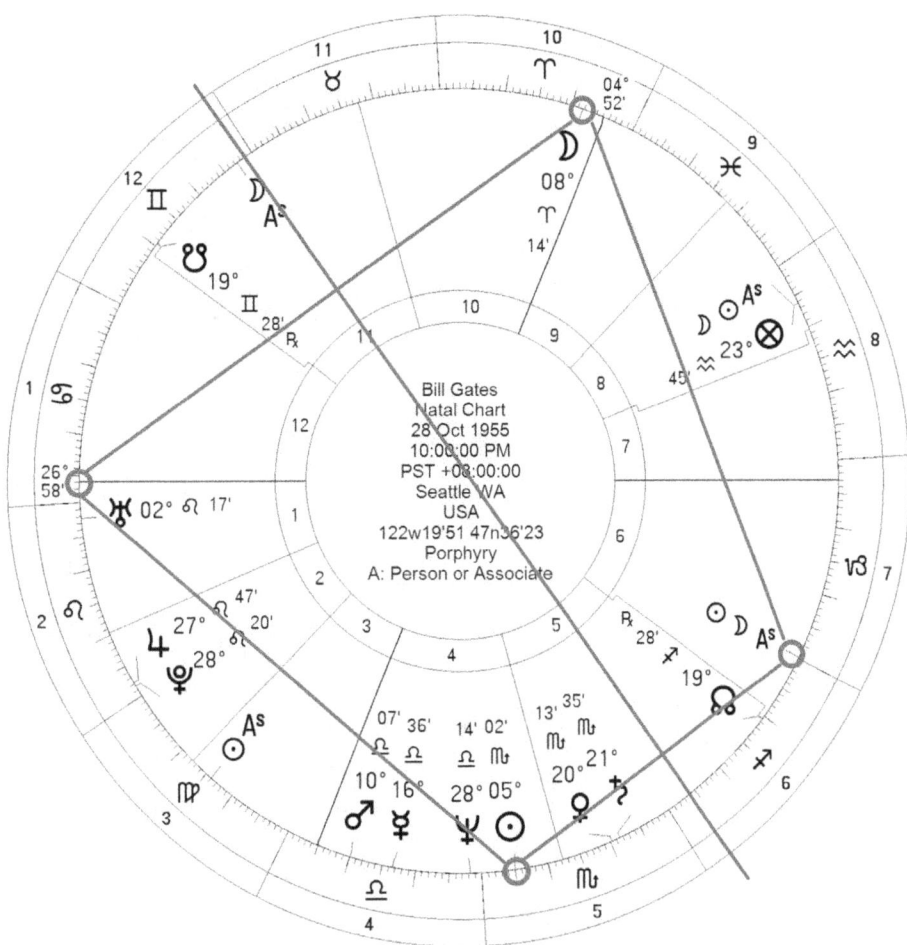

The Lot of Spirit is at 0 Capricorn, a cardinal sign where Saturn is strong as ruler, and Mars has a strong influence here sinced the lot is in the exaltation and triplicityof Mars. In the cardinal signs the Lot is supported by Mars, by Mercury, and by the Moon.

Both Lots have multiple planets in the stakes with them, and planets in the stakes intensify how a Lot expresses.

We see that Mars is an important planet for both of the Lots. We have the tight 3/8 aspect to Fortune, and we have Mars strong by dignity at Spirit, and square Spirit by sign. Combine this with Mars being angular and ruling the Midheaven, and it is clear that Mars is the dominant planet in the chart.

We mentioned the connection of Mars and Saturn by mutual reception. There is another strong pattern that ties these two planets together, as we see in the next diagram.

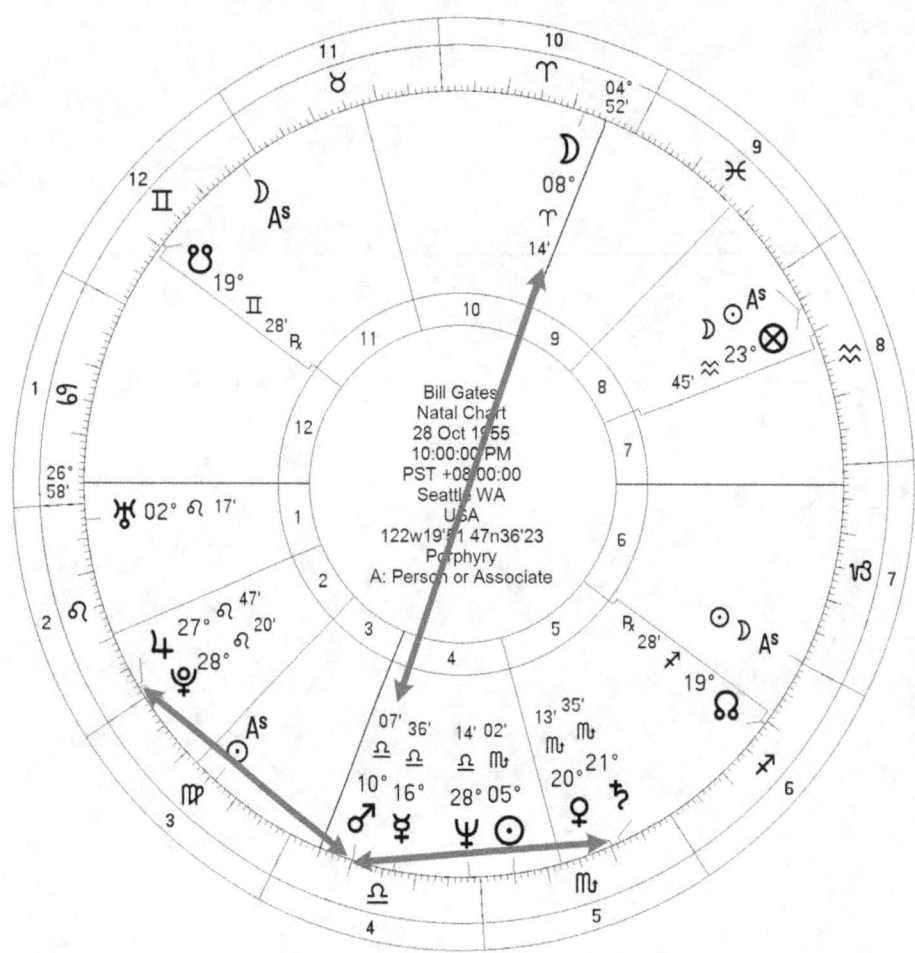

Note in the above diagram that Mars is right on the midpoint between Jupiter-Pluto on one side and Venus-Saturn on the other. All five planets are combined in this configuration, and Mars on the angle is the focus of action. If you mix these 5 planets together with the focus on Mars you get a very good description of Bill Gates, who is very competitive, a fanatically hard worker, visionary, strongly expansive. With Jupiter and Pluto in the second house opposite Fortune, Gates is also extremely wealthy. Both Jupiter and Pluto have a connection with wealth.

There is a final tie-in with Mars and the Lots that involves primary directions.

We mentioned the strong mutual reception between Mars and both Saturn and Venus, and that Saturn is the ruler of the two Lots. Mars is averse those two planets, making no aspect. ***The potential in that Mars-Saturn mutual reception came to fruition during the period that Mars moved into Scorpio by primary direction*** and was then in the same sign with Saturn and Venus, and square to the Lot of Fortune. During that period, in the middle 1970's, Bill Gates founded Microsoft while he was still in college. The primary direction of Mars to Saturn and Venus in Scorpio marks when the fixed sign support for the Lot of Fortune was fully triggered.

Steve Jobs

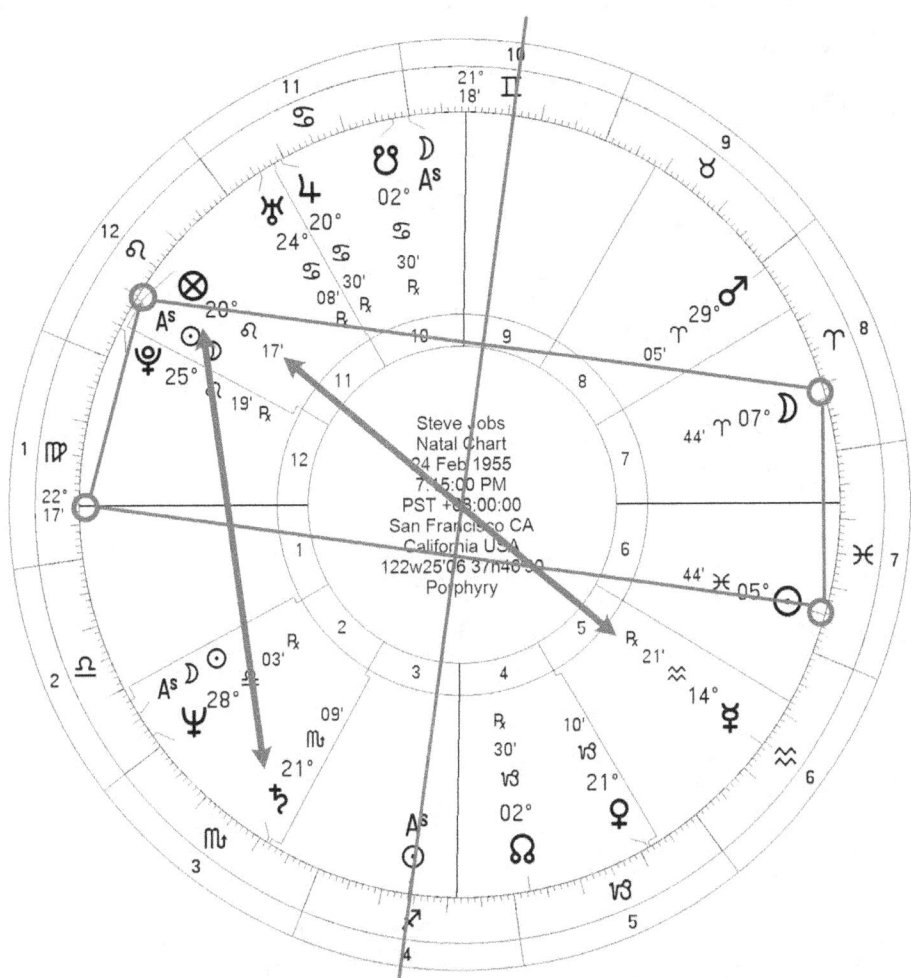

Steve Jobs, Feb 24, 1955, 7:15 PM, San Francisco, CA. Rodden Rating AA.

Steve Jobs is the co-founder of Apple, the pioneer tech inventor who gave us the Macintosh computer, the IPod, ITunes, and the Iphone. He was one of the wealthiest people in the world, known for being brilliant, eccentric and fanatic in his convictions.

In this analysis I am concentrating only on the chart patterns relative to the two Lots, to see if we can find the kind of strength and support we would expect in the chart of a man who was this successful and influential.

First note that Jobs has outer planets conjunct both of the Lots. Pluto is conjunct Fortune and Neptune is conjunct Spirit. In modern astrology this can represent a visionary who had power issues and who completely transformed the culture. Pluto can also be associated with wealth and power. I hesitate placing too much emphasis on the outer planets, so I am just tentatively exploring the symbolism here. I think the overall pattern of the chart stands up without undue emphasis on those two planets.

The diagram above shows the pattern of the Lot of Fortune. Note that the Lot midpoint is strongly angular along the MC/IC axis. Any activation of the Lot would then strongly express professionally in the public arena.

There are two planets strongly configured to Fortune in the fixed sign stakes of Fortune. Mercury in Aquarius is opposite Fortune, and Saturn in Scorpio is square to Fortune. Mercury is important in the chart as ruler of the two angles.

The next diagram is of the Lot of Spirit, and we will see more strong features.

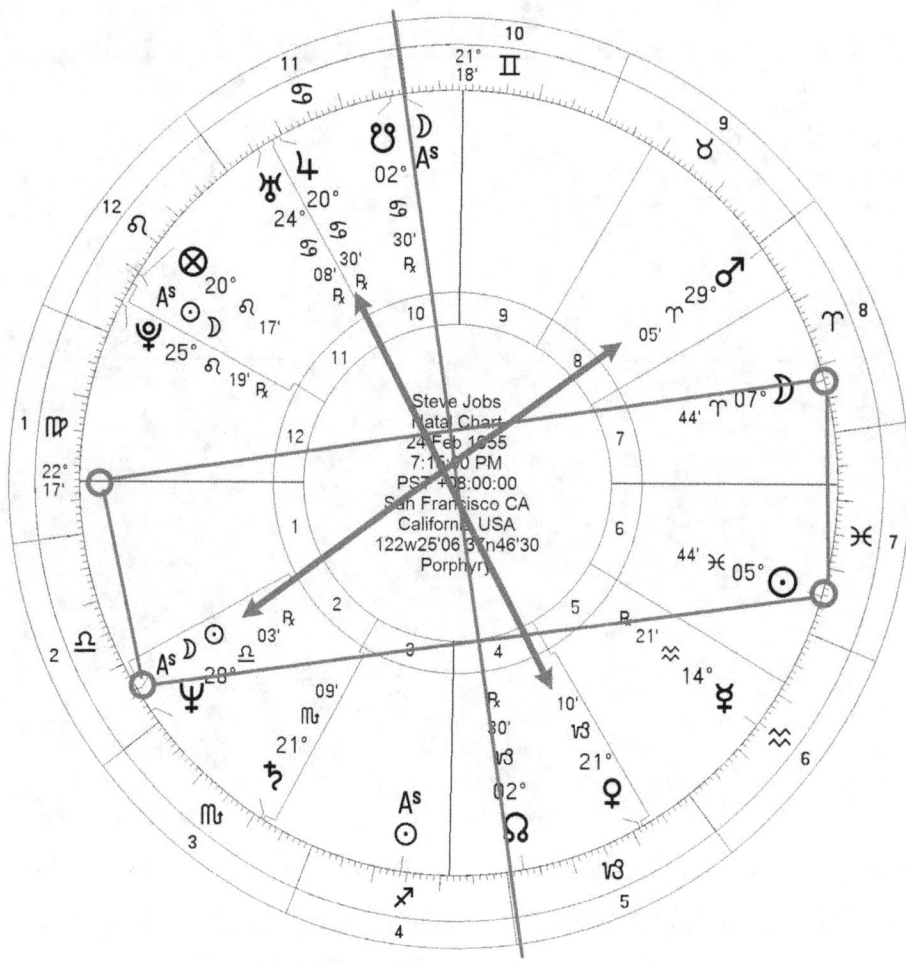

Note that the midpoint axis of this Lot is also strongly angular, falling within 10 degrees of the MC/IC axis.

The Lot of Spirit falls in the second house at 24 Libra, and is conjunct Neptune as we noted. Spirit is strongly supported by planets in the stakes of this cardinal sign. It is opposite to Mars in rulership in Aries, square to exalted Jupiter in Cancer which is conjunct Uranus, and also square to the Lot ruler Venus in Capricorn.

Both Lots are strongly supported by planets in the stakes, both Lot midpoint axes are angular, and both Lots tie into the overall strengths of the chart.

Transits to Lots

This a list of the transit periods of Saturn in square to the two Lots, and what was going on with Jobs during those periods. Some of these periods are more important than others, and most of them are suggestive. Remember that the Saturn transit through a sign takes over two years, and the entire period can be significant.

I am listing the transits to Spirit first. In general they seem to be more important than the transits to Fortune.

Saturn transits to Lot of Spirit

In mid 1975 we have Saturn square Spirit. During this period Jobs and Wozniak were working together, attending home brew computer club meetings, and planning their own computer. Jobs and Wozniak formed Apple in April 1976, at the tail end of this period.

1982 Saturn is conjunct Spirit, and in this period Apple revenue hit 1 billion for the first time.

In 1990 and 1991 Saturn is square Spirit. 1991 was the year Apple and IBM announced an alliance.

1998 Saturn is opposition Spirit. After being out of the company for awhile, Jobs is back as Apple CEO. Apple returns to profitability after several bad years.

2003 Saturn is square Spirit. In this period Jobs starts iTunes, 2004 pancreatic cancer surgery, 2005 expands iPod line. This is definitely a strong and expanding period for Apple and for Jobs.

2011-2012 Saturn is conjunct Spirit. This is the period that Jobs resigned, and died shortly after.

Saturn transits to Lot of Fortune

In 1977 Saturn is conjunct Fortune. Apple incorporated in this period, so this transit is particularly noteworthy.

1984 Saturn is square Fortune. The iconic 1984 Macintosh commercial appeared during the Superbowl in this period

In 1993 we have Saturn opposition Fortune. During this period Jobs was out of Apple, and this was a bad year for the company. I would not call this transit particularly significant at least in professional terms.

2000, Saturn square Fortune, Jobs is back at CEO at Apple.

2006-2007 Saturn is conjunct Fortune. In 2006 Disney bought Pixar, an animation company Jobs co-founded. 2007 was first smartphone.

I want to conclude this section with a diagram that shows the primary directions of Mars during a critical period of the development of Apple.

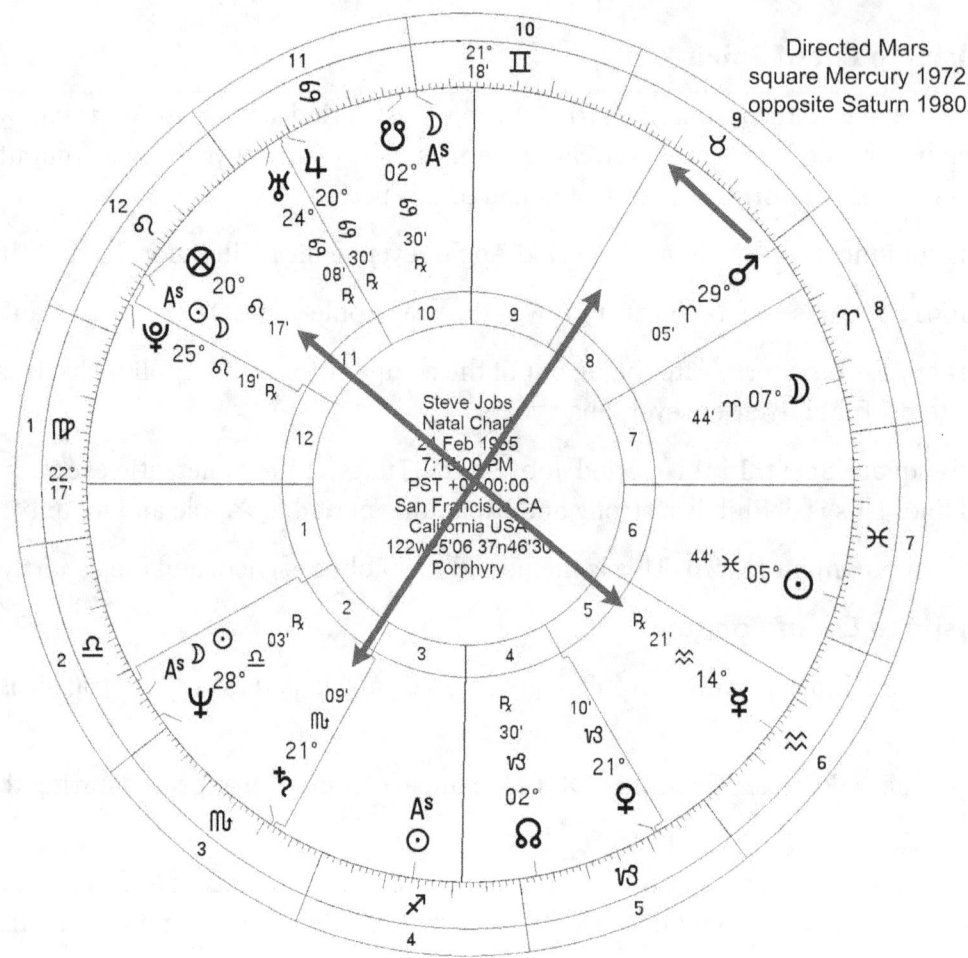

We already mentioned the strong configuration formed by the Lot of Fortune in Taurus opposite Mercury and square to Saturn.

The primary directions of Mars moved into Taurus to complete the cross with Mercury, Saturn and the Lot. Mars directed to square Mercury in 1972 and to opposition Saturn in 1980, strongly aspecting the cross during that whole time frame. The period of that direction, 1972 to 1980, were the critical years in the founding of Apple. It spans the time of Jobs entering college, then founding Apple, all the way to perfecting the opposition to Saturn at the Initial Public Offering of Apple stock in 1980.

Warren Buffett

Warren Buffett is well known for a single thing, being very, very wealthy, very focused on making money, and very, very good at it. Analyzing this chart I kept noticing small things, each somewhat important, and those small things kept adding up, building into a very coherent chart pattern.

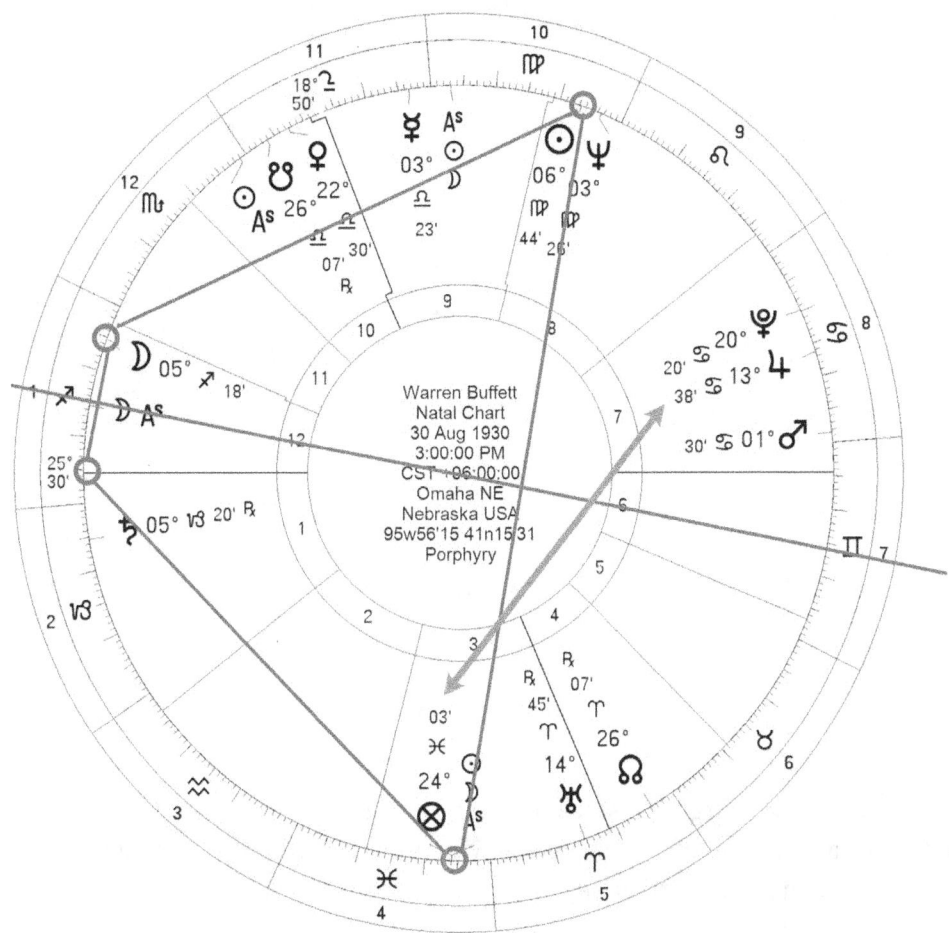

Warren Edward Buffett, August 30, 1930, 3 PM, Omaha, NE. Rodden Rating A.

Starting with the Lot of Fortune, the Lot itself is at 24 Pisces, a mutable sign, and the Lot midpoint is at 15 Sag/Gemini, in the same signs as the Ascendant and Descendant, so the midpoint is loosely angular. The Lot, Lot midpoint, and angles are all in mutable signs.

The ruler of the Lot, Jupiter, is very strong, in exaltation in Cancer, and Jupiter makes a comfortable trine by sign to the Lot. Jupiter is angular and very strong in the seventh house, and note that Buffett's money making strategy often involves close partnerships with others.

The exalted ruler of the Lot, Venus, is very strong, in her rulership in Libra and tightly conjunct the Midheaven.

So both the Fortune sign ruler and exalted ruler are strong, well dignified and angular. Both Jupiter and Venus are benefics and fortunate. The midpoint rulers Jupiter and Mercury are strong and dignified.

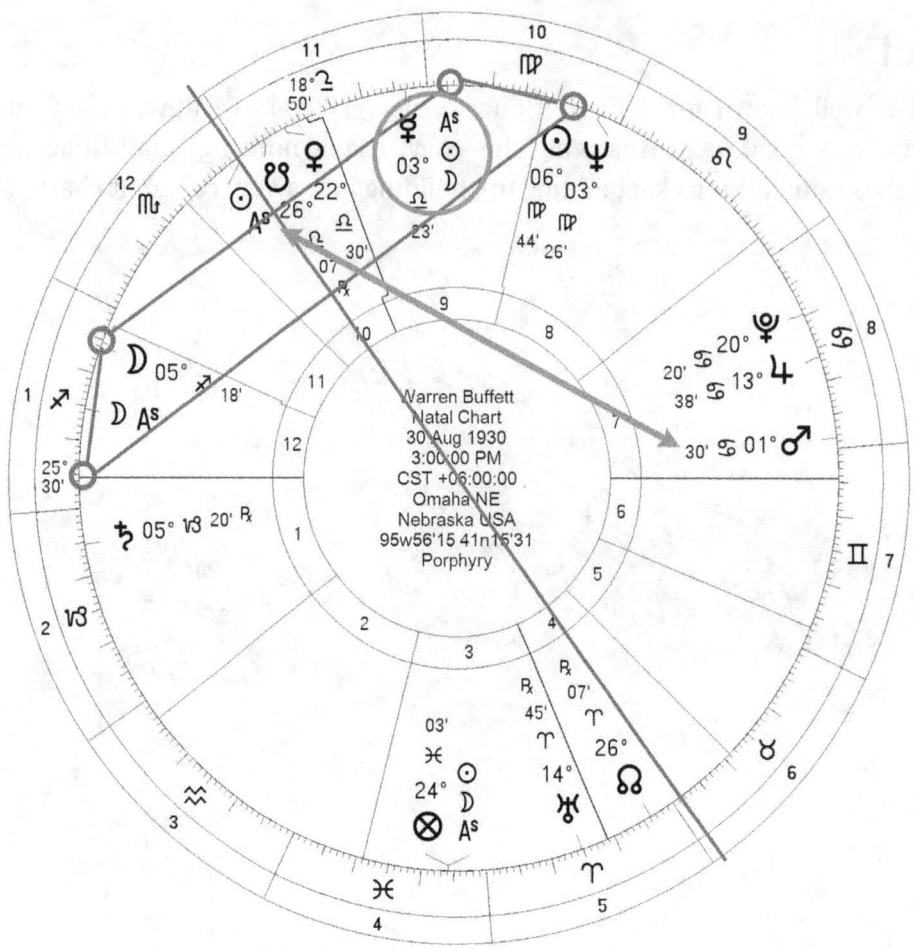

The other Lot, Spirit, is at 27 Virgo, loosely conjunct its ruler Mercury which is at 3 Libra. Mercury is stronger than it looks at first glance. Along with having triplicity dignity in an air sign, it is in the same sign Libra as its ruler Venus, and derives support from its ruler.

The Lot midpoint is at 1 degree Scorpio/Taurus, around 12 degrees from the Midheaven and in a different sign, so very loosely angular. The ruler of the Scorpio midpoint is Mars, very angular in the seventh house. Mars in Cancer is in fall, but Mars has the minor dignities of triplicity and term, and also gains support by being in the same sign as its exalted ruler Jupiter.

The other Lot midpoint at 1 Taurus has its ruler Venus strong, angular and in rulership.

This is starting to add up.

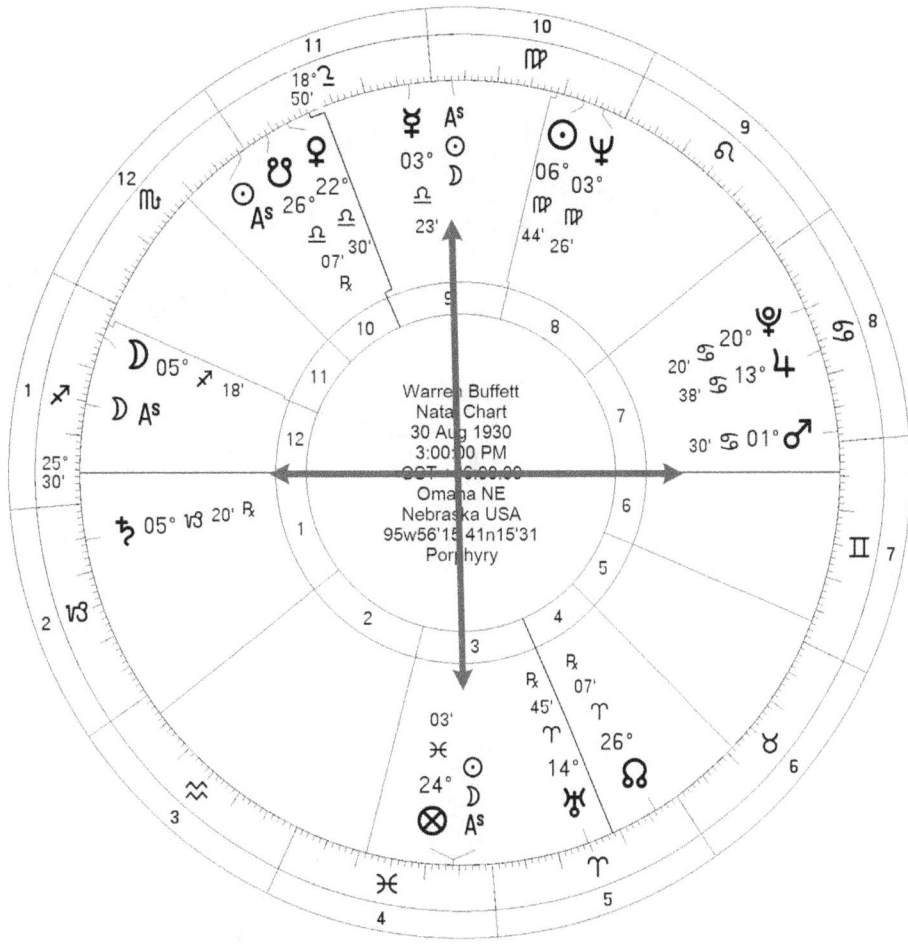

Buffett's lunar phase is very nearly exact first quarter, and this puts the two Lots tightly opposite each other, and tightly square to the Ascendant/Descendant axis. This means that both Lots are tightly angular by sign and aspect.

This cross is very late in mutable signs. An interesting interaction happens in this chart when you look at the numerous planets very early in cardinal signs.

The Lot of Spirit is conjunct its ruler Mercury, and Mercury at 3 Libra is in a tight square with both Mars and Saturn. Mercury is tightly tied to the majority of strong cardinal planets in this chart.

There is another strong aspect pattern involving the cardinal planets, which is illustrated by this next chart.

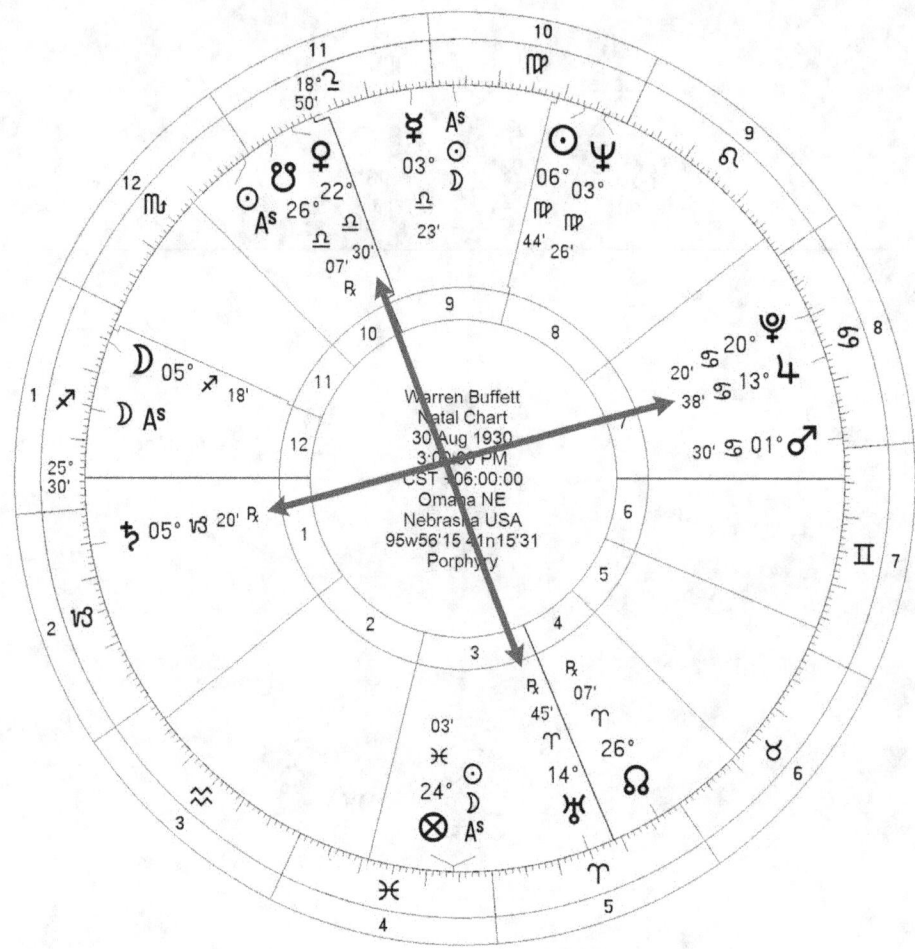

The strongest action is in the cardinal signs of this chart. You have Saturn in rulership in Capricorn, Uranus, Mars, Jupiter in exaltation, Pluto, Mercury in rulership, and Venus in rulership. There is a loose grand cross here that ties together all of these planets. One of them, Mercury, overlaps the opposition between the Lots by its being in conjunction with the Lot of Spirit. Mercury serves to tie the strong early cardinal sign planets in with the two Lots late in mutable signs.

At this point in the analysis I was struck by the fact that quite a few planets are in the early degrees of cardinal signs. An interesting pattern appears when you look at the aspects between them.

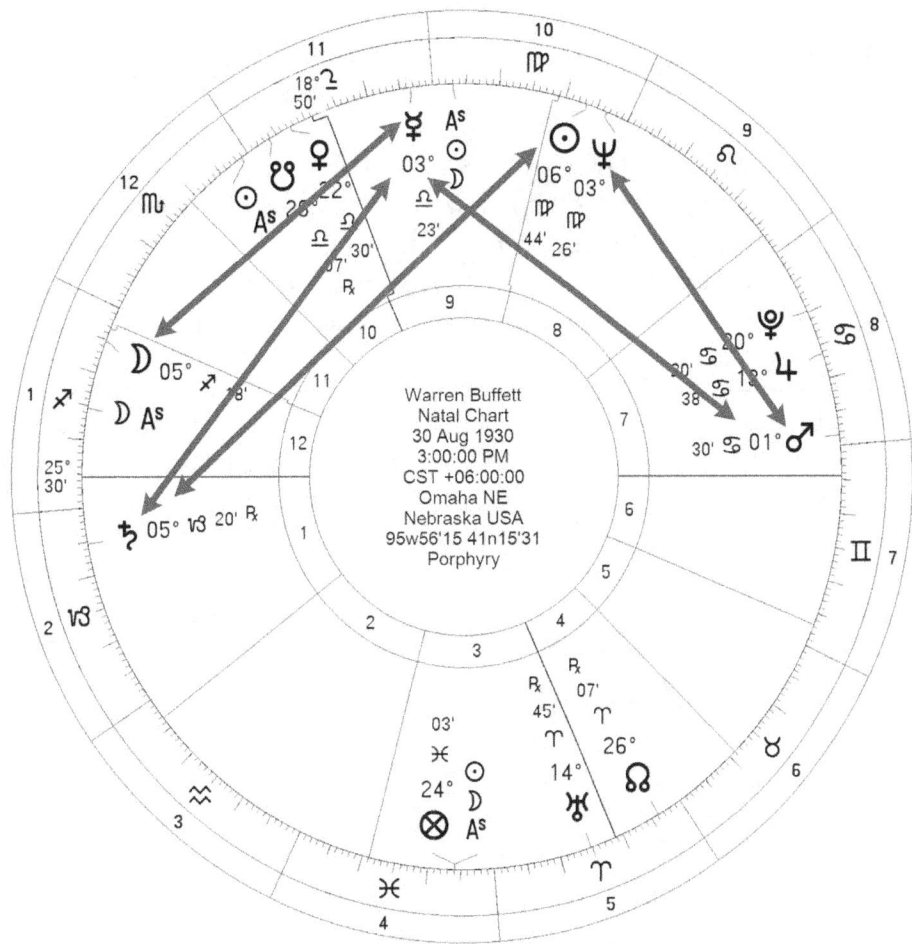

Saturn is square Mercury; the Moon is sextile Mercury; Mars is square Mercury; Saturn is trine the Sun and Neptune; Mars is sextile the Sun and Neptune.

Most of these planets have tight degree aspects to each other, and most of those aspects converge up at the top of the chart at Mercury. Mercury is the planet that rules commerce and exchange of money, and Mercury rules and is conjunct the Lot of Spirit.

I encourage you to go back through this section and watch all of these points build on each other, and the tightly knit final pattern that it creates. It is quite beautiful.

Donald Trump

To say that Donald Trump inspires strong reactions and opinions is like saying that fire gets a little hot sometimes. On the one extreme are those who view him as a strong outspoken leader, determined to drain the swamp and Make America Great Again. On the other extreme are those who react with rage and hatred and view him as a combination of Hitler, Antichrist and Bozo the Clown. (This is being written in late 2018, in the middle of Trump's first term as President of the United States.)

I don't want to take sides in the political war, so please do not assume that this chapter is taking one or other side in that debate. Here I want to look at Donald Trump, the very wealthy businessman who has been very fortunate by pretty much any standard. I want to look at the Lots in Trump's chart with that in mind. He is an interesting and vivid man, and this is an interesting and vivid chart.

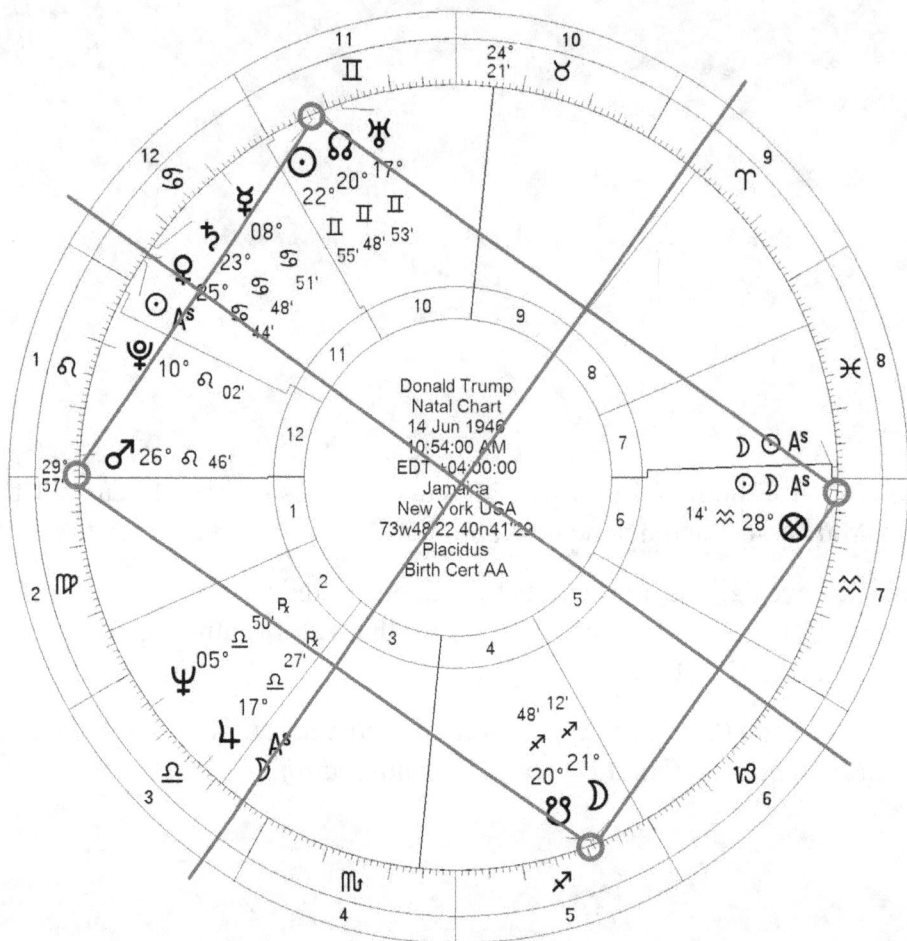

Donald John Trump, June 14, 1946, 10:54 AM, Jamaica, New York. Rodden Rating AA.

Trump was born very near a full moon; in fact he was born very near an eclipse. This puts the two Lots very nearly conjunct on either side of his Descendant, and makes the two Lot structures almost identical, in the shape of a rectangle, with the two midpoint axes at right angles to each other.

76

Mars is right on his Ascendant, the out of sect outspoken malefic in Leo, the man who speaks his mind bluntly and sometimes crudely.

The Sun is on the North Node, which magnifies it, and is conjunct Uranus. This is Trump as surprising, unpredictable, individualistic, sometimes erratic, someone who shakes things up.

The pattern of the Lot midpoints is very important and significant here. One of them is at 25 Cancer, tightly conjunct Venus and Saturn. The other Lot midpoint is at 25 Libra, tight square, and that is loosely conjunct Jupiter in Libra.

Jupiter is the key to the whole chart.

The chart shows Jupiter retrograde, but actually it is almost exactly right at its second station, about to turn direct, which greatly amplifies its effect and importance.

Consider the interaction between Jupiter on one hand, and Venus and Saturn on the other. ***Jupiter is in mutual mixed reception by rulership and exaltation with Venus, and in mixed reception by exaltation with Saturn.***

Those are the 3 planets on the Lot midpoints, the axes of action of the Lot structures, and those planets sit on either side of the Ascendant at about equal distance, focused right at the Ascendant and Mars.

That is a potent combination. You have a strongly emphasized Jupiter, working in tight coordination with Venus and Saturn together. No wonder the man is so forceful and lucky.

It is also worth mentioning that **right on the Ascendant, also conjunct Mars, magnified by that Jupiter-Venus-Saturn combination, is the fixed Royal Star, Regulus.**

Love him, hate him or both, Donald Trump is a distinctive man, and this is a distinctive chart.

Transits to the Lots

Up to this point I have concentrated on the two Lots in natal charts. In the next few examples I want to focus specifically on how the Lots are activated during significant periods of life.

I have chosen some examples of famous people where there is a distinct correlation with critical events in the person's life, and the meaning of transits to the Lots.

In working with celebrity charts I often find that this technique, and astrology timing techniques in general, often do not show the kinds of consistent correlations I get when working with charts of people I know, or working with clients where I can ask questions about specific time periods. Techniques like this are good at pinpointing periods and events that have significance for the person. With celebrity charts we don't always know what is going on with them behind the glare of the media lights, so we cannot see events that are important to them that do not get publicity.

Angela Davis

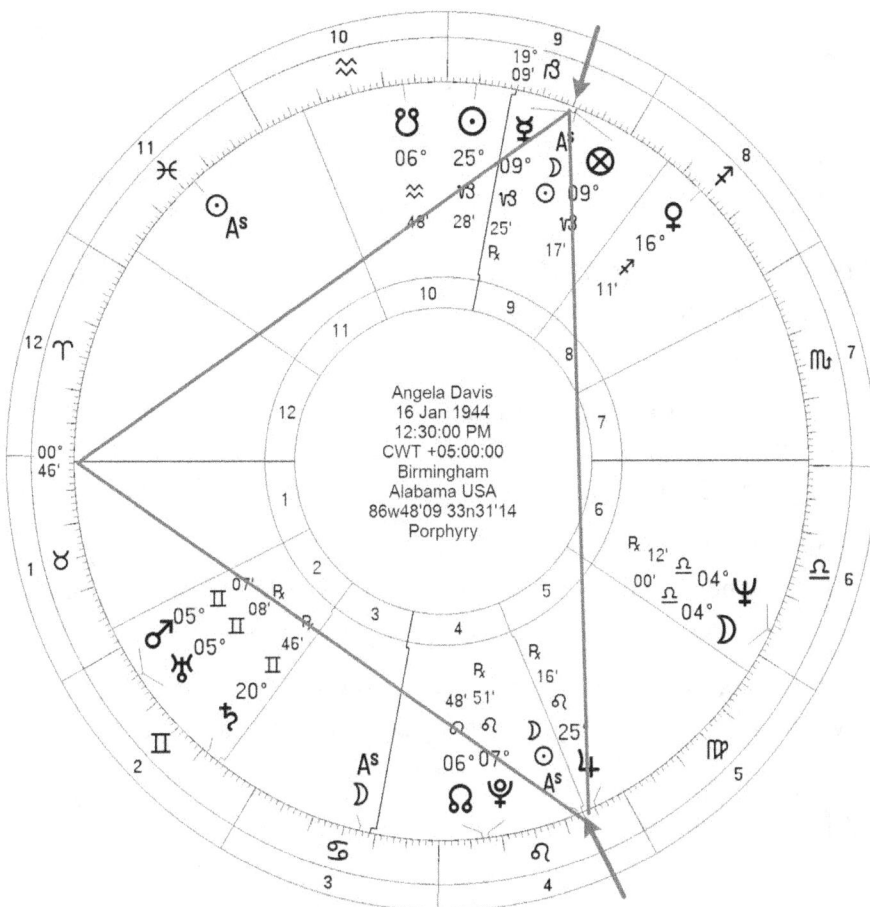

Angela Davis, January 16, 1944, 12:30 PM, Birmingham, Alabama. Rodden Rating AA.

I used the chart of Angela Davis in two of my previous books. Angela Davis is a civil rights activist, feminist, philosopher, professor, and writer. Her chart is a good example of a one-pointed, coherent chart, where everything is coordinated and moving in the same direction. This gives a one-pointed, dedicated, even fanatic quality to her life.

Examining the Lots in her chart takes that coherent, one-pointed quality to a whole new dimension.

Davis has a chart where BOTH of the Lots have natal planets in close conjunction, and the two planets together pinpoint the focus of her life.

Her Lot of Fortune is at 9 Virgo 17, within eight minutes of her natal Mercury.

Her Lot of Spirit is at 22 Leo 15, around three degrees from her natal Jupiter.

I drew the triangle in this chart to illustrate how the Lots are at equal distances from the Ascendant, so the Ascendant is the midpoint of the two Lots.

This means that the Ascendant is the focal point of Mercury plus Jupiter integrating the two Lots.

Mercury plus Jupiter - philosopher, teacher, writer, public speaker who traveled widely.

Arrest and Trial

The most famous incident of her life, that brought her to public notoriety, ties together these associations. Davis was drawn to championing the cause of black prisoners.

Davis grew particularly attached to a young revolutionary, George Jackson, one of the Soledad Brothers, and she worked to help build a mass movement to free the Soledad Brothers who were facing a murder charge inside Soledad Prison.

During an escape attempt, Jackson's brother Jonathan was among four persons killed, along with the trial judge from the Hall of Justice in Marin County, California. After that incident Angela Davis was suspected of complicity, and Davis became one of the FBI's Ten Most Wanted criminals.

Davis hit the headlines after she was accused of being involved in the planning and alleged kidnapping of three San Quentin prisoners, and of supplying the gun that killed four people during the incident. After attempting to go into hiding, Davis was found and arrested.

Her high visibility trial sparked massive public reaction and support, and the movement to Free Angela Davis received worldwide visibility. She was eventually acquitted of the charges.

After that incident, and the publication of her autobiography telling the story, she became a world recognized radical political figure. All of her work after that, including work on prison reform, grew from that incident.

In the following charts we are going to look at the period of her public trial and acquittal.

Angela Davis Trial

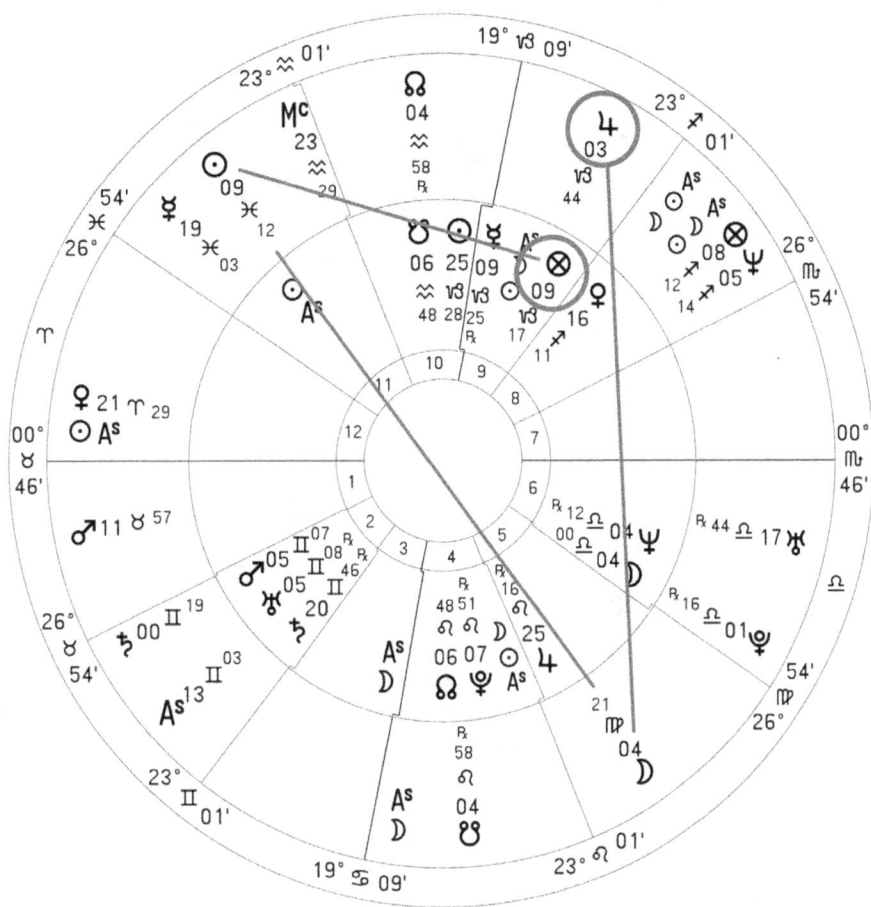

Inner: Angela Davis natal. Outer: Trial start, February 28, 1972.

The natal Lot of Fortune is the focus of the chart this year, and it is in the ninth house, corresponding in government to the judiciary, the courts.

The single most important feature is transiting Jupiter. On the day of the trial it was at 3 degrees Capricorn, within orb of her natal Lot of Fortune and closing in.

The trial coincided with a transit of Jupiter to her Lot of Fortune, and Jupiter is one of the strongest and most important planets in her chart.

Note that on day of the start of the trial transiting Moon was in early Virgo trine transiting Jupiter. I drew up this chart for noon. If the trial started in the morning the aspect was likely near exact when the trial began.

Note transiting Sun in tight sextile to the Lot of Fortune.

The Sun is also approaching the Sun/Ascendant midpoint, the midpoint axis of the Lot of Spirit, the Lot that is conjunct Jupiter.

Angela Davis Solar Return 1972

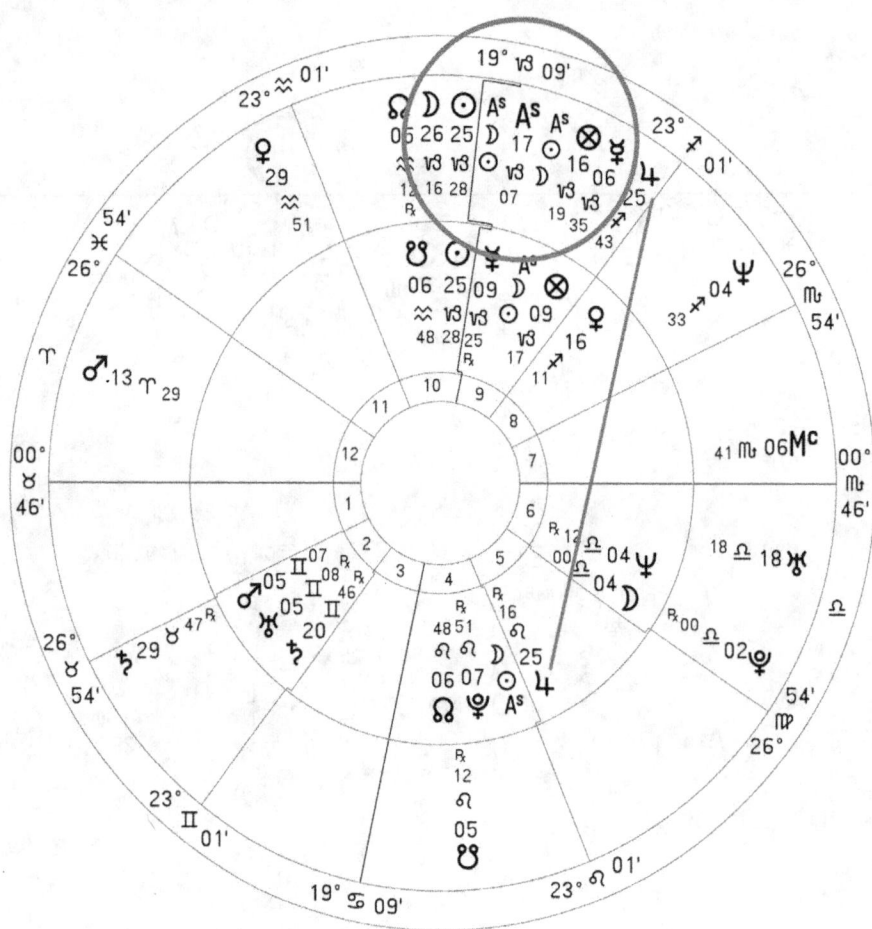

Inner: Angela Davis natal. Outer: Solar Return 1972.

The solar return for this trial year is right on a new Moon, less than a degree after exact. The solar return Ascendant is at 17 Capricorn, within orb of natal Lot of Fortune, and the two solar return Lots are conjunct that Ascendant since it is a new Moon.

Almost all of the action in the solar return is focused in Capricorn up in the ninth house of judiciary.

Solar return Jupiter is at 25 Sagittarius, in a tight trine to natal Jupiter at 25 Leo.

Jupiter and Mercury dominate the action in these two charts, and they are the two dominant planets conjunct the Lots in her natal. This is the year, and the event, where those two planets were activated to their fullest.

Adolf Hitler

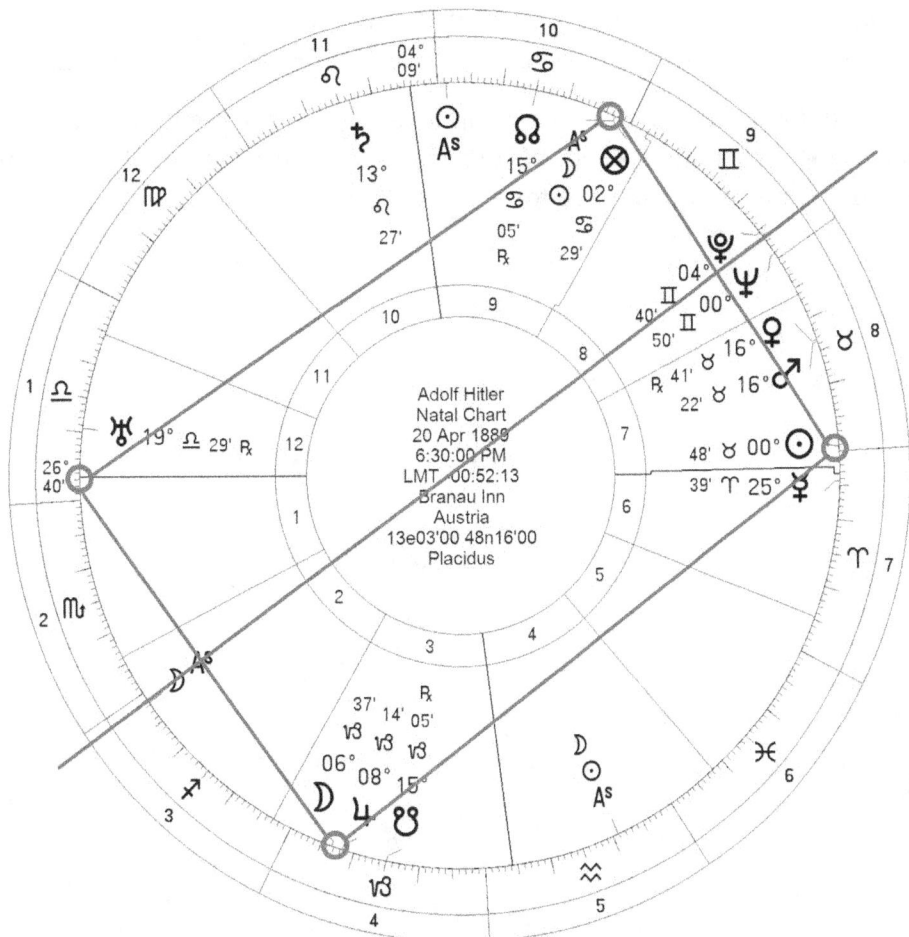

Adolf Hitler, April 20, 1889, 6:30 PM, Branau Inn, Austria. Rodden Rating AA.

We will use looking at the two Lot configurations in Hitler's chart as a way to get at the overall strong points.

The Lot of Fortune is at 2 Cancer. Planets in the stakes of cardinal signs (square and opposite to Cancer) are very important here.

Fortune is opposite its ruler the Moon, which is conjunct Jupiter its exalted ruler, and the Moon is in detriment and Jupiter is in fall. Planets in fall are ignored, not respected, and often have a great need to call attention and respect to themselves. In this case the Moon-Jupiter combination is kind of a bottomless pit of emotional need for recognition.

Remember that debilitated planets can act strongly, but in unbalanced and erratic ways.

The Sun, which is angular near the Descendant, is conjunct Mercury in Aries which is headed towards combustion. However, the Sun receives Mercury in exaltation and triplicity, which lessens the debilitating effect of the combustion. Mercury is also opposite Uranus, an electric and erratic tense aspect. The man was a powerful, persuasive and electrifying orator who exalted his own speech powers, who worked himself into a frenzy in his speeches.

With the Moon-Jupiter combination opposite, and the Mercury-Uranus opposition also in cardinal signs, we have a setup here for strong, extreme, erratic action, driven by powerful emotional need.

The Lot of Fortune midpoint axis is in mutable signs, Sagittarius to Gemini, and runs ninth to third houses by whole sign, eighth to second by quadrant. This can reasonably be interpreted as a connection between 9th house expansion in foreign lands and 8th house death.

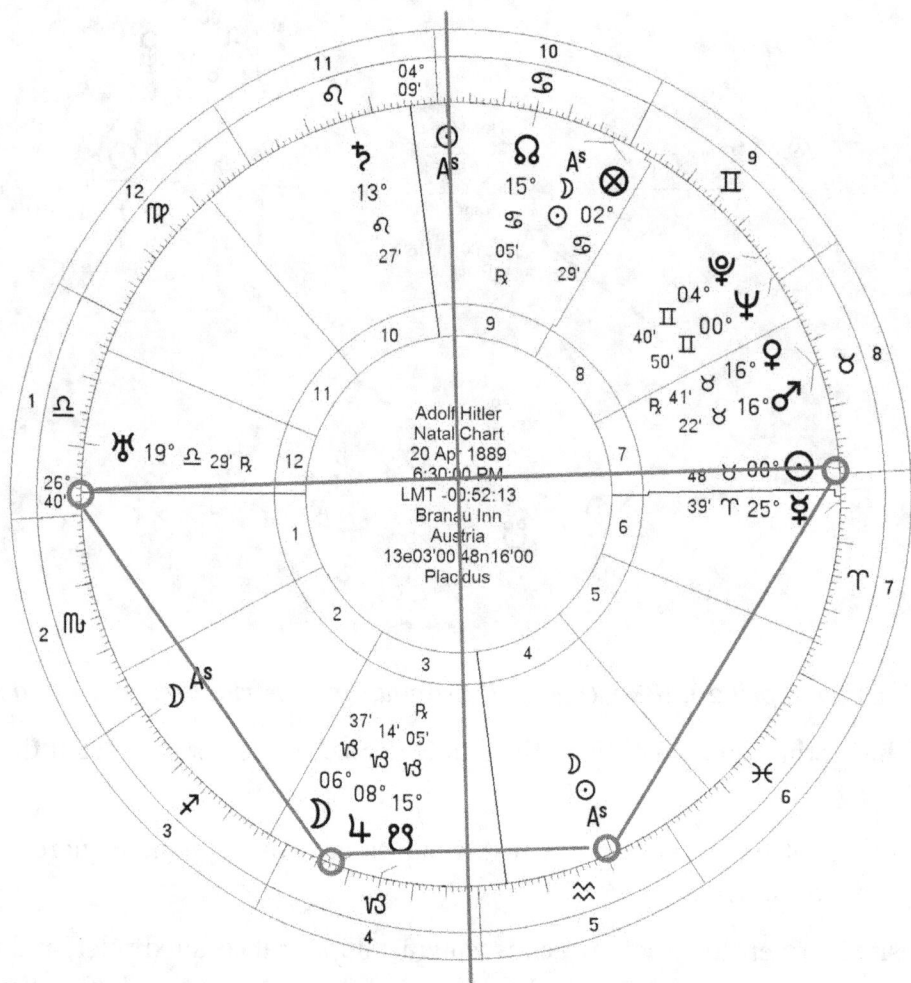

The Lot of Spirit is at 21 Aquarius, opposite Saturn its ruler which is in detriment. Spirit is also square to Venus in rulership conjunct Mars in detriment. The midpoint axis of Spirit is strongly angular, just a few degrees from the MC/IC axis.

Notice that both of the Lots are opposite their rulers which are debilitated. Again, this is a recipe for strong but erratic and unbalanced action.

84

Note both Mars and Venus in this fixed sign configuration are loosely trine Moon and Jupiter, the rulers of the other Lot. With the trine, the two sets of drives work together. We have strong emotion and a need for recognition, combined with frustration and anger.

There is a tight square of Mars and Venus to Saturn, with no reception between the two malefics. I think this Saturn to Mars square may be the single most important configuration in Hitler's chart. Both malefics are debilitated, in harsh aspect with each other, with no cooperation between them. There is the aggression, the need for power and control, and the feeling of struggle against a hostile world.

Since both Saturn and Jupiter are in significant relationships to the two Lots, we should expect to see them prominent in transits and in returns.

It is also worth noting that Fortune is in Cancer where Jupiter is exalted but Saturn is in detriment, and Spirit is in Aquarius where Saturn rules. We can surmise that Saturn transits to the two Lots could differ in effect, with Saturn to Spirit-Aquarius being more positive than Saturn to Fortune-Cancer.

Solar Return 1923 - the Beer Hall Putsch

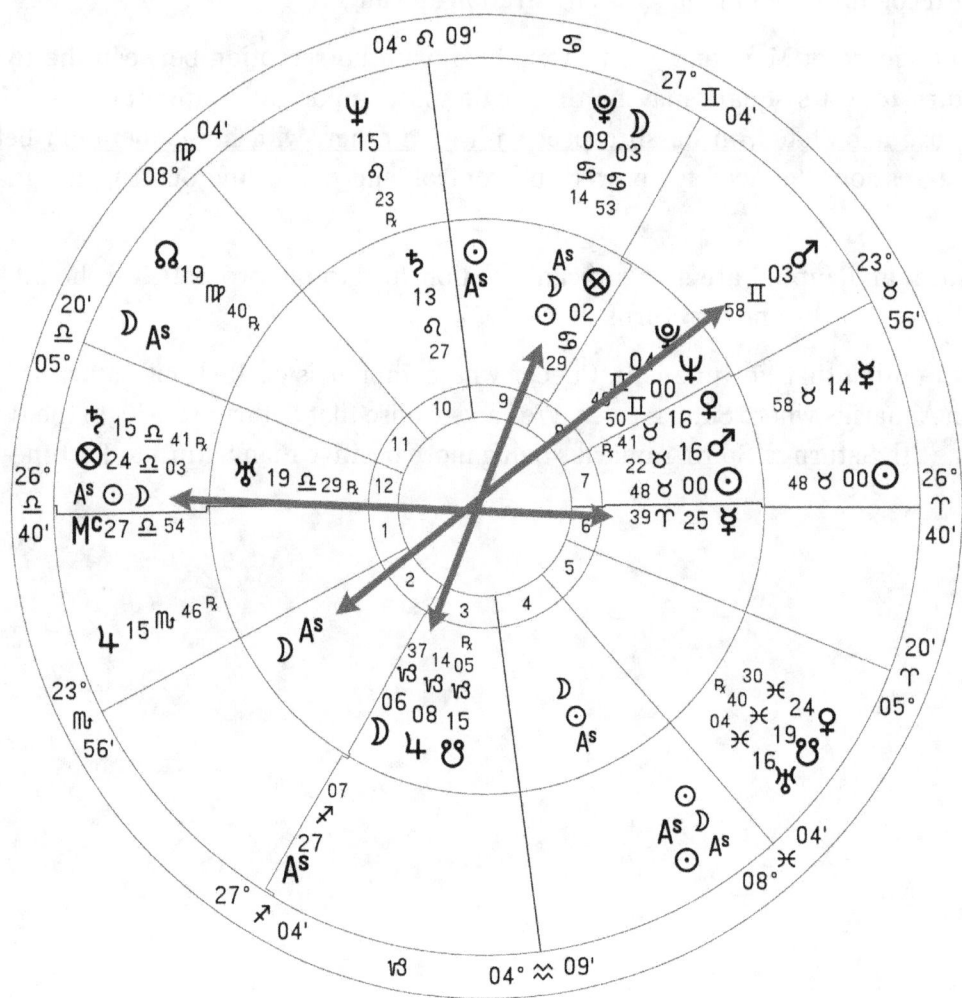

Inner: Hitler natal. Outer: Solar Return 1923.

This biwheel has Hitler's natal chart in the center ring with the solar return for 1923 in the outer ring. Some of the house symbolism here is very descriptive of the year's events.

Solar return (SR) Moon is conjunct Fortune in the ninth house of judiciary and courts. That opposition is angular since the SR Ascendant is at 27 Sagittarius. The Moon - Jupiter opposition to Fortune is strongly activated in the SR.

Solar Return Fortune is in the 12th house conjunct transiting Saturn, and the 12 house connotes prison, and SR Fortune and Saturn are both conjunct natal Uranus and opposite his natal Mercury.

This was the year that Hitler staged a failed attempt to overthrow the government, was arrested, and eventually sentenced to prison (12th). During the trial (9th) he was able to make speeches (Mercury) that helped to increase his reputation.

Note that Saturn is exalted in Libra in the Return and is trine his natal Spirit.

SR Mars at 3 Gemini is tightly conjunct the Spirit midpoint axis.

And finally, SR Mercury at 14 Taurus is on natal Mars-Venus, the two planets in square to Saturn and Spirit. SR Mercury is opposite SR Jupiter in Scorpio, which is also square Saturn.

1933 - Hitler Takes Control of Germany

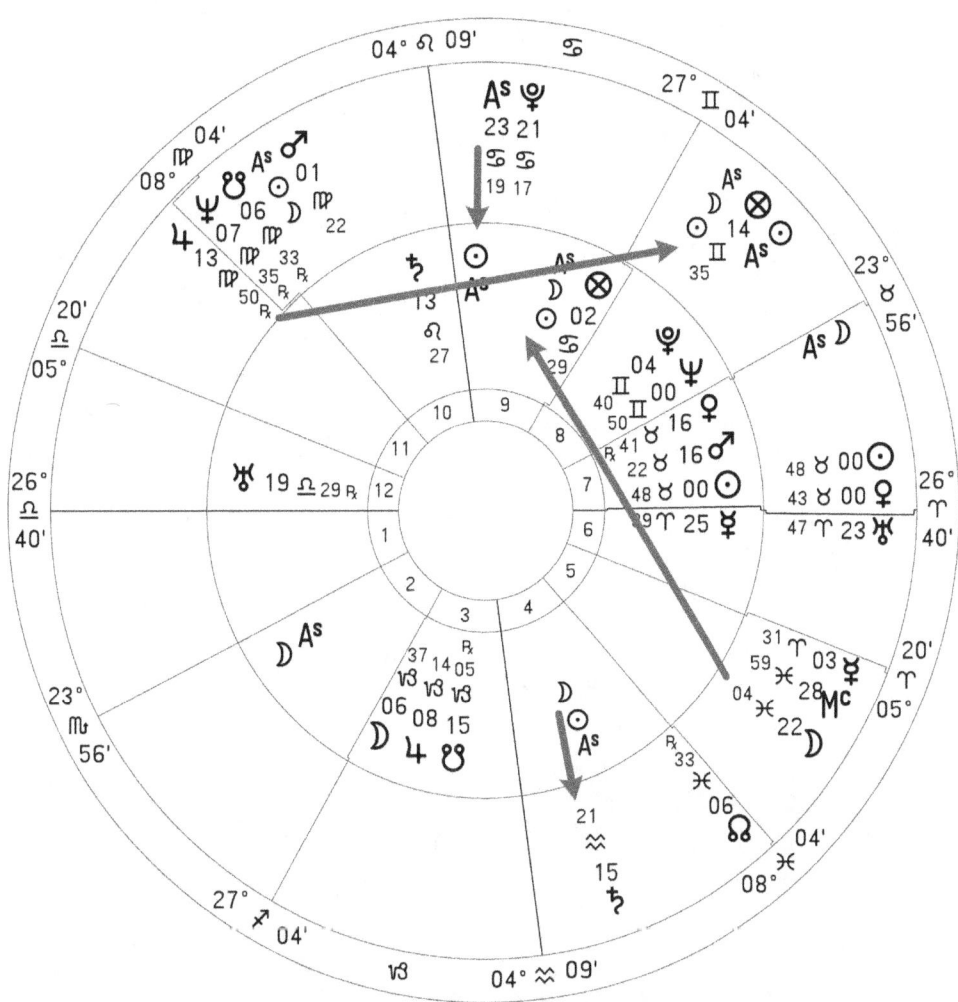

Inner: Hitler natal. Outer: Solar Return 1933.

This diagram is the solar return for 1933. This is the period when Hitler went from Chancellor to absolute dictator in the space of about a year.

We will start by looking at just the Saturn and Jupiter solar return placements. Saturn is transiting conjunct natal Spirit in its ruling sign Aquarius. At the same time, SR Jupiter is in a tight square to Fortune, which is in Cancer where Jupiter is exalted.

Saturn and Jupiter are each activating the Lot where they have major dignity.

The natal Spirit midpoint at 29 Cancer is angular in the return chart, near the SR Ascendant at 23 Cancer. We previously noted that this midpoint is angular in the natal, near the MC/IC axis.

87

The return Moon is at 22 Pisces on the SR Midheaven, and is trine by sign to Fortune in Cancer which it rules, and in tight trine to the Spirit midpoint.

1941 - Invasion of Russia

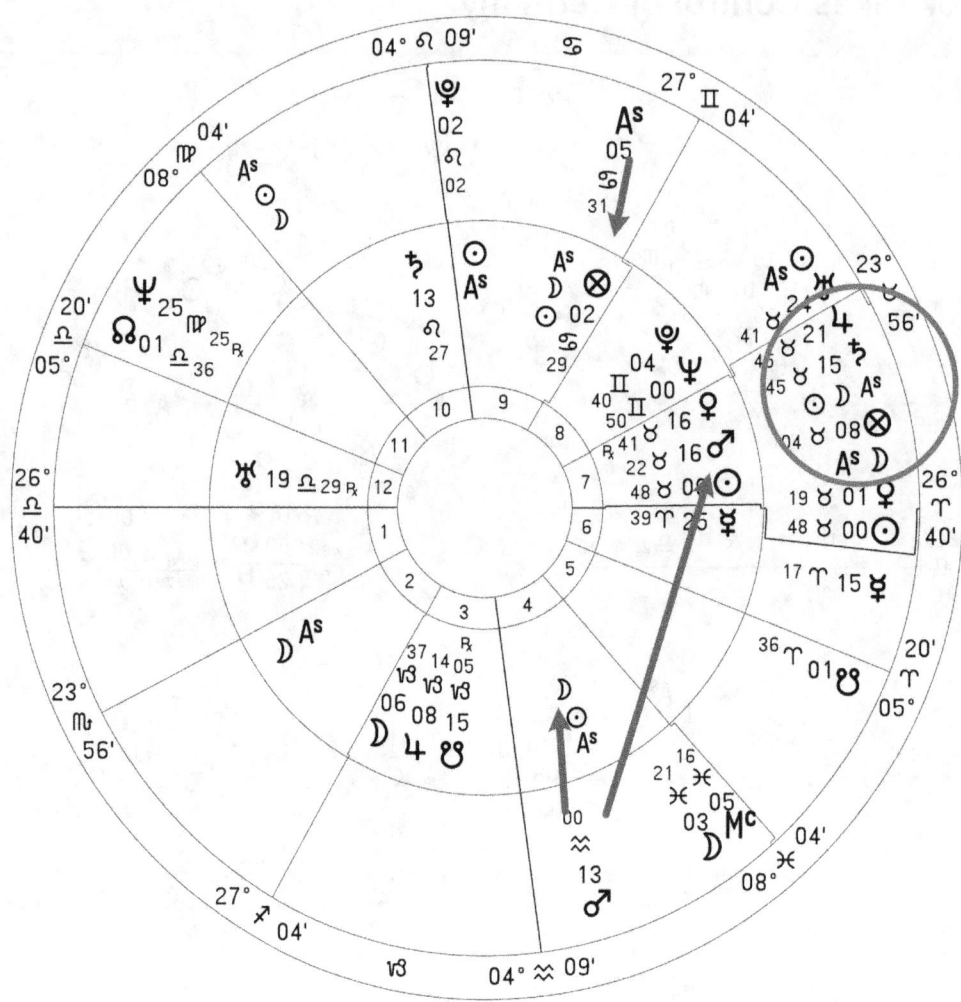

Inner: Hitler natal. Outer: Solar Return 1941.

The invasion of Russia is the single most grandiose and ambitious expansion move that Hitler made. It was the catastrophic collapse of this invasion attempt that decimated much of the German army, and this marked the main turning point that led to the total collapse of Germany a few years later.

Most noteworthy in this Return chart is the cluster of points in Taurus. SR Fortune, Saturn, Jupiter and Uranus are all close together, transiting over the natal Mars and Venus, square to natal Saturn and LOS.

The SR Ascendant at 5 Cancer is on natal Fortune in the 9th house of foreign lands, opposite natal Moon Jupiter which is also activated.

SR Mars at 13 Aquarius is opposite natal Saturn, near Spirit and in a close square to natal Mars and Venus and the transiting group in Taurus.

1944 - Germany Falls Apart, Hitler Dies

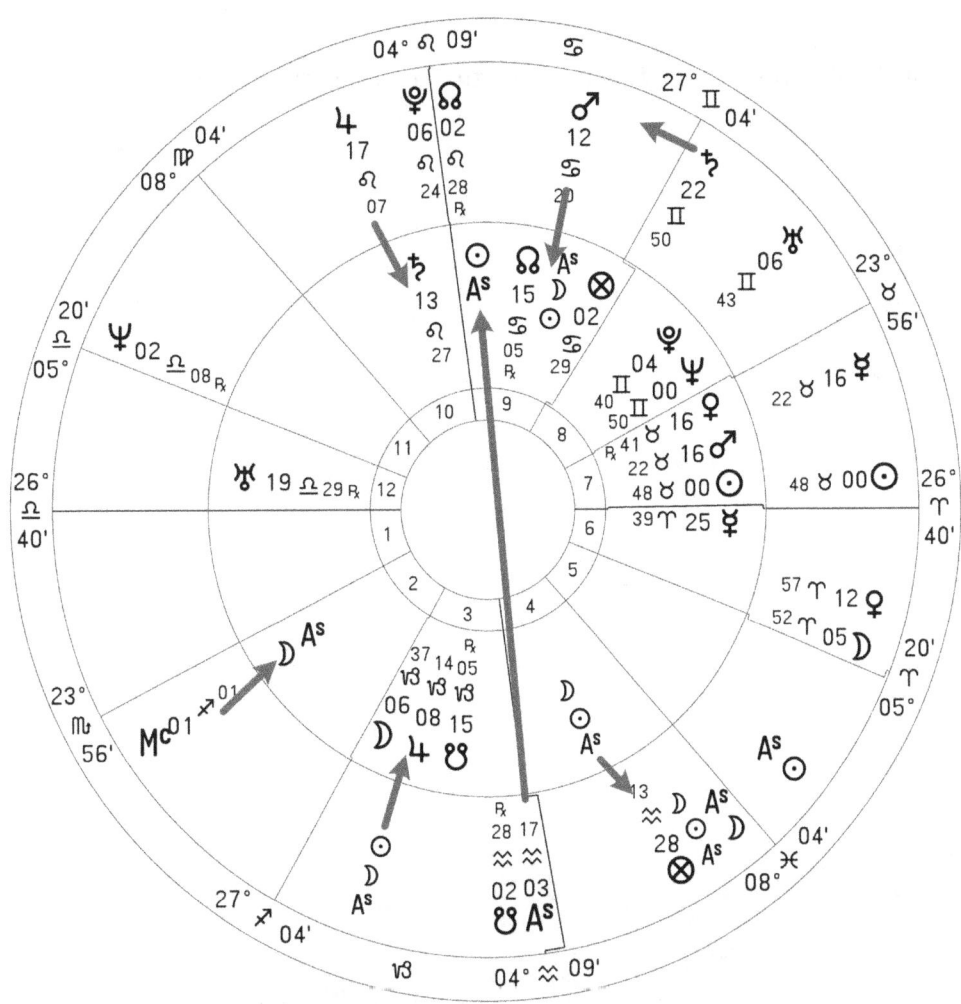

Inner: Hitler natal. Outer: Solar Return 1944.

SR Saturn is late Gemini, and will be transiting into Cancer later in 1944 and through 1945. This Saturn transit through Cancer marks the period of the final collapse of Germany and of Hitler's suicide. Saturn is in detriment transiting the sign of Hitler's Lot of Fortune throughout this period.

The other malefic, Mars, is also in Cancer in the Return, near his natal Fortune, and Mars is in Fall in Cancer. **Both malefics are transiting the Lot of Fortune together in a sign where they are both debilitated.** Both Mars and Saturn are debilitated in the natal, and here they come to their final fruition.

While that Saturn and Mars combined transit is the single most important factor here by far, there are a few other points that are worth noting.

Solar Return Jupiter is in Leo opposite Spirit, and conjunct his natal Saturn.

The SR Ascendant at 3 Aquarius is conjunct the midpoint axis of natal Spirit and on the natal MC/IC axis.

And finally, the SR Midheaven at 1 Sagittarius is on the Fortune midpoint axis.

Margaret Thatcher

Margaret Thatcher, the "Iron Lady", was the first woman Prime Minister of England and the longest serving PM in the 20th century, from 1979 to 1990. She was politically conservative, and her leadership style was strong, severe and uncompromising.

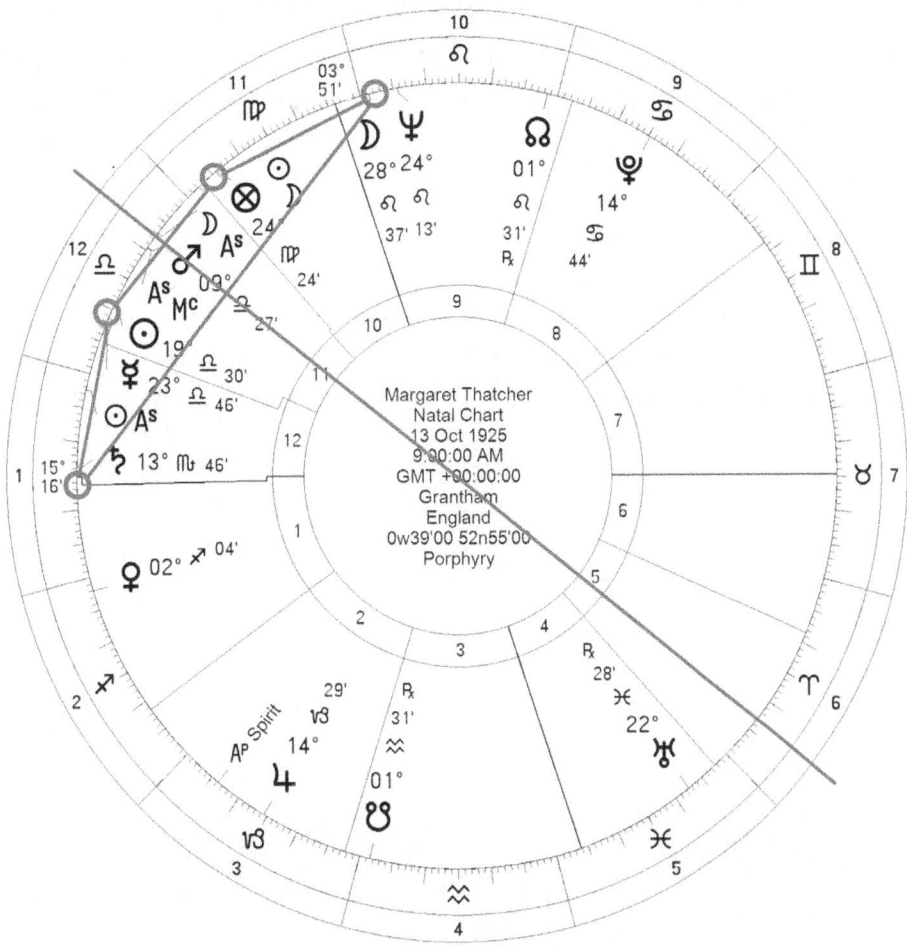

Margaret Hilda Roberts, October 13, 1925, 9 AM, Grantham, England. Rodden Rating A.

First, note conjunctions to the points involved in the Lots. Most notably, Saturn is tightly conjunct the Ascendant, and the Moon and Neptune together are conjunct the Midheaven. In addition, the Sun and Mercury are conjunct. All of these planets are activated when either Lot is activated, and having Saturn, the Moon and Neptune on angles gives them extra strength.

The Lot of Fortune, shown in the above diagram, is at 24 Virgo, in quadrant 10th house, and whole sign 11th house. Mercury rules Fortune, both the Ascendant and Midheaven are in the bounds of Mercury, a minor dignity having to do with how things are implemented. As a political figure much of her work was done in Mercurial ways, involving speaking and writing. It is also important that her prime political issues focused on the economy, and Mercury is related to all commerce.

Mars is conjunct the Fortune midpoint, meaning when Fortune is triggered, it expresses through Mars. Along with being Lord of the Ascendant and Saturn is Scorpio, Mars has a very important mutual reception relationship with Saturn, rulership to exaltation. We have a mutual cooperation between these two planets that will come to fruition during the period that Mars moves into Scorpio by primary direction.

The Lot itself is in the triplicity and terms of Mars, further accentuating its importance.

Having Mars at the Fortune midpoint axis also puts Mars at the midpoint of Saturn and Ascendant on one side, and the Moon, Neptune and the Midheaven on the other. The Moon/Neptune in Leo gave her a forceful charisma, and it is a charisma driven by Mars, a personal presence that could be very strong, even belligerent.

The Lot as a whole is focused more on Mars than on Mercury. Even though much of her work was Mercurial in the sense of being done by words and persuasion, it was Mercury at the service of Mars and Saturn which set the tone. Her speaking style was known for being forceful, direct, one-pointed and organized. If you look at the events related to Thatcher's Lot transits they are largely political, have to do with persuasion, and often involve speeches, campaigning and writing.

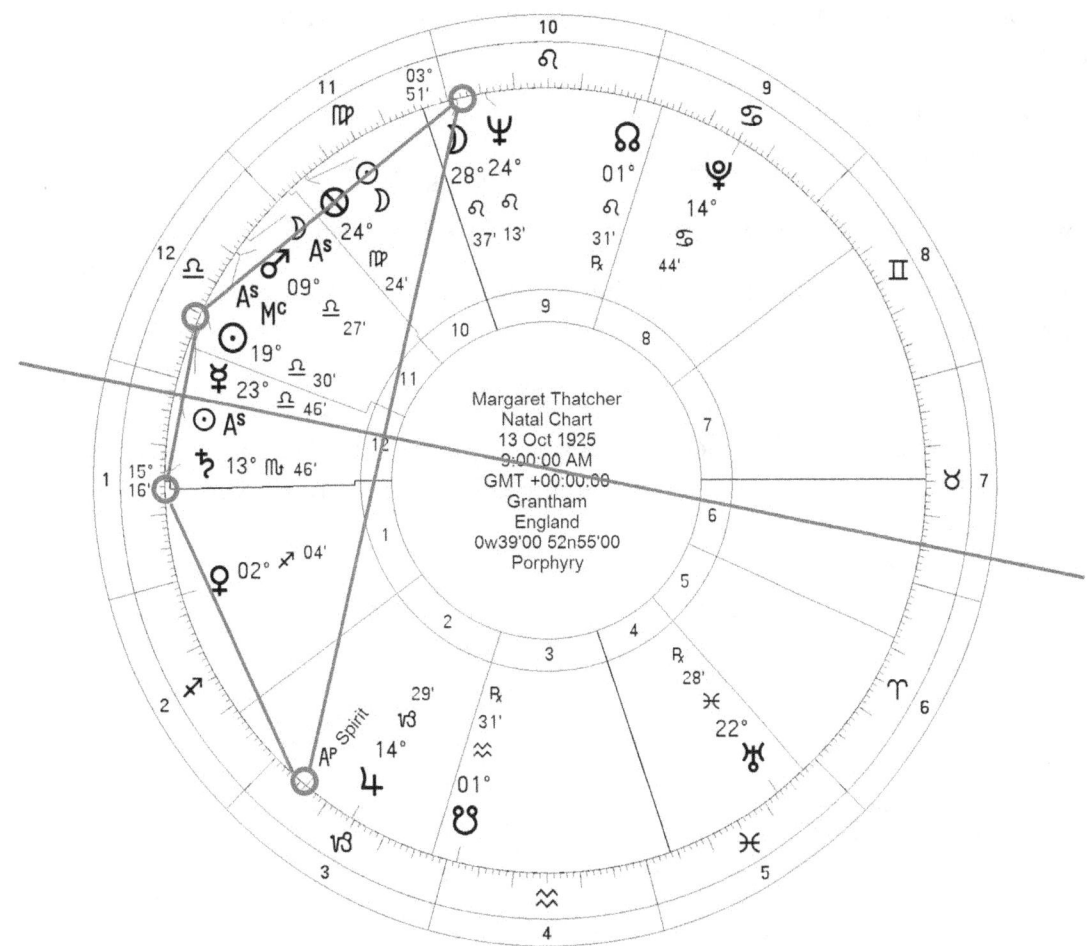

The Lot of Spirit is at 8 Capricorn and, Jupiter is loosely conjunct with an 8 degree orb. Jupiter in this chart is weak by dignity, being in fall. Being in Capricorn this Lot is ruled by Saturn and Mars. The Lot midpoint is in Scorpio, also ruled by Mars.

Both Lot structures emphasize the importance of Mars.

Also note that this Lot is in the bounds of Mercury, as are the Ascendant, Saturn, the Midheaven and Mars itself. We have multiple indications with both Lots that Mercurial processes are her mode of acting in the world, and that completely fits her focus and her style.

Transits to the Lots

Here is a list of hard transits by Saturn to the Lot of Fortune for the most active period of her life. I could find significant political events for almost all of these, and a few are very striking.

1950 conjunction - Completed her MA at Oxford, and also fought and lost as a Tory political candidate.

1958 square - Selected for candidate in Finchley April 1958, and made a major speech that helped put her on the map politically.

1966 opposition - Moves to the Shadow Treasury team as part of British cabinet, highly unusual for a woman at that time.

1979-89 conjunction - elected Prime Minister.

1987 square - Won her third general election by a large majority.

1995 opposition - the second volume of her autobiography was published.

2003 square - This was an eventful period. She published a book on International relations, and her husband died in June 2003.

We will close this section with a closer look at the solar return for October 1978, active the year she was elected Prime Minister, 1979. There are several significant Lot correlations here.

Inner: Thatcher natal. Outer: Solar Return 1978.

The solar return Ascendant is 2 Libra, conjunct the Fortune Lot Midpoint at 6 Libra and near natal Mars.

The solar return midpoint for the Lot of Spirit is at 10 Libra, conjunct natal Mars at 9 Libra.

Solar return Fortune at 11 Taurus in on her natal Descendant, opposite natal Saturn and Ascendant. On the same axis, conjunct her natal Ascendant is solar return Mars and Uranus. Mars and Saturn, her two strongest planets, are both activated in this pattern.

Solar return Spirit at 22 Aquarius, opposite natal Neptune/Moon, one of the points that are part of both Lot patterns.

The Lot of Fortune midpoints for the two charts are conjunct on natal Mars.

And finally, solar return Saturn is transiting in Virgo, the sign of her natal Lot of Fortune, throughout this period that she was elected prime minister. In this case a Saturn that is strong in the natal chart expresses in a strong and positive way when transiting the Lot of Fortune.

It is worth noting that 1980, the first full year that Margaret Thatcher was in office, was a year of a Grand Conjunction of Jupiter and Saturn. These take place every 20 years and are significant as markers for mundane events and periods.

This particular grand conjunction took place at 9 degrees Libra.

In Thatcher's natal chart her Mars and her Lot of Fortune midpoint are conjunct - at 9 degrees Libra.

Personal Chart Examples

In this section we will look at the chart of some people I interviewed who shared their chart and their life experiences with me.

There are several points that stand out in these examples.

- It is noteworthy that I did not find any people where transits to the Lots were not significant.

- With all of the people I talked to, transiting conjunctions were consistently important. The other hard transits varied in importance.

- Saturn transits were consistently important, while the effects of Jupiter transits were not as consistent.

- In some charts the themes and effects of the two Lots were similar. In others, the effects of transits on the two Lots were very different in effect, or one Lot would be significant while the other would not. When only one Lot was important, it was not always the case that Fortune was the active Lot and Spirit not very active. (Note that, being a traditional astrologer, I use the traditional formula for Fortune and Spirit where I reverse the two Lots in night charts.)

- I did not find any consistent pattern as to a difference of meaning between events related to Fortune and those related to Spirit. I have no specific evidence to point to saying that Fortune always means one set of events, and Spirit another set.

As a general rule, in every case I looked at there was a common theme if you looked at all of the Lot transits together in a single chart. It is also the case that this common theme of the Lot transits coincided with the most important kinds of events and issues in the person's life.

Note that, other than the examples using my own birth chart, I have changed the names and omitted the birth data of all the people in this personal examples section. I received the birth times from the people themselves, so this makes the charts Rodden Rating A or better.

Michael

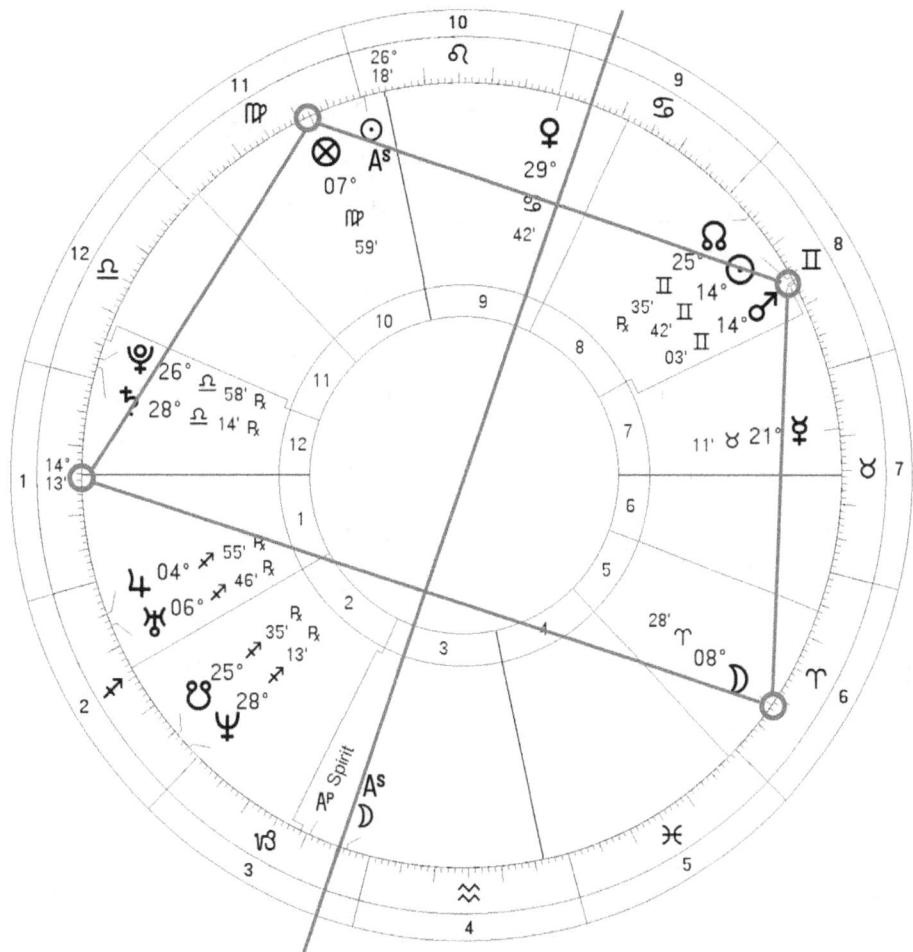

Michael is an educator, artist and astrologer, and is active in the independent theater scene.

General Notes

The Sun in this chart is very tightly conjunct Mars at an orb of 39 minutes. Mars has dignity only by face, and the Sun is peregrine, and they are in the eighth house. Mars is then part of the Lot configuration, but neither Sun nor Mars are in position to express themselves strongly from the weak eighth house. Mars is lord of the Scorpio Ascendant, but averse, making no aspect.

Jupiter is prominent, being the one planet in rulership, triplicity and term, conjunct Uranus in a 2 degree orb. Jupiter is also the rising planet, in the first house by quadrant system.

Before we look at the two Lots independently, note the cross-connections between them. Fortune at 7 Virgo 59 is within conjunction range of the Spirit midpoint at 29 Leo 28. Starting with the other Lot pattern, Spirit at 20 Capricorn 28 is very near the Fortune midpoint at 26 Capricorn 21. Each Lot is near the midpoint of the other Lot, which likely means that they activate each other. Given this connection we should expect the transit themes at the two Lots to be very similar.

Fortune

We will start with Fortune at 7 Virgo 59, with the Lot midpoint at 26 Capricorn/Cancer. The Lot of Fortune pattern is pictured in the chart on the previous page.

The Lot is in the tenth house by quadrant and the eleventh by whole sign, and it is angular, within 10 degrees of the Midheaven. Given the angularity we should expect transits to Fortune to have themes of career and public visibility. Since the Lot itself is in the eleventh house we should see events involving groups of friends.

The Lot is in a mutable sign, and it is affected by the five planets in mutable signs. Jupiter, Uranus and Neptune are all in Sagittarius, and Mars and the Sun are in Gemini. With that many planets in the stakes of Fortune we should expect transits to this Lot to have a strong affect.

The Lot midpoint at 26 Cancer is very close to Venus at late 29 Cancer, in the ninth house. This means that the Lot could find expression in areas related to education (9th) or the arts (Venus) or to both together.

Finally, note that Venus, on the Lot midpoint, rules the seventh house. We will find close relationship themes showing up repeatedly.

Lot of Spirit

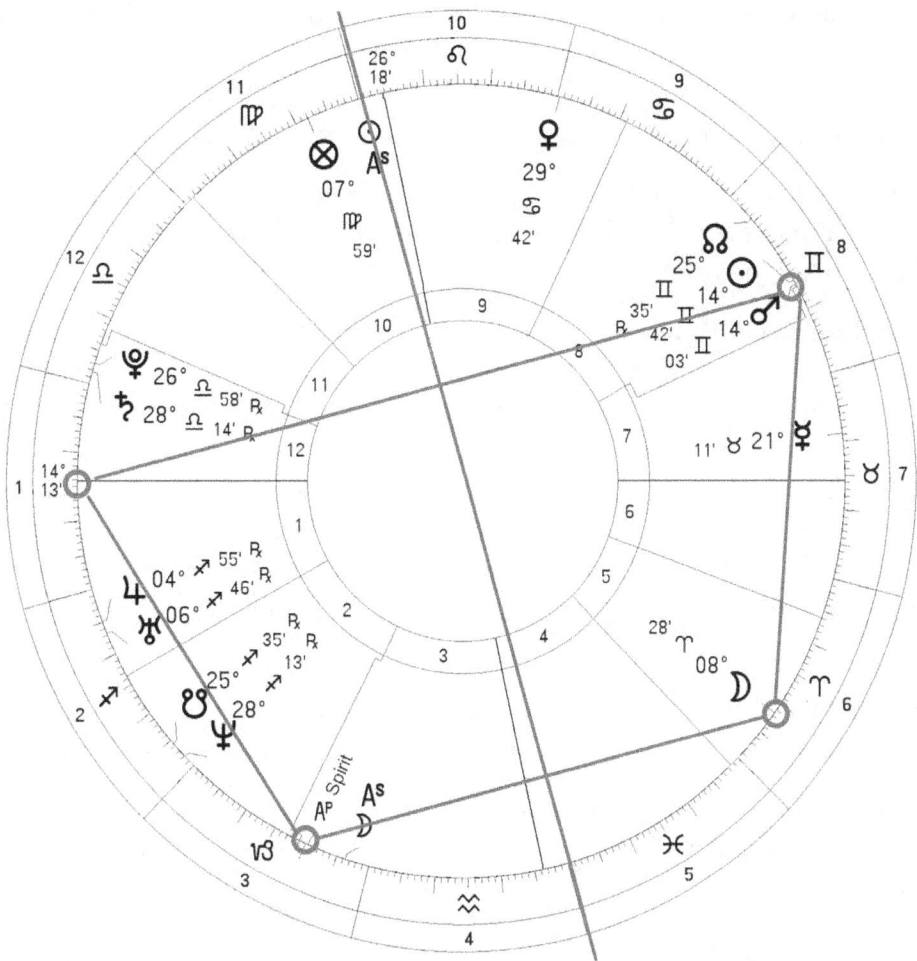

The Lot of Spirit is at 20 Capricorn 28, and the Lot midpoint is at 29 Leo 28, Leo/Aquarius. Spirit in late Capricorn is in the third house, and this can tie in the theme of education we saw with the other Lot midpoint in the ninth house. The Spirit midpoint at very late Leo/Aquarius is tightly conjunct the MC/IC axis, and we already noted it is close to the Lot of Fortune.

Spirit is in a cardinal sign, and is in a tight square with natal Saturn and Pluto, both in Libra, where Saturn is exalted. The Moon is also in the cardinal sign Aries. Again we find that the Lot is in the stakes with strong planets which will affect how the Lot plays out.

Themes of Transits

With the transits of Saturn to Fortune, the main themes were the starting and ending of relationships, and sometimes both at once. Saturn transits involved forming relationships that didn't last, or ending one and starting another. Sometimes this involved relationships where there is tension or discord. This makes sense of Fortune in a mutable sign affected by Mars in the mutable stakes.

One of the Saturn transits involved relationships with two teachers, who were very important, and who shaped Michael's vocation as teacher. There are also cross themes throughout connecting teaching and family as forming similar kinds of bonds.

Given how strong Jupiter is in this chart, it is not surprising that the transits of Jupiter to Fortune were consistently positive. All the Jupiter transits involved work in a group where Michael felt like he fit really well, and felt at home. This included a great relationship with teacher, and good relationships with his own students. One of the Jupiter transits involved a really good theater role where oddball Michael felt like he fit, like he belonged there. This is an important theme in Michael's life, and is related to the Sun-Mars combination in the eighth house. Eighth house planets can be experienced as not fitting, or not being able to easily assert themselves, and not feeling in control. In Michael's life even those places where he feels like he fits tend to be oddball, out of the mainstream communities or roles.

Transits of Saturn to Spirit were consistently difficult. These transits involved hard years at school, or relationships ending, and they also included Saturnian themes of taking responsibility.

With the transits of Jupiter to Spirit we again have themes of relationship experiences, and again were mostly positive. Again, appropriately for the overall chart, even the relationships have an outcast or rebel theme to them.

Lots and Synastry

It is worth mentioning that, throughout the instances described here, one particular close friend kept coming up over and over. This was an ongoing close relationship starting during his school years, that overlapped into work in theater and in the arts. This was a turbulent relationship that stayed very close until his friend moved to another city.

In the close friend's chart, the friend's Lot of Fortune is in very early Virgo, right on Michael's Lot midpoint for Spirit, near the Midheaven, and near the Lot of Fortune. Given that synastry, connections with his friend included both a close personal dimension and a public performing dimension. That relationship knits together many of the ongoing themes we have seen in looking at the transits.

Selene

Selene's life is all about the community of women. Her life partner is a woman, and the communities she is most dedicated to are women's communities. She has a very strong sense of caring and maternal service in how she relates to people.

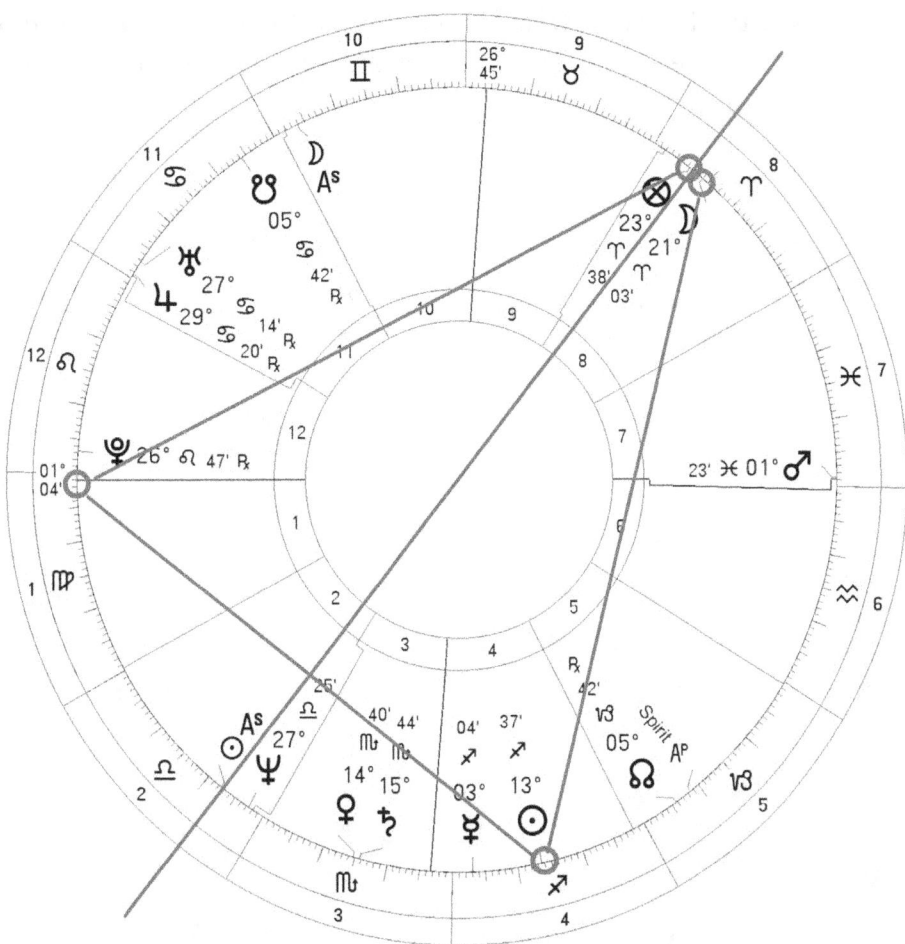

Lot of Fortune

The Lot of Fortune is in the eighth house, and is conjunct the Moon. This makes the Moon the dominant planet in her chart. Selene identifies with the Moon, and the theme of her life is all about relationships with women and groups of women, where the groups are like family and call forth a family obligation.

The Moon rules the sign Cancer, her eleventh house of communities and extended family. In this house is Jupiter, which is exalted here and conjunct Uranus, both planets being retrograde. This is a night chart, so the Moon is the ruling light, and Jupiter is out of sect. I think that Jupiter plus Uranus retrograde here is related to the high value, the exaltation, of her women's community, a community which views itself as outside of societal norm. With one significant exception, the events and stories she told me were all about women.

Jupiter in turn rules her seventh house, and the most angular planet is Mars in Pisces right on the seventh house cusp. Mars takes on added importance by being the sign ruler of the Moon. This is very appropriate for the great value she places on the relationship with her long term life partner.

In this chart the themes of the Lot of Fortune are more about the houses connected to the Lot ruler than to the eighth house itself. Death was not a significant theme in the Lot related events which she described.

The Lot of Spirit

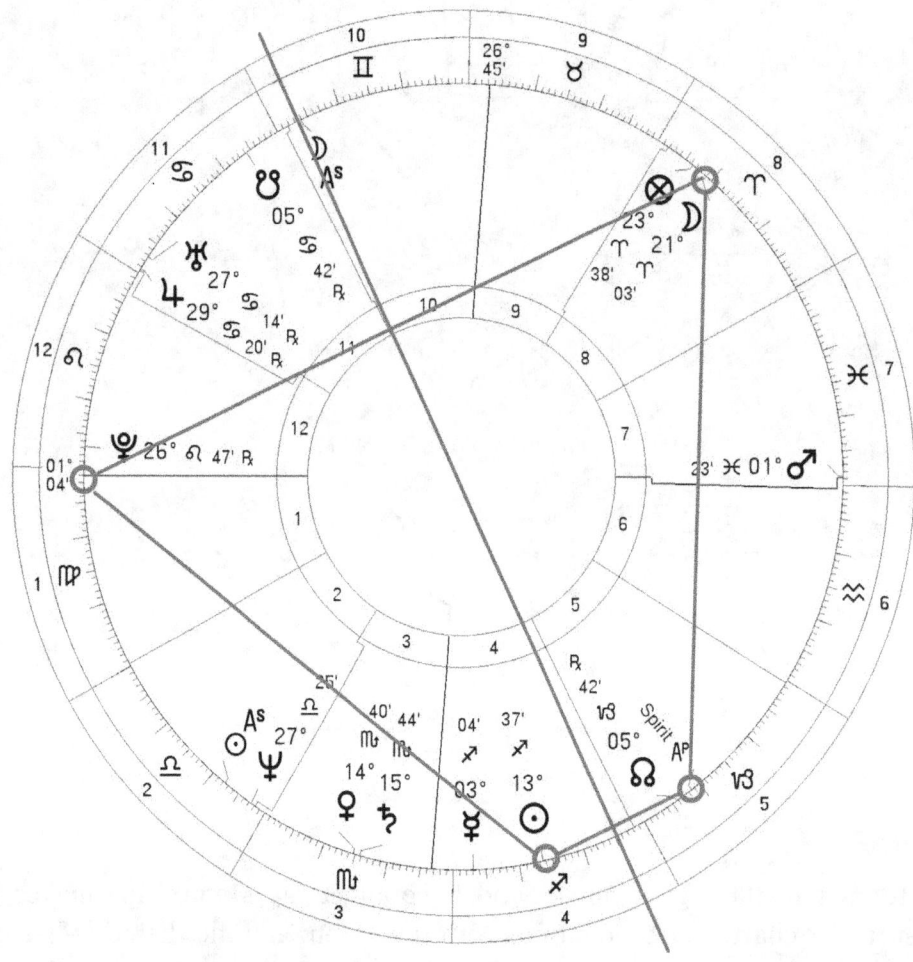

The Lot of Spirit is at 9 Capricorn and is in the fifth house, conjunct her North Node. The nodes are connected with the Moon, and I often find the Nodes to be related to significant relationships.

The Lot of Spirit midpoint is in late Gemini/Sagittarius.

Lot of Spirit ruler Saturn is in bad shape. It is peregrine in Scorpio, and is conjunct Venus in fall.

The location of the Lot in the fifth house ruled by Saturn is related to an important life situation. Selene assumed responsibility for the son of her sister, who had died some years earlier. Selene has no children of her own, but she was responsible as a mother to that young man. This fits well with the Lot in the house of children ruled by the planet of responsibility and care.

Note that both of the Lots are in cardinal signs, so the planets in cardinal signs should strongly affect the Lot events. We have already looked at the Moon in Aries, and Jupiter and Uranus in cardinal Cancer in the eleventh house. You can argue that those three cardinal sign planets define the main themes of the chart.

The one other cardinal planet is Neptune, in Libra in the second house, opposite the Moon by sign. This is a difficult placement. The two main rulers of Libra, Saturn and Venus, are both weak by dignity and are averse the house, making no aspect. Second house finance themes are a consistent problem area in her life.

Lot Transit Themes

In this chart the two Lots are square to each other in cardinal signs, so the hard aspects to the two points overlap. Because of that the transits to one Lot also affect the other.

Saturn transits were mostly about friends, and groups or communities of friends. In some cases the themes were about stresses and conflict, and in others the themes were commitments and responsibilities.

This included the time of college, a period of going off on your own. For this period Selene spoke of the difficulty of getting along with the group of friends she lived with, and the challenges of finding her group. There were also stories of fights with sisters and friends, and these are conflicts within a family or close group, not wars with an outsider.

Some of the Saturn transits involved changes in work, either starting new jobs or having jobs end, and it was during one of those new jobs that Selene met her life partner.

It was during a Saturn transit that Selene had a major family fight with her sister, and her sister died before they could be reconciled in person. In a later Saturn period her sister's son moved in to live with her, and there were conflicts with her partner about how he should be parented.

Jupiter transits were mainly good, and were mainly about people, including making a connection in a relationship, moving in with her main life partner.

One of the Jupiter transits involved a fortunate money related event, a large gift of money from a friend.

Summing up, the themes of the Lots in her chart, the main themes of her life, all revolve around the affairs of the Moon, the planet conjunct Fortune. For Selene this means close personal relationships and groups of women. In this chart looking at the Moon, its rulerships, planets in aspect to it, makes more sense of the chart than anything else. Again this confirms the pivotal importance of a planet when it is conjunct a Lot.

Rachel

This is the chart of a woman who was raised a member of the Christian cult named the Children of God. Her life story revolves around being raised in that exclusive community, and having to leave the group as an adult, go off into the world, and find her own community, her own spiritual path and her own relationships.

In this discussion I will focus only on the description of the Lots, and show how they vividly reflect the main themes of her life.

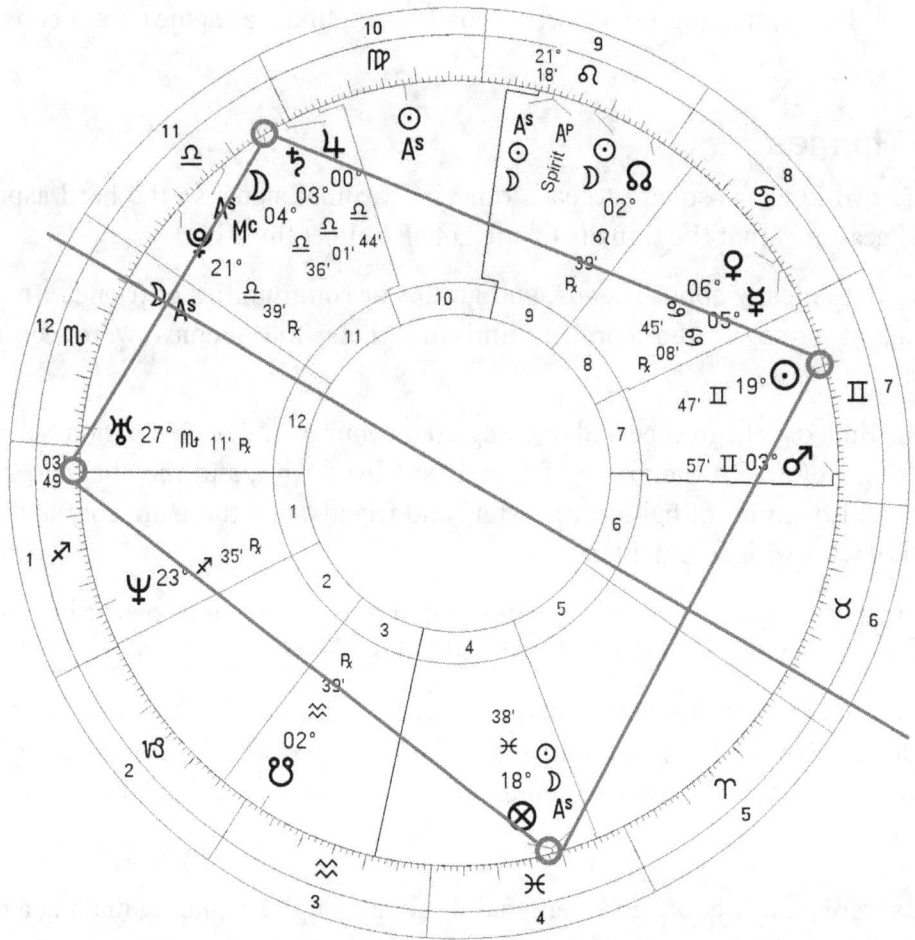

The very important key to both Lots, and the whole chart, is the distinctive conjunction of Jupiter, Saturn and the Moon, in Libra in the eleventh house of communities and groups. Saturn is very much the strongest planet by dignity, being in exaltation and triplicity, and its own terms.

Since the Moon is part of that conjunction it is part of both Lot structures.

Saturn exalted here is the authoritarian leader of the cult who proclaimed himself a prophet of God and laid down the law to be followed. Saturn here is conjunct Jupiter, natural ruler of churches and religion. They are both conjunct the Moon which is the people controlled by the church, under the shadow of the leader - and the conjunction is in 11th house of communities.

Since Jupiter is ruler of the Ascendant, in traditional astrology Jupiter is the planet representing Rachel herself.

Lot of Fortune

The Lot of Fortune, shown in the above chart, is at 18 Pisces, in the fourth house of family. The Lot ruler Jupiter is part of the conjunction, and Jupiter also rules the Sagittarius ascendant - home and family (fourth house) controlled by the religious (Jupiter) community (stellium in eleventh). Issues of home, family and religion dominate the Lot.

Since Jupiter also rules the Ascendant these same issues are the core of her identity. Finding her own spiritual path that gives her life meaning is the center of her life.

The Sun at 19 Gemini is tight square to the Lot and is in the seventh house, and finding her primary relationships is one of Rachel's main life themes. With Sun tightly square Fortune, any transit that activates Fortune will also make a hard aspect to the Sun.

The midpoint axis of this Lot is 5 Scorpio/Taurus and runs from twelfth to sixth houses. Mars and Venus are the rulers of the signs in this axis, and Mars is conjunct the Descendant. Twelfth house themes of hidden community are important, and seventh house themes of primary relationships keep coming up.

Lot of Spirit

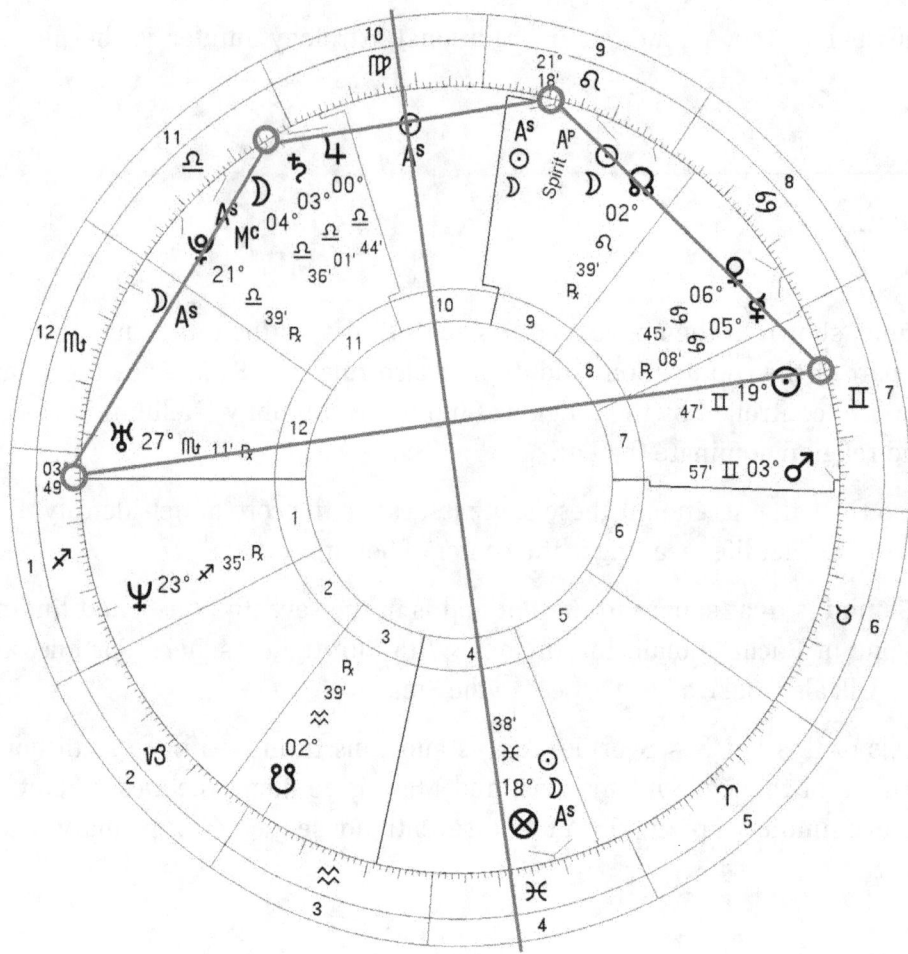

The Lot of Spirit shown here is at 19 Leo, in the ninth house of religion, and conjunct the Midheaven at 21 Leo.

Note that the midpoint axis of this Lot, at 12 Pisces/Virgo, is six degrees from Fortune. The midpoint of Spirit (ninth house religion) and the Moon Jupiter Saturn conjunction (eleventh house groups) controls the other Lot in the fourth house (home, family).

The cult had a strong missionary focus that involved travel, both ninth house activities.

Transits to the Lots

These are the main themes of the Lot transit periods, the kinds of events that came up over and over. The themes for the two Lots are similar, which makes sense since we saw the connection of Fortune with the midpoint of Spirit. The two Lots are intertwined. You will see the core themes that we already focused on in the Lot descriptions.

Moving around came up repeatedly, which is a ninth house travel theme.

This moving included changes in the church communities. During these moves groups shifted, changed size, and changed membership. Moving between communities came up repeatedly.

This is related to issues of belonging, being in and out of groups. She experienced being kicked out of some groups, and welcomed into others. Eleventh house issues of group membership were a repeating theme.

There were also stories of changing homes, which is a fourth house Lot of Fortune theme. There were stories being forced to leave, of being homeless, finding new homes, finding a home on her own, and of finding a home with a new partner.

The Lot transit periods often marked significant developments in primary relationships, good and bad. This involved starting new relationships, ending old ones, and crisis points in relationships and family.

A strong core theme running like a golden thread through the transits, and coming into focus in later ones, is the need to find her own religion, her own spiritual path. Finding her spiritual path, her family, her home and her relationships are all tightly intertwined.

Deborah

This chart is a good example of a situation where you need to take the entire chart pattern into account when interpreting the Lot.

I will look at rulers, aspects and aversions, planets in stakes, the main other aspects, and the order in which aspects perfect.

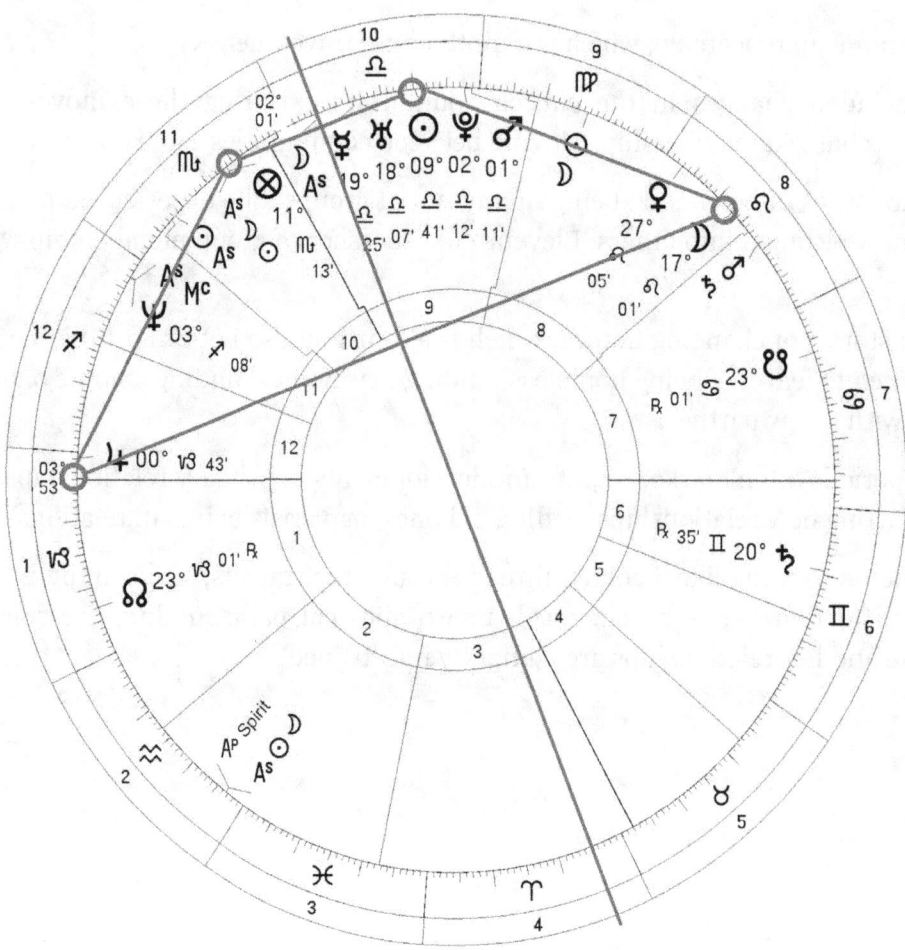

General

The most noteworthy feature of the chart is the stellium in Libra. The order of the planets by degree is, first Mars and Pluto, then the Sun, then Uranus and Mercury. The order of those planets is important.

Looking at Rulerships, there are two important major mutual receptions. Most important is the trine with mutual reception between Saturn and Mercury, and keep in mind Mercury is the final planet in the stellium sequence in Libra. There is also major mutual reception between Sun in Libra and Venus in Leo.

108

Jupiter is conjunct the Ascendant, so it is activated with the two Lot patterns. Jupiter is in Capricorn in fall and is in a tight square with the out of sect malefic Mars which is in detriment in Libra.

The Sun is in fall, in the middle of the Libra stellium, at the midpoint of Mars and Pluto on one side, and Mercury and Uranus on the other. That is a very stressful midpoint, with the turbulence and even violence of Mars and Pluto on one side, combining with the edgy, erratic Mercury Uranus combination. Put the meanings of these 5 planets together and you have a fighter who deals with difficult turns of fortune with a strong sense of individuality, fighting for her own selfhood.

The Moon is peregrine in a loose square to Fortune, and that square will end up being very important.

The vulnerability in this chart is physical and emotional, especially the Moon. The strength is with intellect, maturity and perspective, expressed by Mercury and Saturn together.

Because of their degree placement and aspects, one of the Lots ends up being associated with the vulnerability, one with the intellectual strength and maturity.

Fortune

Fortune is at 11 Scorpio, loosely angular near the Midheaven. The most important feature of Fortune is that it is in aversion to most of the planets in the chart, including all of the strong planets. Aversion, a lack of aspect by sign, creates situations with lack of communication, areas that are out of control. Fortune is averse the entire stellium in Libra, and is also averse Saturn in Gemini.

The ruler of Fortune is Mars, averse the Lot, not aspecting it. It is out of sect, a night planet in a day chart, and is in detriment. Mars is also part of the Libra stellium and conjunct Pluto. Note that Mars is the lead planet in the stellium, meaning that it will be the first to be activated by transits. By whole sign Mars rules the fourth and eleventh houses. Some of the transit events involved moving, or buying a house, or taking out own mortgage. Fortune is in the tenth house by quadrant, and career issues came up repeatedly. Being debilitated and averse, Mars gives no support to the Lot.

The other planets in the stakes to Fortune, the fixed signs square to the Lot, are Venus and the Moon in Leo, and motherhood and health themes came up over and over. Venus is also tightly opposite Spirit. The Moon is the earlier planet of the two and is weak, while Venus is at a later degree and has tmutual reception support from the Sun.

Note that the Mars/Saturn midpoint at 11 Leo is in a hard square to Fortune, so anything that aspects Fortune aspects that point. In traditional terms, the interaction between the two malefics, Mars and Saturn, is often a key factor in the worst difficulties that people experience.

The Fortune midpoint is at 25 Libra, trine to Spirit at 26 Aquarius, near Mercury and also part of the grand trine with Saturn and Mercury. This will be very important when we look at Spirit. Because of their sequence and this relation, the events of the Fortune transits are followed by, and feed into, the subsequent Spirit transits.

Spirit

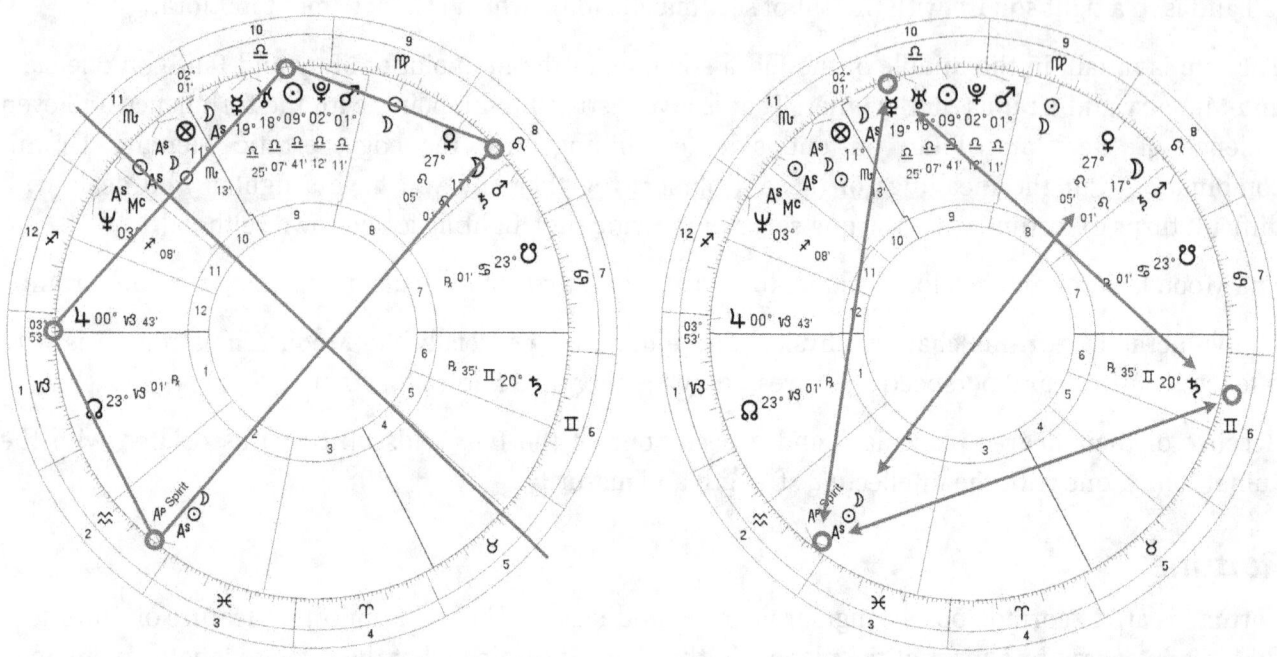

The left wheel shows the Spirit Lot structure, and the right wheel points out some very important aspects to Spirit. Spirit is at 26 Aquarius, a fixed sign. It is ruled by Saturn which is trine the Lot in Gemini. Spirit is also trine Mercury, and with Mercury and Saturn in trine with mutual reception, Spirit gets major support from those two planets.

Spirit is tightly opposite Venus, which has the mutual reception with the Sun in Libra.

The Lot of Spirit midpoint is also in fixed Scorpio, a few degrees later than Spirit. Both the Lot of Spirit itself, and the Lot midpoint, are at later degrees than Fortune. Transits to this Lot always come after transits to the other, so this Lot acts as a sequel.

Transits to Spirit complete that grand trine w Mercury and Saturn. Those three together give a kind of harvest of wisdom, going through difficult times in order to learn from them and write about them. Note that with Capricorn rising Saturn is lord of the Ascendant. In traditional terms, Deborah is Saturn, and that harvest of wisdom is a focal point of her life.

Transits to Lots

In this case the transits to the two Lots had very different tones. The Saturn transits to Fortune were pretty consistently difficult, ranging from challenging to dreadful. Transits of either Jupiter or Saturn to Spirit were consistently remembered as positive times. In this case the planets being aspected along with the Lot are very important.

Order of Transits

The order of planets, and the order that transits perfect, is critical here.

Fortune is 11 Scorpio and the Moon is at 17 Leo, and both the Lot and the Moon are weak and unsupported, so any planet that makes a hard aspect to the Lot will then make a hard aspect to the Moon. For instance, if Saturn were transiting Leo, it would make a hard square to Fortune at the same time it was approaching conjunction to the Moon. The two weak points are hit in close sequence.

Once past the Moon, hard aspects to Spirit activate the Mercury-Saturn trine, and also make a hard aspect to Venus, which has the mutual reception support from the Sun. Spirit gets much more support at time of activation from the strongest planets in the chart. The strongly supported Spirit transits help with dealing with and integrating the difficult events of the Fortune transits.

All of the Saturn hard aspect transits to Fortune were eventful times, but this is a case where the conjunction strongly stood out. The Saturn transit to conjunct Fortune in Scorpio was described as an ENORMOUS big year (her words), that included the following events:

- In a court battle she got custody of her daughters from her ex-husband.

- Her mother was terminally ill, and during this period she visited her mother for last time, who died shortly after.

- She became very sick and almost died from an auto-immune disorder. One one of the dates when the Saturn conjunction to Fortune was exact she was in the hospital, at the low point in life, sick enough that she realized was probably going to die.

- She did slowly recover, and later that year was married to second husband.

- Also late in this period, in December 2013 first cousin was brutally murdered.

- And finally, also late in this period, she changed her name.

By contrast, the transits to Spirit by both Jupiter and Saturn were mostly described as good times, when things were being resolved and going well. These included periods of creativity, when she was involved in art, or in one important period when she began writing her memoir. The Spirit transits thus often involved processing events that occurred at the Fortune transits. We can see the support of the Mercury Saturn trine here.

Natal Chart with Lot of Fortune - Charles Obert

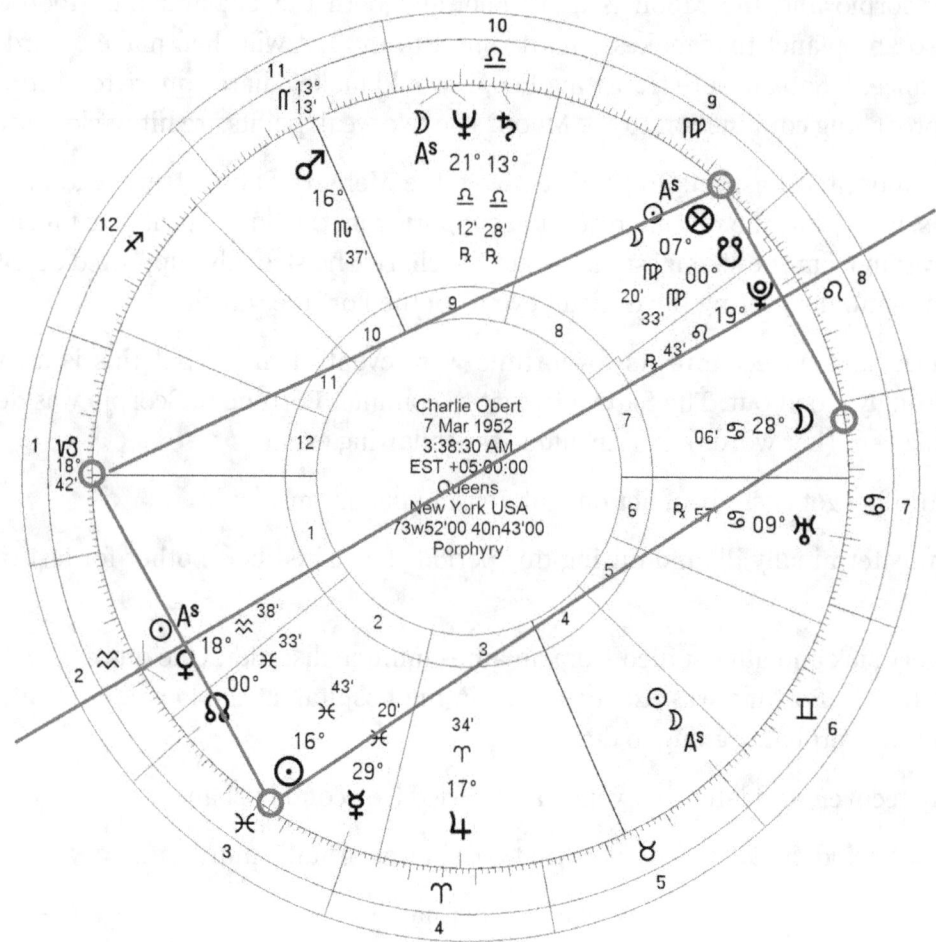

Charles Obert, March 7, 1952, 3:38 AM, Queens, New York. Rodden Rating AA.

This is my natal chart showing the Lot of Fortune pattern. I want to go into this example in a fair amount of detail, since I obviously know this life from the inside. Just as I found that it was much easier and more consistent to make sense of the Lots in the charts of people I could talk with, I can confirm the meaning of the Lot transits since I can speak from the perspective of what is meaningful to me.

Note first that the Lot itself is in the eighth house by quadrant, and the ninth house by whole sign. Eight house has connotations of death, of inheritances, and issues with other people's money, especially that of the partner. Ninth house connotes religion, higher values, teaching.

The ruler of the Lot, Mercury, is in very poor shape, in detriment and fall in late Pisces. It is opposite the Lot by whole sign, second house by quadrant, third house by whole sign.

The planet Mercury is very fluid, and it takes on the characteristics of the planets which closely aspect it. In this chart Mercury makes one very close aspect, an applying trine to the Moon, in rulership in Cancer in the seventh house, so emotions and primary relationships have a strong influence on

Mercury here. Since Mercury rules both of the Lots in this chart, it makes sense that many Lot related events concern my primary relationships.

The Lot itself is loosely conjunct the South Node, which diminishes things and connotes loss.

Overall the Lot and its ruler are in pretty weak shape, and we should expect in general that times the Lot is triggered are mostly difficult.

It is worth noting that the Lot midpoint line is 18 Aquarius / 18 Leo, which is conjunct my natal Venus in Aquarius, natal Pluto at the other, and both are square natal Mars at the Midheaven. The line runs from second to eighth houses whole sign, first to seventh by quadrant. Looking at the transits, the one time this midpoint was important was when the Lot itself was being triggered by transit.

Any time that Lot is triggered, Venus and that entire T square structure gets triggered along with it, and that is one of the strongest aspect patterns in the chart.

Given that background, we will examine the transits of Saturn and Jupiter to the Lot.

Saturn Transits to the Lot of Fortune

Before we consider the Saturn transits it is worth considering the condition of Saturn in the chart. Saturn has some major debilities here; it is out of sect, a day planet in a night chart, and it is retrograde. On the other hand it has major dignity of both exaltation and triplicity in Libra, and it is in mutual reception with Venus in Aquarius, with the two connected by a tight trine aspect. My experience with Saturn here is that it is difficult, often creating delays and pressure, but it is always fair. Saturn periods often involve hard work, and with the trine to Venus in the second house it often involves earning money by that work. We can expect similar effects when Saturn transits the Lot, periods that are mostly difficult, involving hard work, but often with good effects sometimes including earning money.

Note that the Lot of Fortune is in Virgo and Saturn itself is in Libra. This means that the period of Saturn transiting the Lot is closely followed by the Saturn return period. This makes for a pretty stressful and significant period of around five years, and that matches my experience with those times.

I want to look just at the conjunctions here, since there is a pretty clear pattern of significant activity at these times.

First Conjunction

The first conjunction was mid to late 1978 and 1979. This was an important period involving commitment and responsibility. I was engaged in 1978 and married in Spring of 1979, and in fall of 1979 I entered seminary for a two year period, planning on becoming an Episcopal priest. I left seminary after completing two years, and a couple of years after that my marriage fell apart. I view the period as one of hard work and stressful commitment to things that did not work out. That makes sense given that the Lot is in a mutable sign with a mutable debilitated ruler.

It is also worth noting that during this period my wife's younger sister died of cancer, which put a great deal of stress on our relationship. We have ninth house themes with seminary, and eighth house themes with death. It was a very Mercury period with seminary, but one where I had little control and didn't feel like I fit, which matches Mercury in detriment and fall.

This period, and the Saturn return right after it when I left seminary, is one of the two most stressful periods in my life. The other one is the second conjunction.

Second Conjunction

This conjunction was first exact in fall of 2007, and continued on into 2008. Late 2007 was when my wife was diagnosed with stage 4 breast cancer, and treatment continued on into the next year. It was also during this period that I started a major teaching job doing computer training. Again we have eighth and ninth house themes, eighth with the illness that led to my wife's death, and ninth with my teaching job.

It is also worth noting that my wife's death involved collecting from a substantial life insurance policy that helped me financially. That ties in the second house theme, which is where the Lot midpoint conjuncts my natal Venus. Jupiter was in Aquarius transiting the Lot midpoint around this time. I checked the dates of other transits to the Lot midpoint and this is the only significant event I found. It appears this midpoint is important when the Lot itself is being activated. The midpoint by itself does not seem to be a major event point for transits.

I had noticed that Venus was always involved in my major relationships, and the Lot configuration helps to explain that.

Jupiter Transits to the Lot of Fortune

Jupiter in the natal chart is in a fairly weak position. It is down at the bottom of the chart in Aries where it has only minor dignity by triplicity. On the plus side it has a major mixed mutual reception with the Sun in Pisces, but the two planets are averse, making no aspect. On the minus side it is in opposition to Saturn and Neptune. It is around 30 degrees prior to the IC so it is cadent and weak in terms of angularity.

The Lot of Fortune is in Virgo, where Jupiter is in detriment. This could make its effect in that house weaker or more irregular.

We will see that the Jupiter conjunctions in my life are often times of increased activity, but none of them are what I would call very fortunate. A planet that is weak in the natal chart produces weak or mixed results in transits.

First Conjunction

The first major Jupiter conjunction to Fortune in my adult life was late 1979 into and through the first half of 1980. Fall 1979 is when I entered seminary, and the first year was hard work, but was also very fulfilling. Seminary is a ninth house kind of pursuit and it also fits the nature of Jupiter.

Note that Jupiter and Saturn were both transiting through Virgo in this period, so there are themes of both of the planets. There was hard work and pressure, but work that was very rewarding and related to what I thought was my vocation. It was definitely an important period of increased activity.

Second Conjunction

The next conjunction was 1991 into 1992. This is the period when my father died. Fortune is in the eighth house of death, and my natal Jupiter is in the fourth house of the father in traditional astrology. Shortly before he died my father did give me a small inheritance, which is an eighth house topic, but it was tied to a financial obligation he asked of me, so it promised more than it delivered, which is characteristic of planets in debility.

Third Conjunction

The next conjunction was around 2003. Job wise my employment was intermittent as was my income, but it was a very creative period. I was very involved with my dancer wife, playing music for her and her belly dance group. I taught myself oud and cumbus (pronounced jumbush), which are middle eastern instruments used with the dance music. This was also a period where my wife and I were teaching local community education classes in drumming for belly dance music. Teaching and education, ninth house themes, are common threads in many of the activations of this Lot.

Fourth Conjunction

Jupiter transited through Virgo again in 2015. This was a big year for me. I published my first astrology book in Spring 2015, and began teaching for Kepler College later in the year. Teaching picks up the ninth house theme of the Lot.

Natal Chart with Lot of Spirit - Charles Obert

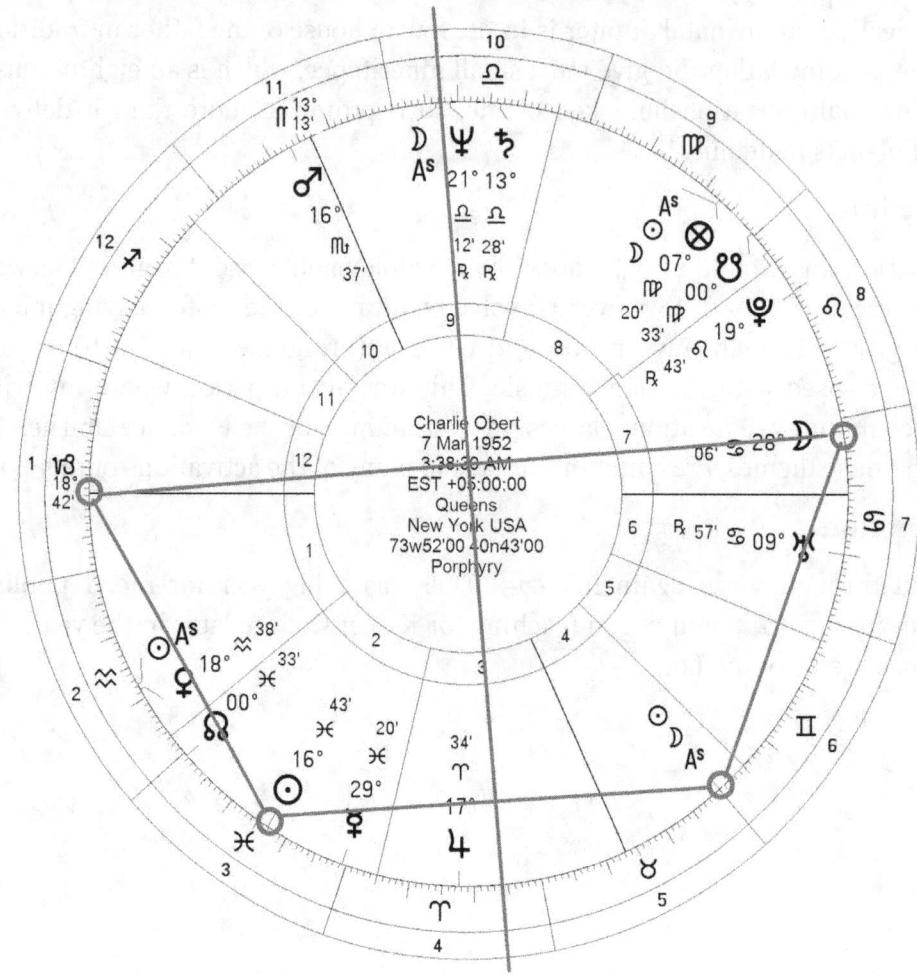

The Lot of Spirit in my natal chart is at 0 degrees Gemini, fourth house by quadrant and sixth house by whole sign. The ruler of the Lot is Mercury, who rules the Lot of Fortune also. When the same planet rules both Lots it is likely that the ruling planet takes on increased significance. Mercury has always been one of the most important planets in my chart, and I have often wondered why since it is weak in several ways, in detriment and in fall, in late degrees of a sign, and weak by angularity. Mercury ruling both Lots helps explain its importance in this chart.

Note that the Lot midpoint in this chart is at 23 Libra, just a few degrees from my natal Neptune in the ninth house by quadrant, tenth by whole sign. The mixture of Mercury, Neptune, ninth and tenth houses fits me as a person who wanted to be a priest, always assumed I would have a spiritual vocation, and ended up a teacher and astrologer.

Even though the Lot is in the sixth house by whole sign, none of the transits I tracked coincided with any major illness. So far I have been very fortunate and have been healthy for almost my entire adult life.

Saturn Transits to the Lot of Spirit

First Conjunction

The first conjunction to this Lot by Saturn was in 1971 and 1972, around my second year of college. I view my college period as a pretty dismal time. I do not think I was a good student even though I ended up with decent grades, and this was a period of serious drug use. It is possible that the Neptune connection with the midpoint of this Lot is related to that. I cared nothing for worldly values and was interested in philosophy and religion.

Second Conjunction

This conjunction was in late 2000 into 2001. This was a very significant period, one where my wife and I moved for the first time in 15 years, and bought our first house. We will see later on that this period coincides with a significant Jupiter transit to the Lot of Spirit.

Jupiter Transits to the Lot of Spirit

First Conjunction

The first Jupiter conjunction in my adult life was in 1976 into 1977. This is the year I had my first teaching job, at a little school in Saint Paul Minnesota named Guadalupe Area Project (GAP), that worked with high school age students who had failed the regular school system. This was hard work with very little income, but the work coincided in many ways with what became my life vocation. It was during my time teaching at GAP that I decided I wanted to be a priest some day. Again both spirituality and education are themes.

This was a low paying job where I had no authority and little recognition, so it was a sixth house kind of job.

Second Conjunction

The next Jupiter conjunction was late 1988 into 1989. This coincides with my second wedding, and it was a period I was very involved with Minnesota Renaissance Festival. I was also doing some of my first computer classes, and teaching is the area that ended up being my main vocation. I would call this a mostly positive period.

It is worth noting that my wife's Sun is at 0 Gemini, tightly conjunct my Lot of Spirit. It fits that a Jupiter transit to her Sun and my Lot would coincide with our wedding. (I will consider our synastry in a later section of the book.)

Third Conjunction

The next conjunction was in late 2000 into 2001. Saturn was also transiting the Lot of Spirit at this time. This is when my wife and I moved and bought our house. It makes sense that a time when both planets transited this Lot would be an important time. As I mentioned previously, it fits that this was a major event with my wife, and her Sun is conjunct the Lot.

Fourth Conjunction

The next conjunction was 2012. This was a very busy and productive year for me with astrology. I was education coordinator of the local chapter of the NCGR astrology organization, and I also started and helped to lead a traditional astrology study group. A previous transit to this Lot also involved the theme of teaching.

It also worth mentioning that I met a person who is now a very close friend of mine, who has a significant planet at 0 Gemini, right on the Lot of Spirit. Transit to this Lot marked a time of increased work and involvement with this friend.

Summing Up

If I considered these transits by conjunction to the Lots, in general I would call them important periods, or at least periods of increased activity. The most negative events took place during Saturn transits, though even the Saturn transits often had positive effects.

There are common themes to all of the Fortune transits, involving death, spirituality, religion, and teaching, and some of those themes also came up during transits to Spirit.

The Lot of Spirit seems to have a special significance to major relationships in my chart, close friends and marriage partners.

Not surprisingly, the themes of the Lot transits are what I consider the main themes and subjects of my life. If you want to know what is important to me in my life, look at the themes of my two Lots.

Solar Returns - Charles Obert

In the previous section I went into detail with my own chart, to show how the Lots worked in the context of my natal chart, and how that correlated with Saturn and Jupiter transits. In this chapter I want to look at solar returns for four of the most pivotal years of my life, to see where the Lots fit in these, and to look for common patterns in all of them.

This exercise makes one of the main points I learned from examining the Lots, that each chart has its own characteristic way of "lighting up" with the Lots. We have to set aside isolated rules and consider the Lots in context to really make sense of them, but once we have that context, the Lots are extremely important, characteristic and meaningful. They really do give us clear information on our particular Lot in life.

Note that I often abbreviate Solar Return as SR.

1985 - I Meet My Second Wife

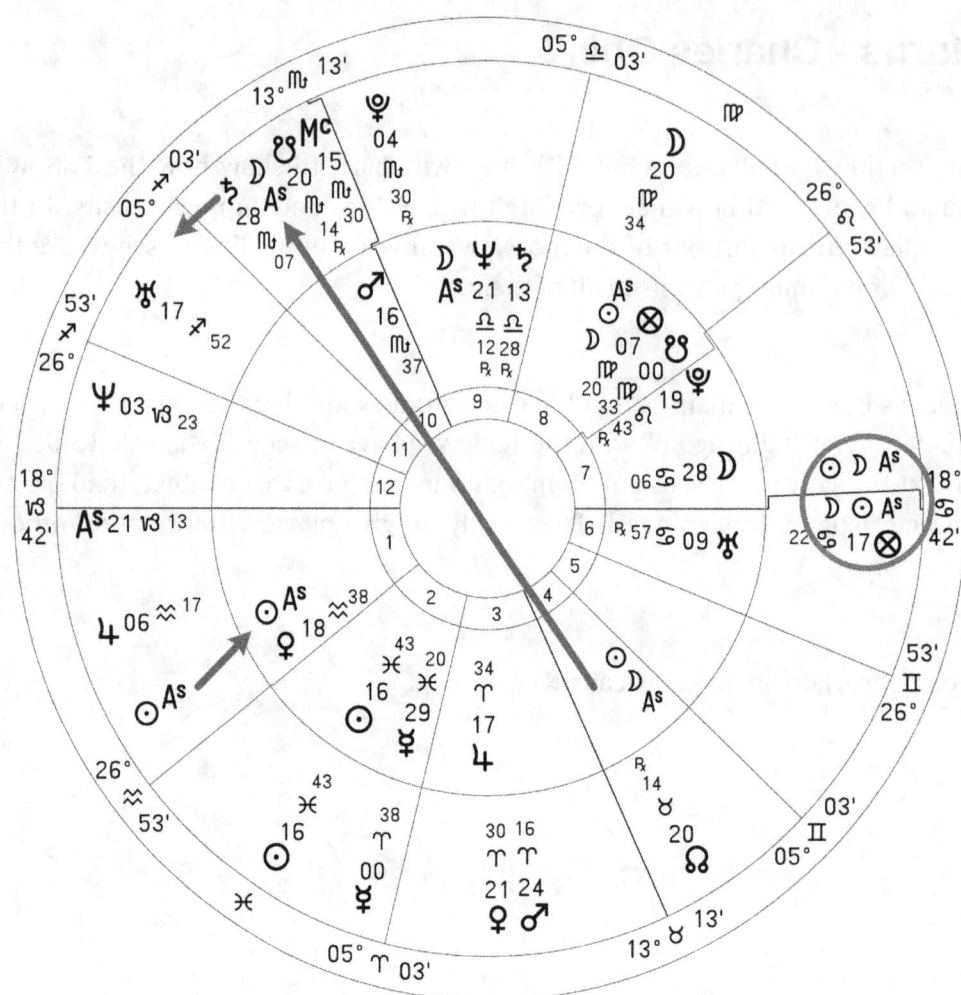

I consider this to be one of the peak years of my life, the year that I met my second wife. We first connected in Spring of 1985, near my birthday, and we moved in together in November.

That year my solar return was very near a full Moon, which means that both of the SR Lots are near the SR Descendant, and the SR Ascendant was less that 3 degrees from my natal, so they share the same angle. Both Lots right on the seventh house axis is a good vivid marker for major relationship.

The full moon in this chart is in Virgo, the same sign as my Lot of Fortune.

The Sun/Ascendant midpoint in the return is 18 Aquarius, EXACTLY conjunct the midpoint of Fortune in my natal. We will see that this Aquarius/Leo/Scorpio configuration is prominently active in all of these returns. That configuration seems to be one of the most important in my chart.

Saturn in the return is in late Scorpio, again in the fixed sign stakes. Saturn moved into Sagittarius late in the year, to oppose Spirit and square Fortune, right around the time we moved in together in November.

The SR Moon/Ascendant midpoint is at 20 Scorpio, on my Midheaven and Mars, and square the other midpoint axis.

The main action here is on the Venus/Mars square, which is appropriate for a major love affair.

I track profections also, and the profected sign of the year is Libra, meaning that Venus is Lord of the Year, the featured planet. That ties in tightly with the Lot midpoints.

1988 - Marriage

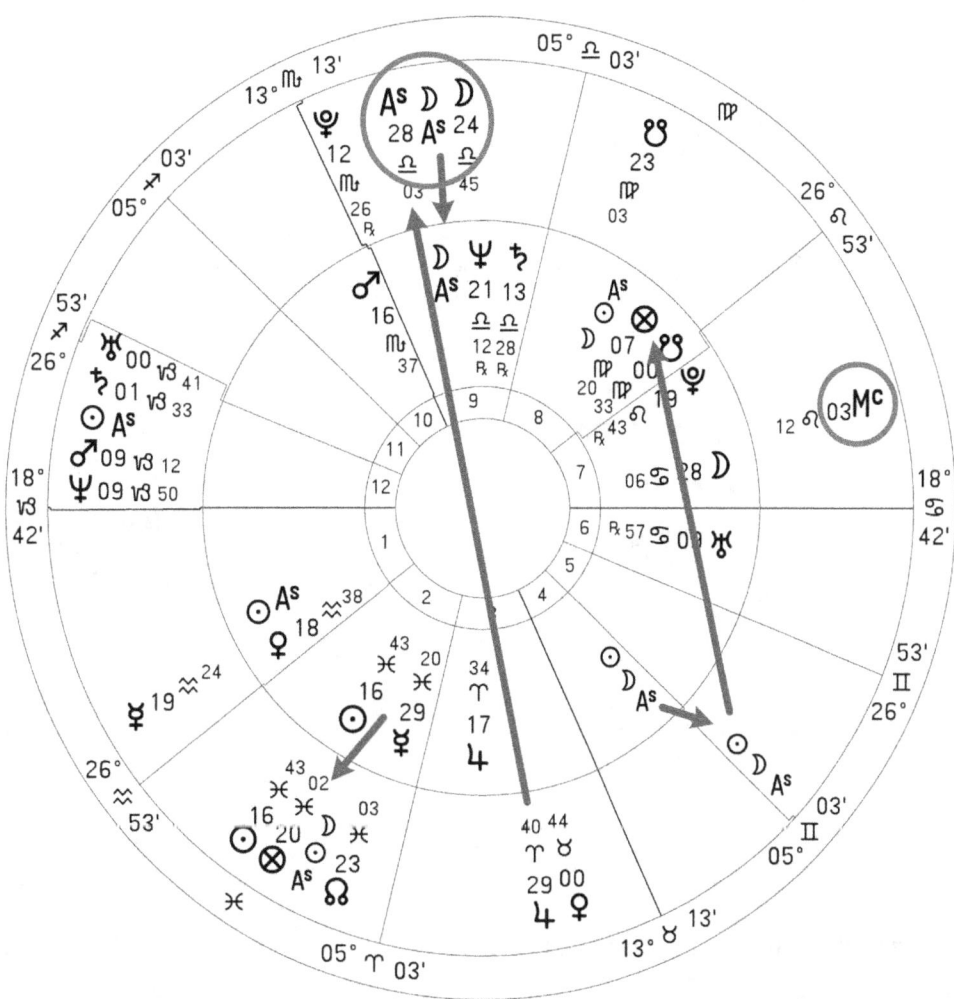

This the year we were married, in character, at the Minnesota Renaissance Festival, at a highly public wedding.

First note that the SR Midheaven is in the seventh house, and the SR Ascendant is up in the tenth house, with the SR Moon and Moon/Asc midpoint both on the Ascendant, and this configuration is appropriate for a public wedding.

SR Spirit is at at 6 Gemini, conjunct natal Spirit, and in tight square with natal Fortune.

SR Fortune is at 20 Pisces, conjunct my Sun, opposite natal Fortune.

Finally, note that Jupiter is at 29 Aries, right on the SR Descendant, In a tight conjunction with SR Venus in early Taurus, her ruling sign. Jupiter is about to move into the sign of Venus, and both of these benefics are conjunct in the whole sign 4th house. The SR seventh is the natal fourth, a very appropriate combination for bringing the relationship home.

2007 - Wife's Cancer Diagnosis

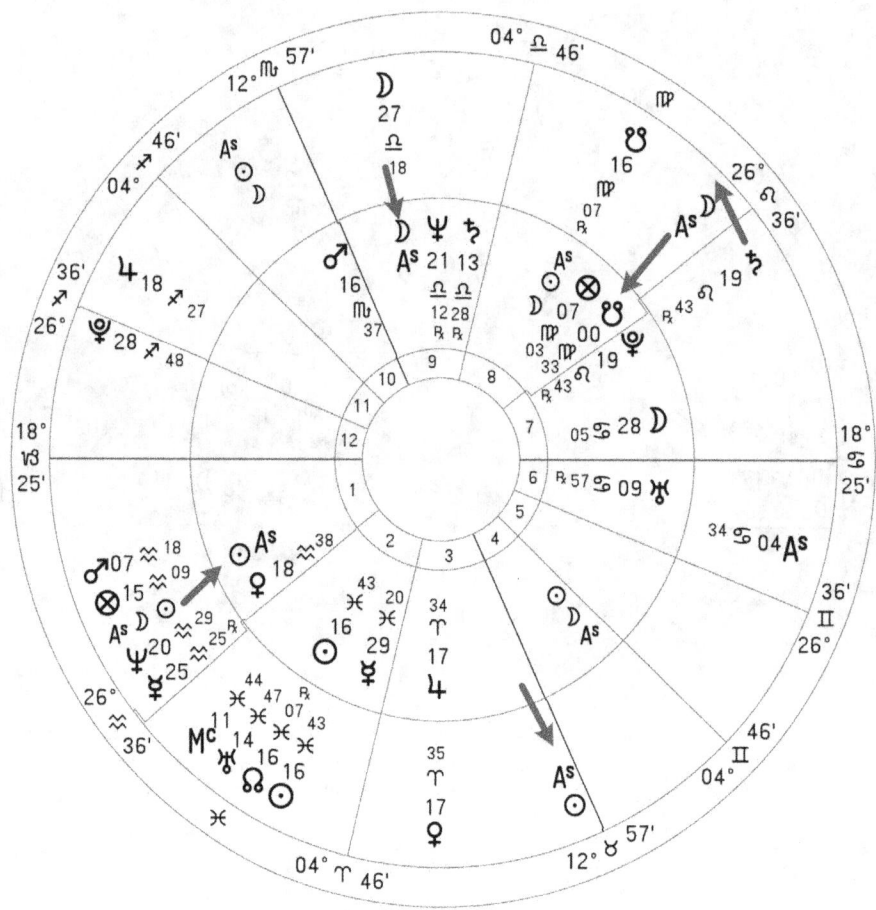

It was late in 2007 that my wife was diagnosed with stage 4 lung cancer. She died two years later.

Most notably, SR Saturn is at 19 Leo, on that same Leo/Aquarius/Scorpio configuration. Saturn transited into Virgo late in 2007, conjunct Fortune and square Spirit, when we got the cancer diagnosis.

SR Fortune is at 15 Aquarius, conjunct Venus on that same fixed sign configuration.

SR Moon/Ascendant midpoint is 0 Virgo, conjunct Fortune and tight square to Spirit.

SR Spirit at 24 Scorpio is in a loose square to Saturn, and part of that same fixed sign configuration.

2009 - My Wife's Death

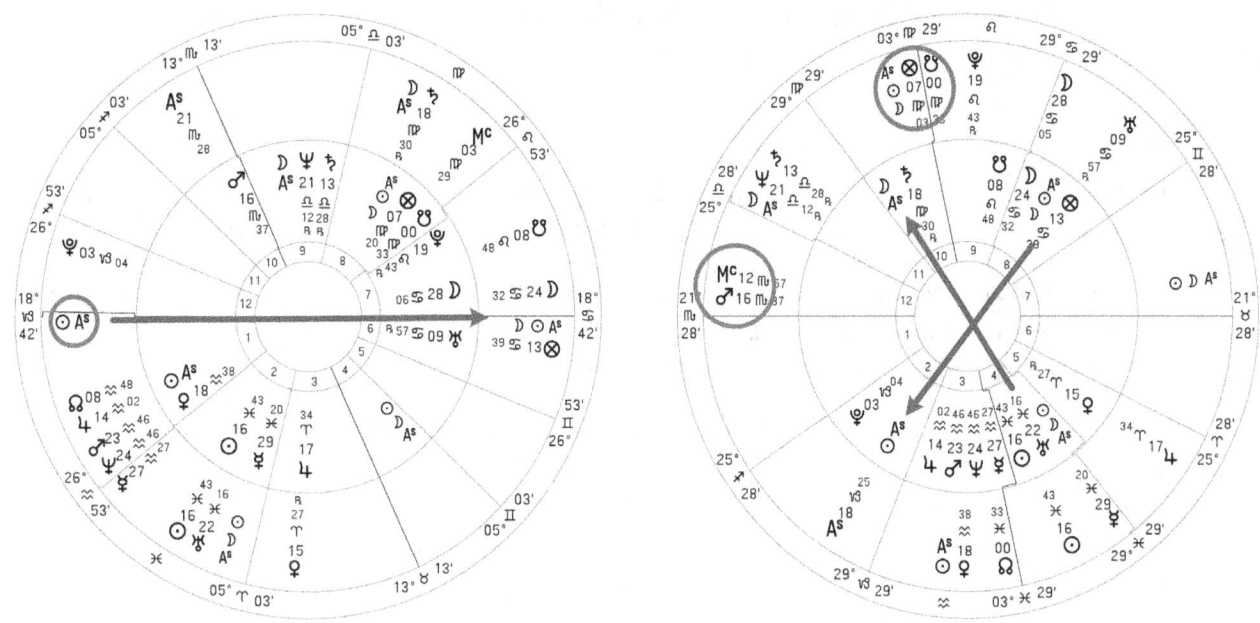

This was the year of my wife's death. It was a very public period, as we opened our home to visitors during the last few months of her life, and we also held a public memorial service for her while she was still alive.

There are two views shown here. The left chart has my natal in the middle and the SR around the outside, and the right chart switches the two and puts the SR in the middle. This points out a couple of very striking angular configurations, which are appropriate for an important and very public year.

SR Fortune is at 13 Cancer just below the Descendant, and tight square to natal Saturn.

SR Moon is at 24 Cancer, again near the Descendant, and also near my natal Moon.

SR Spirit at 29 Pisces is exactly conjunct natal Mercury, ruler of both my Lots.

SR Sun/Ascendant midpoint at 19 Capricorn is dead on my Ascendant.

SR Midheaven at 4 Virgo is conjunct Fortune, appropriate for a very public death, and natal Fortune is in the eighth house by quadrant, ninth house by whole sign. The meanings of both houses apply here.

My natal Midheaven is in the SR twelfth house.

And finally, the SR Moon/Ascendant midpoint at 23 Virgo conjunct SR Saturn, still in the sign of the Lot.

Client Session Example - Eric

I want to close this section with an example of how the use of the Lots is central to the reading. The entire reading was structured around the Lot configurations.

Life Context

To introduce this chart session, I want to quote from the initial contact email I received. In the first sentence he is referring to a podcast interview I did with Chris Brennan in May 2018.

> *"I also want to thank you for the comments you made addressing the fact that each of us faces adversity and we often turn to astrology and astrologers when that happens. However, often astrologers fail to acknowledge the presence of "adversity."*
>
> *It has seemed to me that astrologers can be unwilling to acknowledge that adverse events outside of a person's control can, and quite frequently do, happen to people. Astrologers and other counselors can at times even leave the client feeling blame and shame and at fault for "creating" their adverse circumstances. Your naming this phenomenon provided relief for me because until you said it, I hadn't realized how much I have been carrying the blame, shame, and fault for my current state of affairs. I hope we can have an opportunity to talk about this further."*

There is a specific adverse event Eric is asking about, that I will describe after we first look at the natal chart with the Lots in mind.

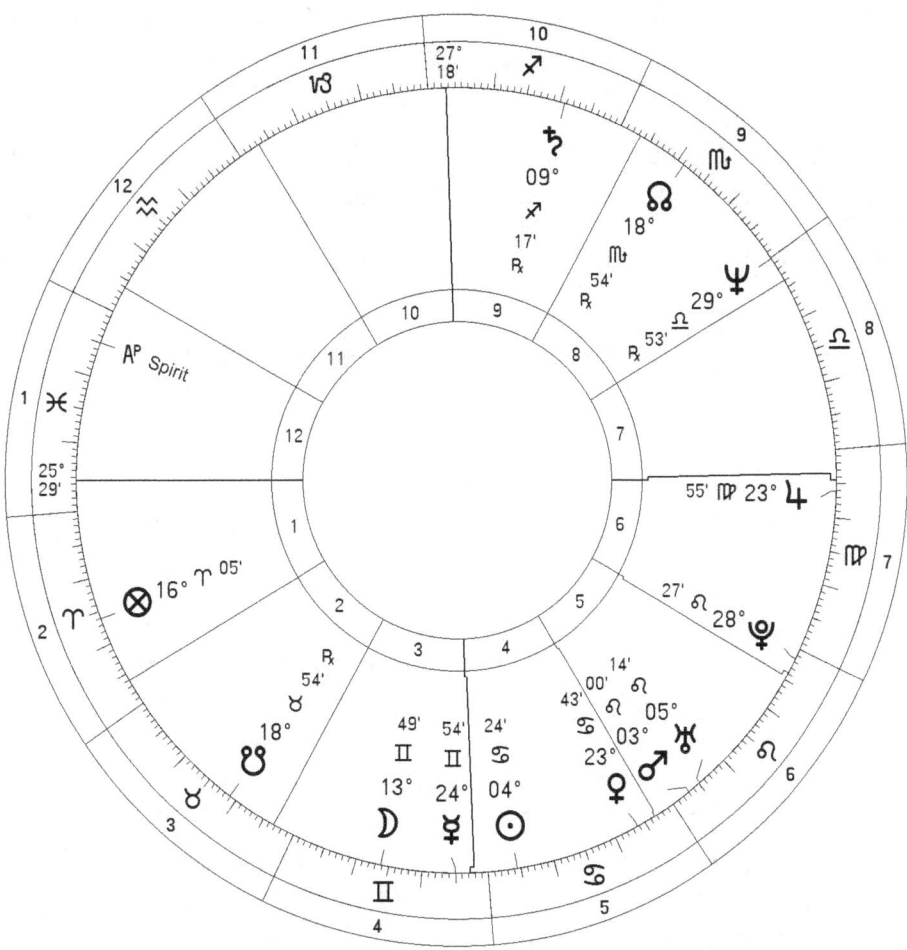

In this reading I used just the Lots themselves without the Lot midpoints, so I am showing just the chart without the Lot diagrams drawn in.

Lot of Spirit

In this chart Spirit is the most critical and active of the two Lots.

Note that the Lot of Spirit is at roughly 5 Pisces, a mutable sign. Most of the rest of the chart is in mutable signs, including all 4 angles, the Moon and Mercury in Gemini, Jupiter in Virgo - and our friend Saturn at 9 degrees Sagittarius, retrograde. This is a night chart, and Saturn being a day planet is especially problematic.

Jupiter, ruler of the Ascendant, is in detriment, and makes a tight square with its ruler Mercury in Pisces. Mercury is tightly angular and is the final dispositor of the chart, directly or indirectly ruling all other planets.

The Moon is very weak in Gemini, the 12th sign from its home sign. Moon and Mercury together represent Eric's mind and how he uses it, with Mercury being the dominant. Moon is also very late balsamic phase, headed towards a new Moon 21 degrees away, and near moving under the rays.

In late phase Moon charts it is often the case that the theme of the person's life is less about action and more about meaning, making sense of things. That is especially the case here, with the central importance of Mercury in the chart.

Mercury is under the rays of the Sun, but is protected by being in its own sign. Mercury is also final dispositor and in a tight square with Jupiter ruler of Ascendant.

The most threatening planet in the chart, Saturn, is opposite the most vulnerable planet in the chart, the Moon.

When the Lot of Spirit is triggered, so are Saturn, Jupiter, Moon, Mercury, and all four angles.

Lot of Fortune

The other Lot, Fortune, is in Aries, ruled by Mars which is peregrine in Leo and conjunct Uranus, which is not a good combination for stability or predictability. In the Cardinal signs we have the Sun and Venus.

Looking at both Lots, all of the traditional planets except Mars are in mutable and cardinal signs. Any event that triggered both lots at once would set off almost the entire chart.

The Accident

This is Eric's description of a traumatic accident.

> "One crucial bit of background for the reading: On December 6, 2016 I had an accident following a medical procedure: I had a seizure and fell, and sustained a severe Traumatic Brain Injury and neck injury. I was unconscious for 2-3 hours.
>
> In the reading, I am seeking greater understanding about the event described above, why I am here now, and some guidance about whatever future time I have in this incarnation—purpose, meaning, what do do and how to do it. Since I survived—or returned—I am now on the long road to recovery."

When I read this, even before I looked at the charts, I decided to check if there was Lot involvement, since this is exactly the kind of event that can happen when a Lot is triggered by Saturn or other stressful planets.

And that is exactly what we see here in the chart.

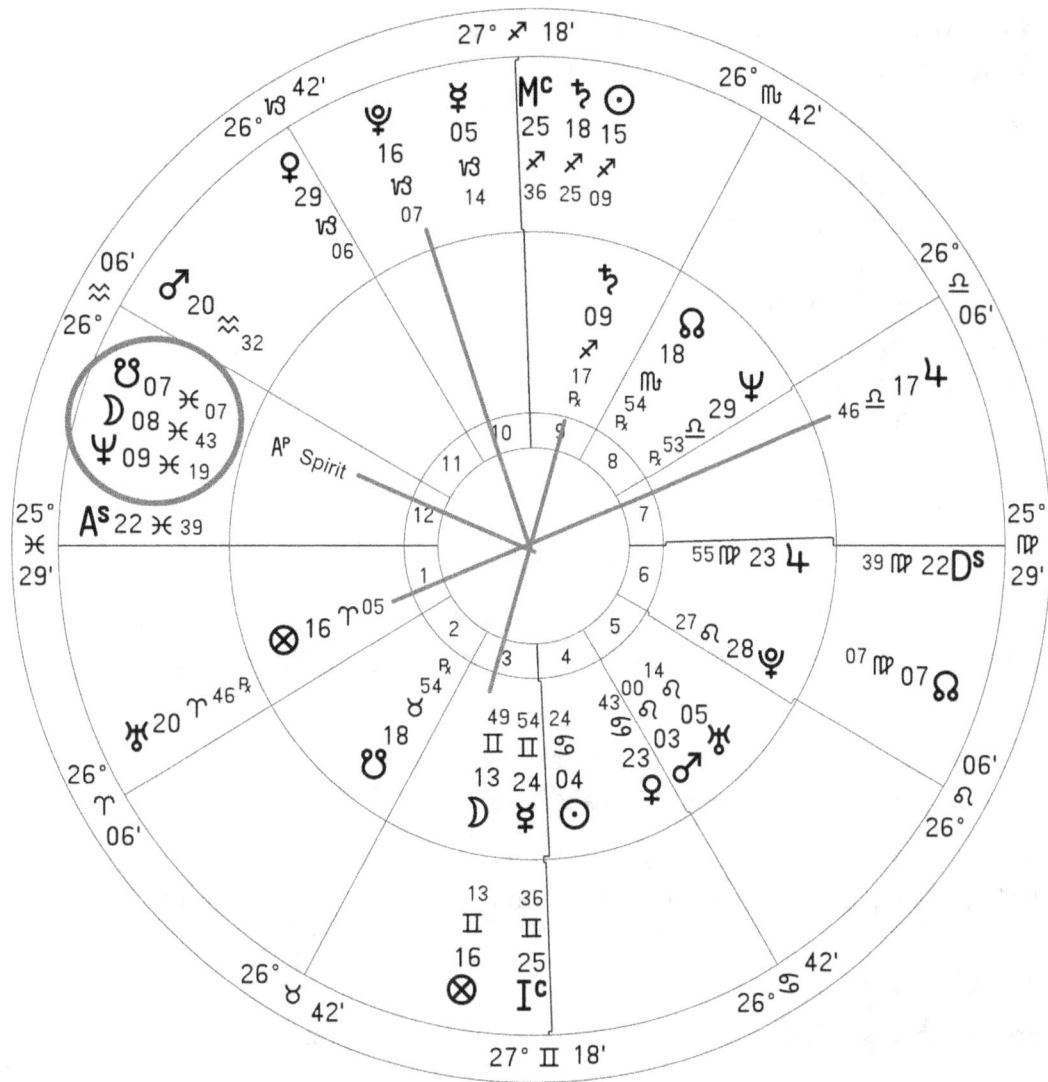

Looking at the slower moving planets first, note that Saturn is in Sagittarius, in a mutable sign square to the Lot of Spirit. This accident is happening during Eric's second Saturn return.

Jupiter is at 17 Libra, just past exactly conjunct Fortune. If you include the outer planets, Uranus is retrograde at 20 Aries, moving back towards conjunction with Fortune. Pluto at 16 Capricorn is tightly square Fortune, square transiting Pluto and opposite Jupiter. The Lot of Fortune is under stressful aspects.

And then we come to Spirit. We already noted transiting Saturn in the sign square Spirit. Notice, in Pisces, we have transiting South Node, Moon and Neptune, all within around 2 degrees of each other, and within a few degrees of Spirit.

Transiting Neptune is square natal Saturn within 2 minutes of arc.

This is a good illustration of why planets in stakes to a Lot are so important. If you look at the transiting Moon, which moves roughly a degree every two hours, you have the following sequence of aspects perfecting, one right after the other.

We have in sequence, the transiting Moon:

- conjunct natal Spirit
- conjunct transit North Node
- square natal Saturn
- conjunct transit Neptune
- square natal Moon
- square transit Sun
- square transit Saturn
- square natal Mercury
- opposite natal Jupiter

That is a very strong series of stressful aspects.

If we include midpoints looking at the vulnerable natal Moon, we see that transiting Saturn is at the midpoint of Moon and Mercury. And, the Moon itself is at the midpoint of natal Saturn and transiting Saturn.

The Lot of Spirit is getting hammered, and the natal Moon is getting hammered. Recall that, while all this is going on, Fortune also has stressful transits going on.

This really is a kind of worst case scenario, with both Lots being hit with stressful aspects at the same time, and the Transiting Moon as the minute hand on the clock setting everything off.

Significance

Here is where the Lots as being related to the strokes of fortune becomes critical.

Recall that, at the heart of this reading, we have the need to make sense of a traumatic injury, and how it fits within in his life purpose going forward. In particular, there is the need to deal with the sense of guilt, shame and personal responsibility, the belief that he was in some ways responsible for this happening to him.

The Lots have to do with strokes of fortune, things that just happen to us. They are the luck of the draw, and have nothing to do with guilt or failure. What Eric most needed to hear, in order to move on, was simply this:

The traumatic brain injury is not his fault. He is not to blame.

Fortune, and the Lots, remind us that sometimes things just happen to us. Sometimes we draw a really difficult Lot. This can be frustrating to some, since it is messy, and people don't always get what they deserve one way or other.

On the other hand, this can also be an enormously liberating insight, to realize that when something really catastrophic happens to us, there is no need to make that worse by mixing in blame, guilt and shame.

That was the single most important purpose of this reading, to help Eric thoroughly realize that he could experience the relief of getting past the guilt and shame. I think Eric was at the point of realizing this for himself, but there can be something very validating about hearing it confirmed by someone else.

Once we had reached this point, the remainder of the session was about how to make sense of this accident in terms of how it could fit within his life purpose for the time that remained to him. This places human choice and meaning where we have responsibility and control, in how we choose to respond and work with what life throws at us.

Event Charts

In this section I want to specifically focus on examples where faster moving planets trigger one or both of the Lots in important events.

The Saturn and Jupiter transits we have looked at are obviously related to specific events. Those two planets move slowly enough so that their transits generally mark extended periods rather than specific points in time. To my surprise, I did find examples with the people I interviewed where the date on which a Saturn or Jupiter transits was exact did sometimes correlate with a specific event. As a general rule, though, Saturn and Jupiter transits to the Lots mark periods rather than points.

The other faster moving planets also make aspects to the Lots, but because of their speed these will be shorter periods of time. The faster planets also transit conjunct the Lot much more frequently. The Sun, Mercury and Venus all transit each Lot point once a year, and the Moon transits each Lot monthly. That is why I did not track faster planet transits for most of the examples I studied.

However, it does make sense that a faster moving planet transiting a Lot, especially by conjunction, could mark a specific trigger for events. This is most likely to happen when there are other stressful aspects to the Lot, so the fast transit activates that stress. I will present a couple of noteworthy examples of such event charts here.

Jimi Hendrix

Wild Child of the Sixties, pioneering electric guitarist, composer and flamboyant performer, Hendrix had an enormous influence on pop and rock music. After listening to Purple Haze or Voodoo Child, the surf music of the Beach Boys just doesn't sound the same.

In this example, along with an event chart, we will also look at two solar returns.

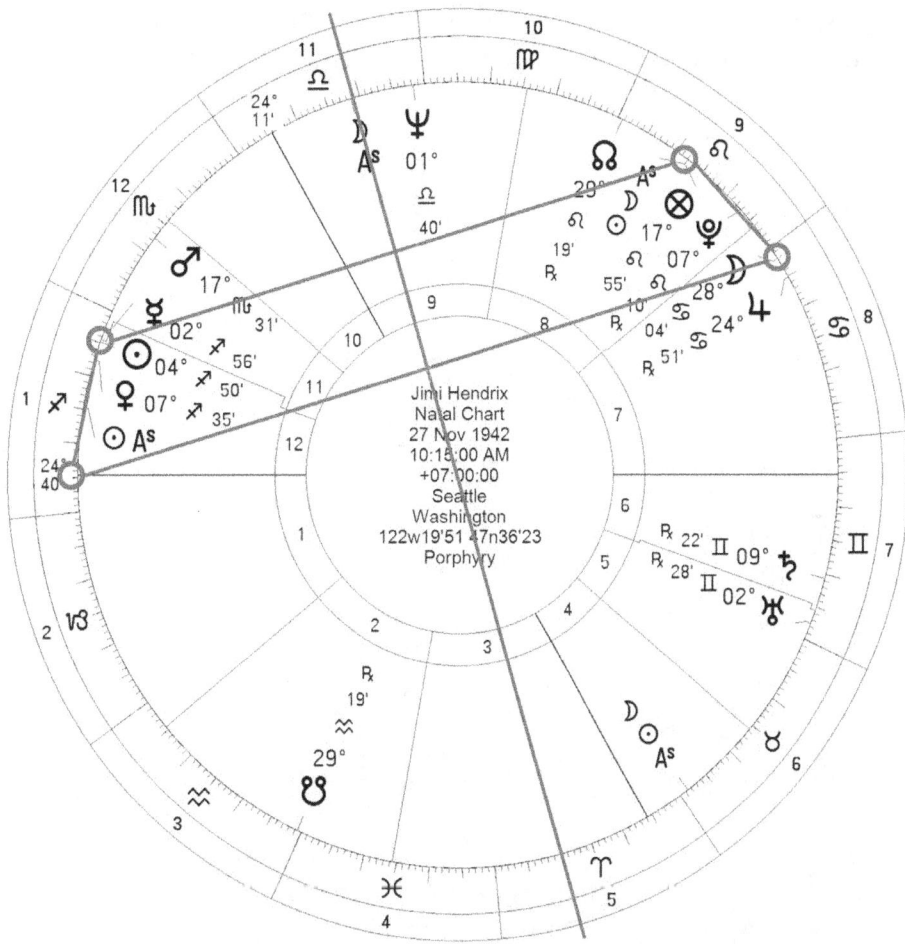

Johnny Allen Hendrix, November 27, 1942, 10:15 AM, Seattle, WA. Rodden Rating AA.

Fortune

The Lot of Fortune is at 17 is loosely conjunct Pluto, in the eighth house by quadrant, and ninth house by whole sign. I personally don't give the Pluto conjunction to the Lot of emphasis here, especially with that wide orb, but I note it since some modern astrologers use Pluto extensively.

There are two important planets that are on the overall Lot pattern. **Exalted Jupiter is conjunct the Moon in Cancer, and Venus and Mercury are both conjunct the Sun.** All of those planets are activated when the Lot is triggered.

That Jupiter Moon conjunction is particularly noteworthy. With both of those planets strong by dignity we have a setup for emotional excess, going to extremes. Jupiter amplifies the Moon.

The Lot midpoint is at 11 Libra, and that point is trine Saturn and sextile Venus, the two predominant rulers of that sign. We will see those same two planets come up again with the other Lot.

Fortune is in a fixed sign, and the one planet in a fixed sign is Mars, in rulership at 17 Scorpio and in a tight square with the Lot. A hard aspect to Fortune also tightly aspects Mars.

When Fortune is activated, this also activates the Ascendant, Sun, Moon, Jupiter, Mercury, Venus and Mars. That is all of the traditional planets except Saturn, and Saturn is trine the Lot midpoint.

Spirit

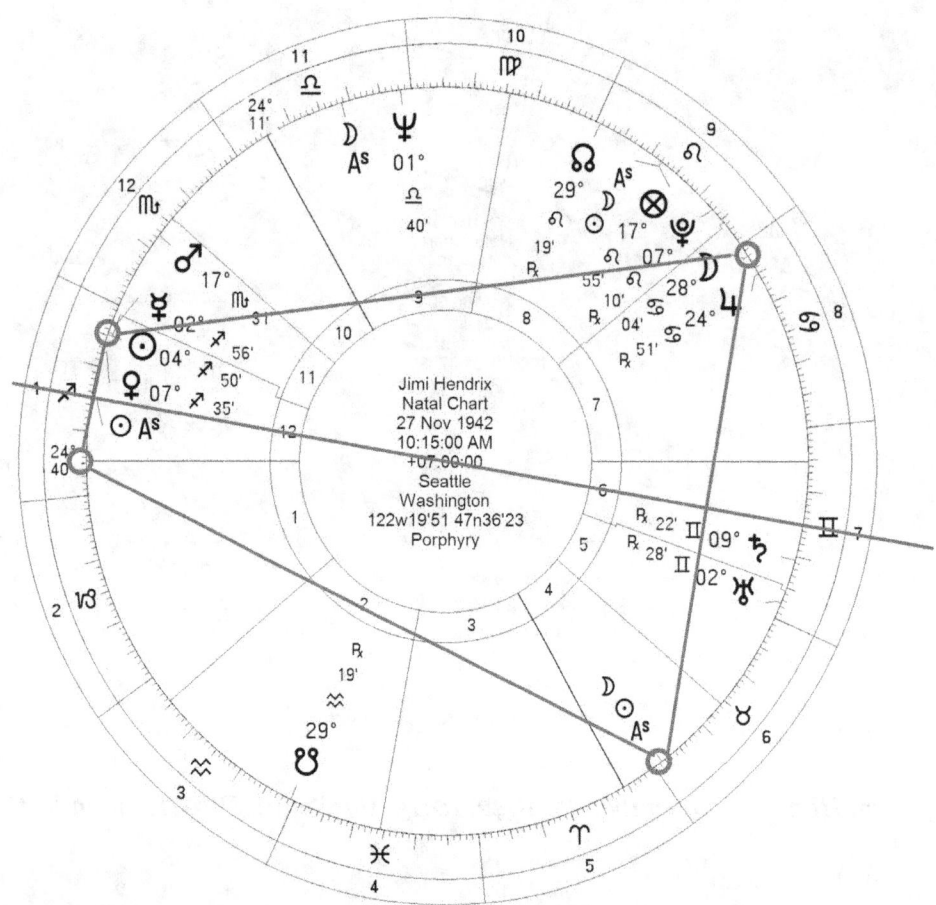

Spirit is in very early Taurus, ruled by Venus and Moon, and on the Lot structure with both of those planets. The Lot midpoint is at 15 Sagittarius, ruled by Jupiter, and in loose conjunction with Venus. In fact, it is at the midpoint of Venus and the Ascendant. Again we see the emphasis on Venus, artistic expression, with all of the wild emotional juice of Jupiter and Moon.

It is also worth noting that the midpoint axis lines up with the two oppositions, Venus to Saturn and Venus to Uranus. The stress of the opposition adds tension, and a strong drive of rebellion against any kind of restriction.

Note that the two Lots are in a loose square, so any hard aspect to one Lot effectively hits the other one at the same time.

1966 Solar Return

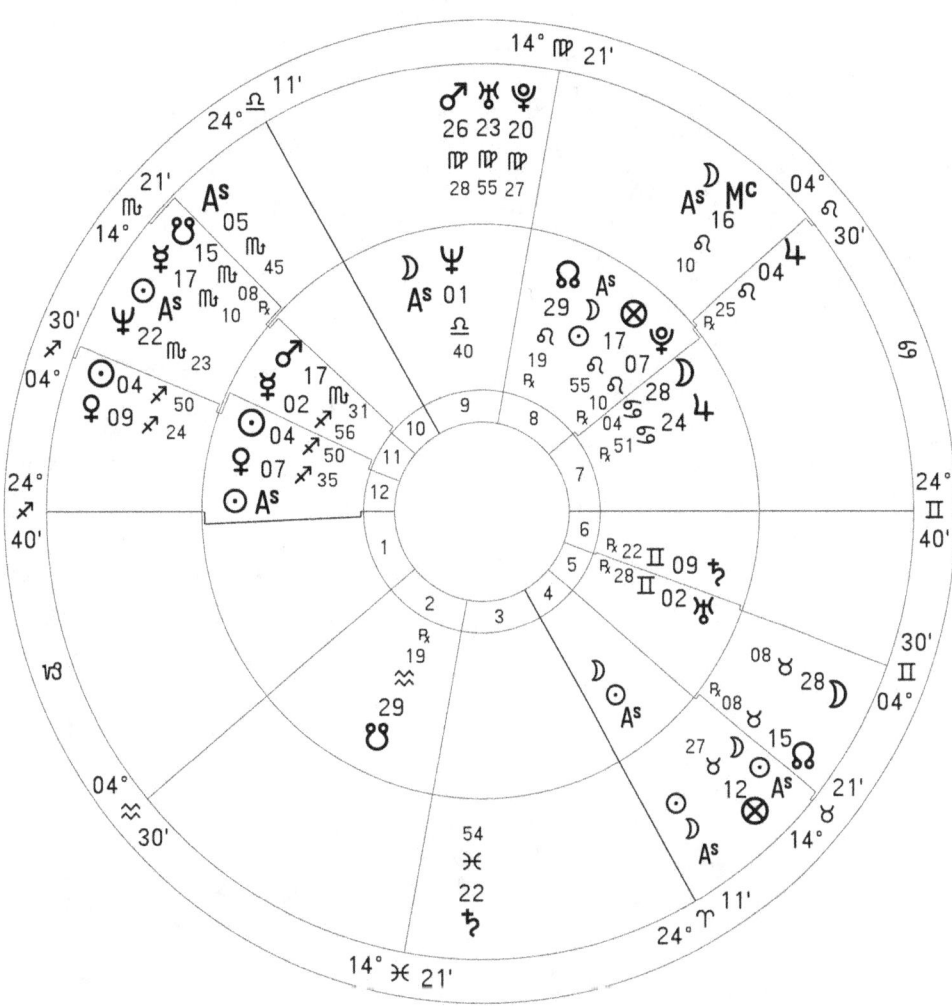

Inner: Hendrix Natal. Outer: Solar Return 1966.

This is the solar return 1966/67, the year that Hendrix hit it very big in USA and worldwide.

Jupiter is newly in Leo approaching Fortune and squaring Spirit, and transiting Leo during his peak year. Jupiter is very strong in this chart, so we would expect its transits to be strong and positive.

There is also activation of the Lots by the solar return angles; the solar return Midheaven is conjunct Fortune, and that point is the solar return Moon/Ascendant midpoint.

Natal Spirit is conjunct return Fortune, and both are those are angular on the return Descendant.

Fortune in the return is at 12 Taurus, in the same sign as natal Spirit.

Both Lots are in fixed signs, and fixed signs are angular in the return.

1969 Solar Return

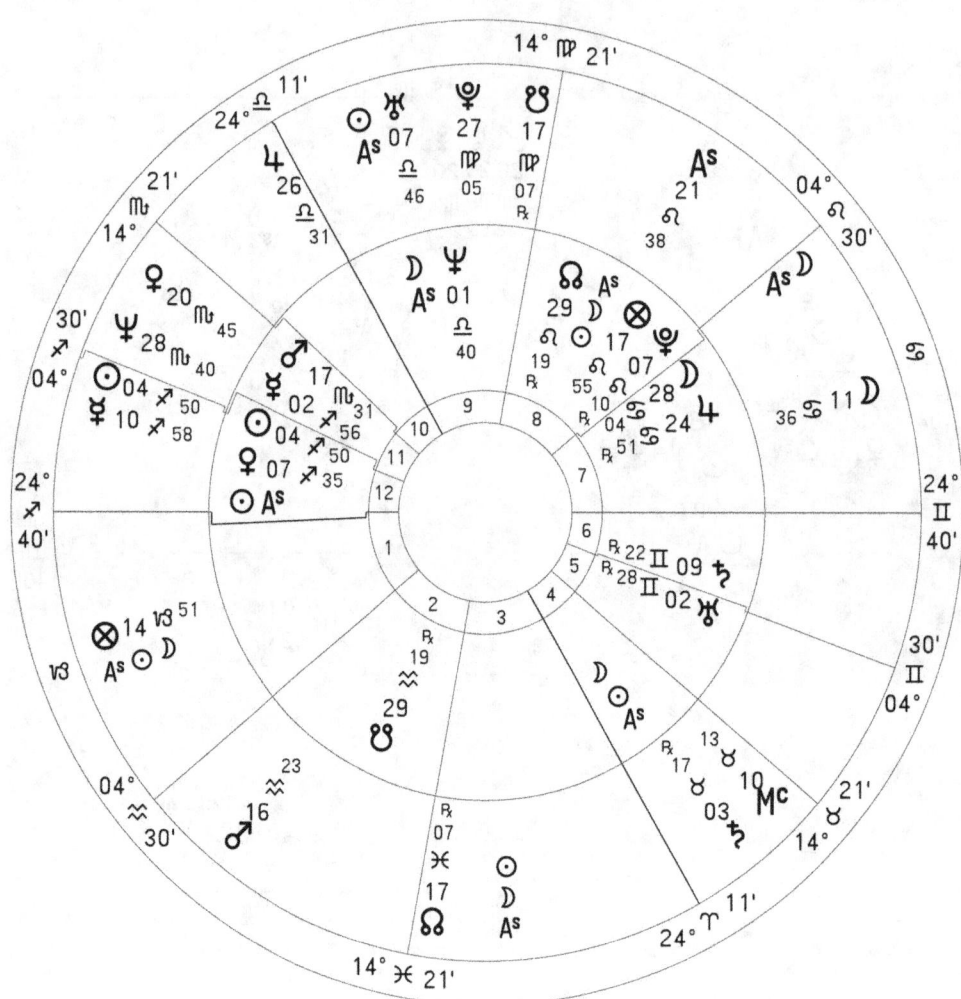

Inner: Hendrix Natal. Outer: Solar Return 1966.

This is the return for 1969, for the last year of Hendrix's life.

Most noteworthy - **Return Saturn is dead on the Lot of Spirit. Saturn was transiting in hard aspect to both Lots the year he died. Also, Jupiter will soon enter fixed sign Scorpio and transit opposite Spirit and square Fortune.**

Both outer planets are transiting the two Lots at the same time, and both outer planets are peregrine in the return chart.

Return Ascendant is conjunct Fortune within 4 degrees, so both Lots are triggered by conjunction in the return this year.

We also see Lot midpoint axes line up here; the natal Moon/Ascendant point is conjunct the solar return Sun/Ascendant. Solar return Moon/Ascendant is conjunct natal Moon.

Return Mars is in fixed sign Aquarius, square natal Mars, tightly opposite Fortune.

Looking more closely at Saturn, we see it at fixed sign 3 Taurus conjunct Spirit and approaching conjunct the return Midheaven and square natal Fortune. The Lot is getting hard transits by both malefics, both Mars and Saturn.

There is also an important house connection here. The solar return Ascendant is in the natal eighth house conjunct Fortune, and return Spirit in Pisces is the return eighth house. That is two eighth house connections.

The Death of Jimi Hendrix

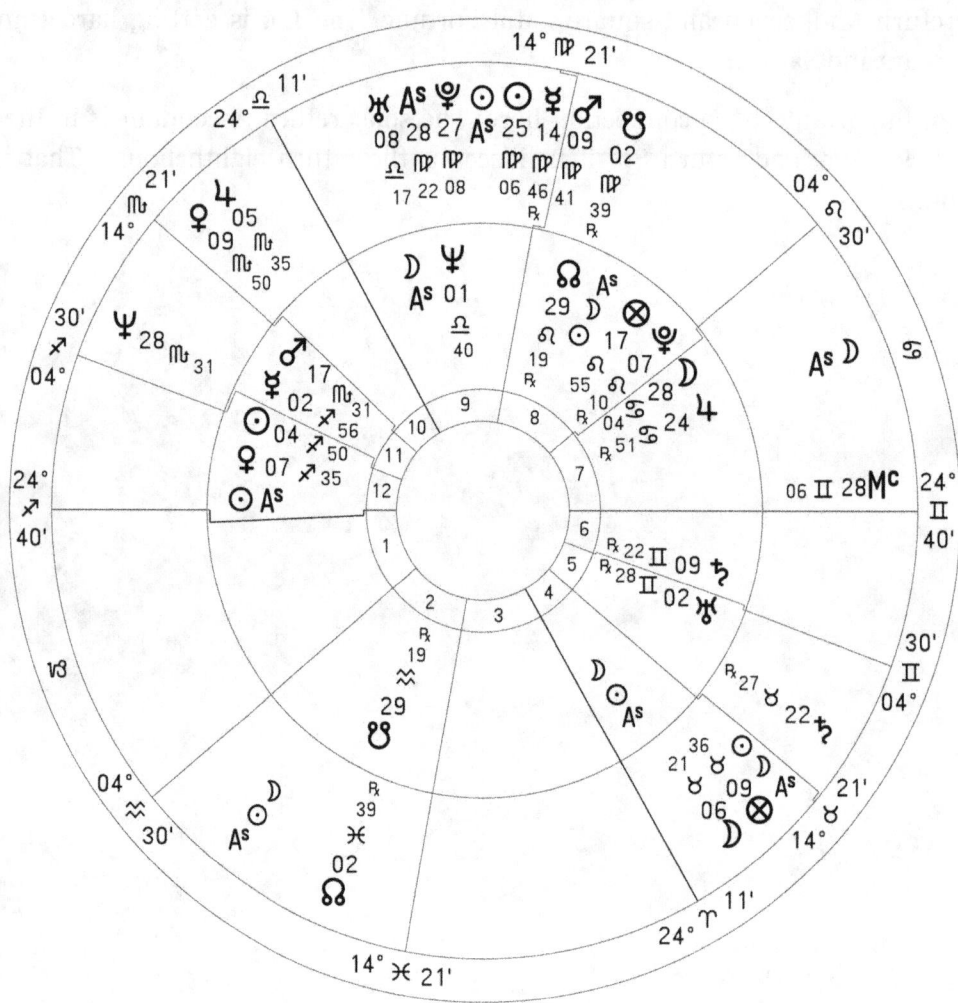

Inner: Hendrix Natal. Outer: Hendrix Death, September 18, 1970.

I drew up this chart for the morning that Hendrix was found dead, choked on his own vomit. There is still some speculation as to whether this apparently accidental death was a murder.

On the day of his death the Moon/Ascendant midpoint for Fortune was conjunct transiting Uranus.

Transiting Jupiter is at 5 Scorpio and Venus at 9 Scorpio. Both are opposite Spirit and square Fortune. In Scorpio Venus is in fall and Jupiter is peregrine, so two planets inclined to excess in the natal chart are in bad unbalanced shape here.

Transiting Mars is making hard square to natal Saturn. Transiting Saturn, still in a fixed sign, is opposite natal Mars. We have hard aspects between the two malefics.

Most interesting in terms of timing, the transiting Moon is shortly past conjunct natal Spirit. It is likely the Moon was conjunct the Lot very near the time he actually died. I ran this chart for 7 am the morning he was discovered dead, and the Moon would have been exactly conjunct Spirit roughly 10 hours before, or around 9 pm in the evening. It is possible that the Moon transit was the exact trigger of the death.

To test that I ran the transits for 9:30 pm the evening prior.

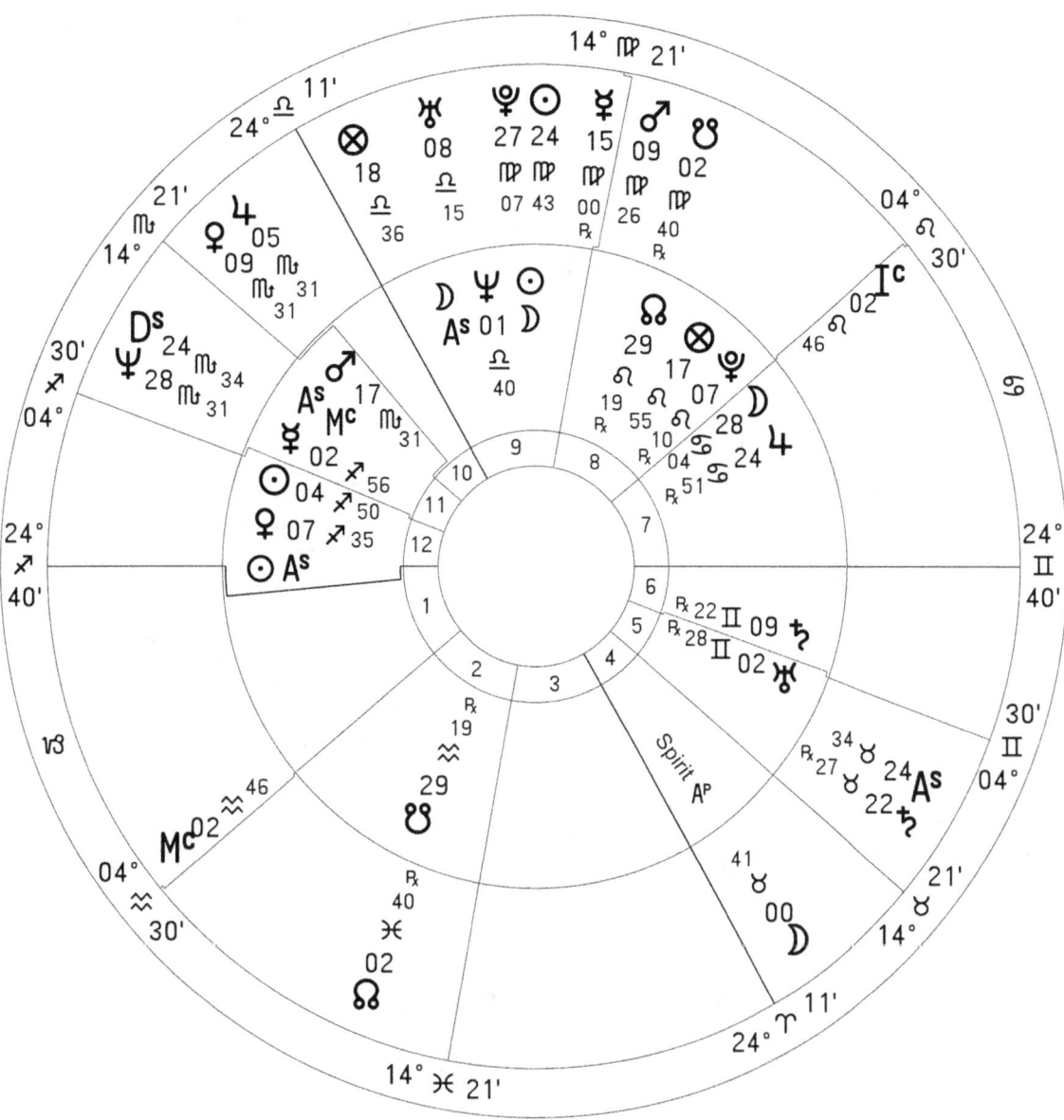

Inner: Hendrix Natal. Outer: Estimated Death time, 9 PM Sep. 17, 1970

At that time the transiting Ascendant is also in the vicinity of Spirit, the Moon is right on Spirit, Saturn is on the Ascendant, Neptune on the Descendant. The transiting IC would be conjunct the other Lot, Fortune, about an hour later.

Pope Francis

I am using this chart example to show the fascinating interaction between the natal chart of Jorge Bergoglio, and the exactly timed chart of the moment the white smoke went up and he was officially proclaimed Pope Francis.

We will start with the natal chart examining the Lot of Fortune.

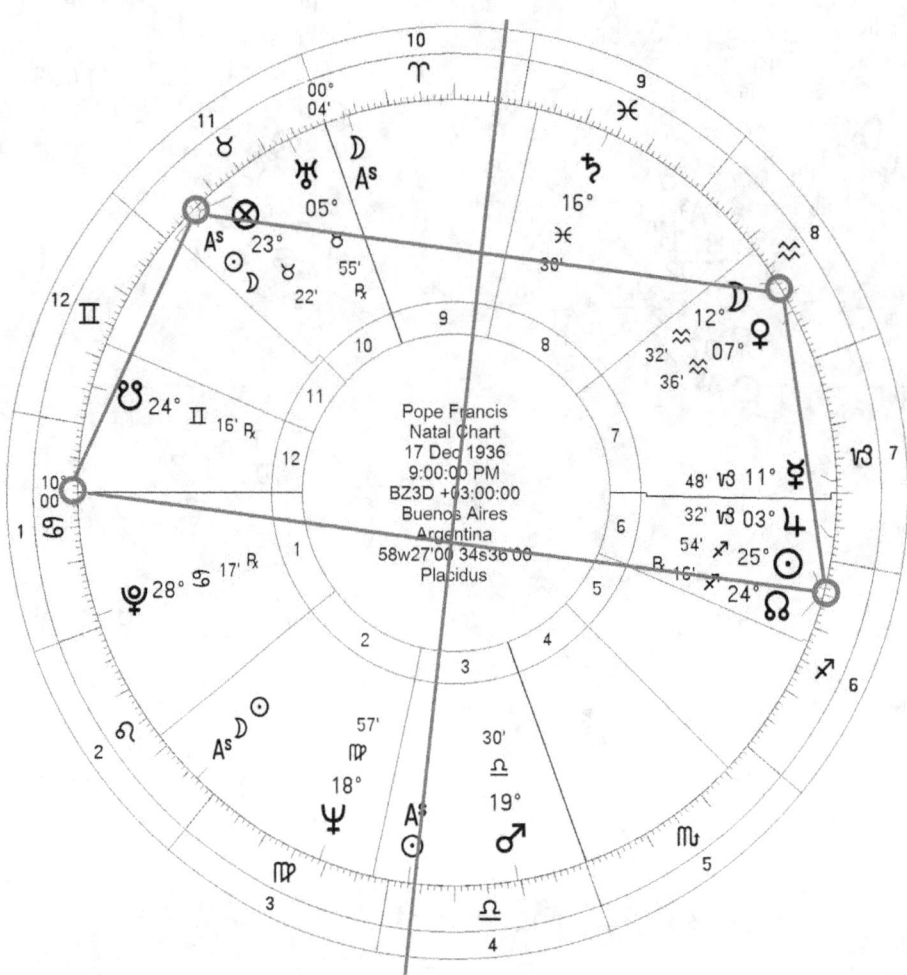

Jorge Mario Bergoglio, December 17, 1936, 9 PM, Buenos Aires, Argentina. Rating AA.

Fortune is at 23 Taurus, a fixed sign. Its sign and exalted rulers, Venus and the Moon, are conjunct in Aquarius, a sign ruled by Saturn, and both planets are square the Lot by sign. The Lot midpoint is very early Libra / Aries, which again emphasizes Venus and Saturn having major dignity in Libra. Being conjunct the Moon, Venus is part of both Lot structures.

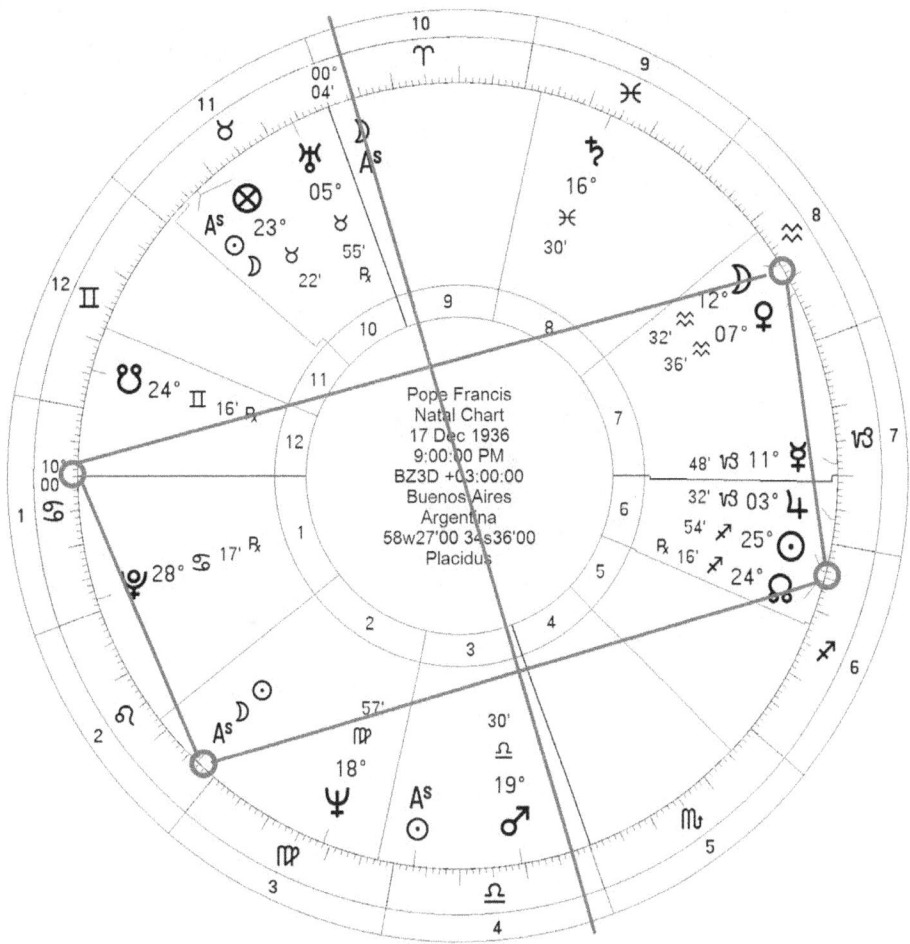

The Lot of Spirit is in late Leo, in a fixed sign and near square to Fortune. Its ruler the Sun is trine the Lot, and the Sun is in late Sagittarius conjunct Jupiter which is in early Capricorn and in fall.

The midpoint of Spirit is in very late Libra and is angular, very near the MC/IC axis.

With both of the Lots in fixed signs, transits by Jupiter and Saturn through fixed signs should be important. It is also noteworthy that Saturn and Jupiter are both weak, but have a strong mixed major mutual reception, and you can trace the rulership of all other planets back to these two. Saturn and Jupiter together in this chart are the Church, and Bergoglio's life is as a servant of the Church.

Bergoglio becomes Pope Francis

This next chart is a biwheel showing Bergoglio's natal chart on the inside, surrounded by the chart of the moment he died as individual man Jorge Bergoglio and was reborn as Pope Francis.

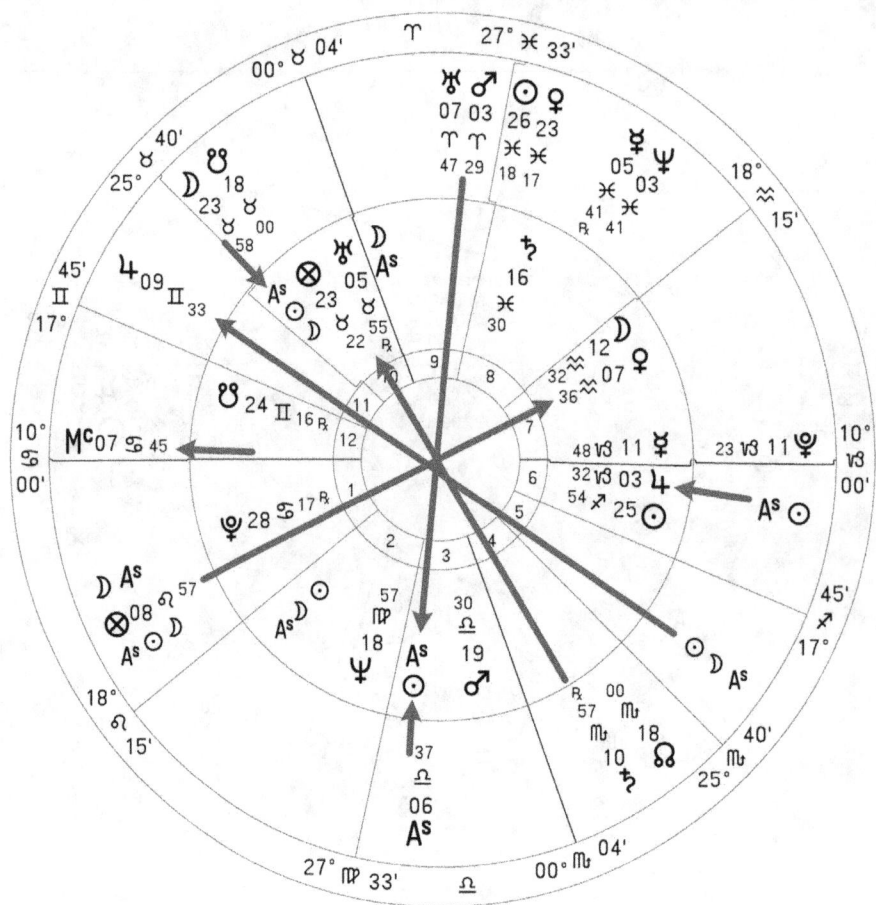

Inner: Bergoglio. Outer: Francis declared Pope, March 16, 2013, 7:06 PM, Vatican City.

The most striking conjunctions in these two charts are the most ephemeral and fast moving timing points.

The white smoke went up when the Moon was tightly conjunct natal Fortune 1/2 degree past exact. Given that the smoke had to go up AFTER the vote had been taken and the decision made, it is quite likely that the vote happened when this aspect was closer to exact.

The Ascendant at the election announcement is conjunct the Sun/Ascendant midpoint for the same Lot, Fortune. This is about 4 degrees past exact, about 16 minutes of clock time.

The Ascendant and Moon aspects to these two points on the natal Lot of Fortune configuration were exact within around 45 minutes of each other. It is within that window of time that Francis was elected Pope.

Fortune in the papacy chart is in Leo, same sign as Spirit in the natal, and it is in a hard opposition to natal Moon and Venus. Transiting Saturn is 10 Scorpio, opposite Fortune, square Spirit, and square natal Venus and Moon, opposite elected Moon.

Papacy Venus in Pisces is conjunct the Sun, and conjunct natal Saturn.

The papacy Sun/Ascendant Midpoint for Fortune is at 1 Capricorn right on natal Jupiter.

Lot of Spirit of the papacy chart is 4 Sagittarius, opposite Jupiter at 9 Gemini in detriment.

Papacy Mars and Uranus are in Aries on the Fortune midpoint, and right on the Descendant of the papacy chart. Having Mars and disruptive Uranus right on the Descendant, the point of open enemies, is unsettling.

And finally, note that the Midheaven at election time is right on Francis' natal Ascendant.

There is one other interesting point about timing, and this is related to primary directions.

The Lot of Fortune is in Taurus, and the two dominant rulers are the Venus and the Moon, which are conjunct in the natal chart. In minor dignities, Fortune is in the bounds of Saturn - **and the Moon and Venus both direct into that set of Saturn bounds, and to conjunct Fortune, in the period 2016 through 2020.** This is arguably the period right when the defining issue of his papacy, the clergy sex abuse scandal, is coming to a head. This is likely the single biggest challenge he faces in his papacy, and thus in his entire life.

I find that to be a very suggestive piece of timing, having the Lot of Fortune rulers directing to conjunct the Lot at a defining moment of a person's life.

Synastry

This part of the study of the Lots is turning out to be consistently important and interesting.

I find that significant cross aspects to Lots between charts of people in close relationships show up very consistently and very often. This is such an important factor, that I would now wonder about the closeness or significance of a relationship between people where I do not see any correlations with these Lots or their related points.

Synastry - Charlie and Cindy

This is the third of a group of chapters where I go into detail on my own chart situation to show how much light the Lot structures can shed on overall chart meaning. Here I want to look at the synastry of my chart with that of my second wife, Cindy, who was the center of my life for 24 years.

I am going to concentrate only on the interaction between the Lot structures. I think that the importance of the Lot midpoints is particularly noteworthy here.

Cindy Lots of Fortune and Spirit

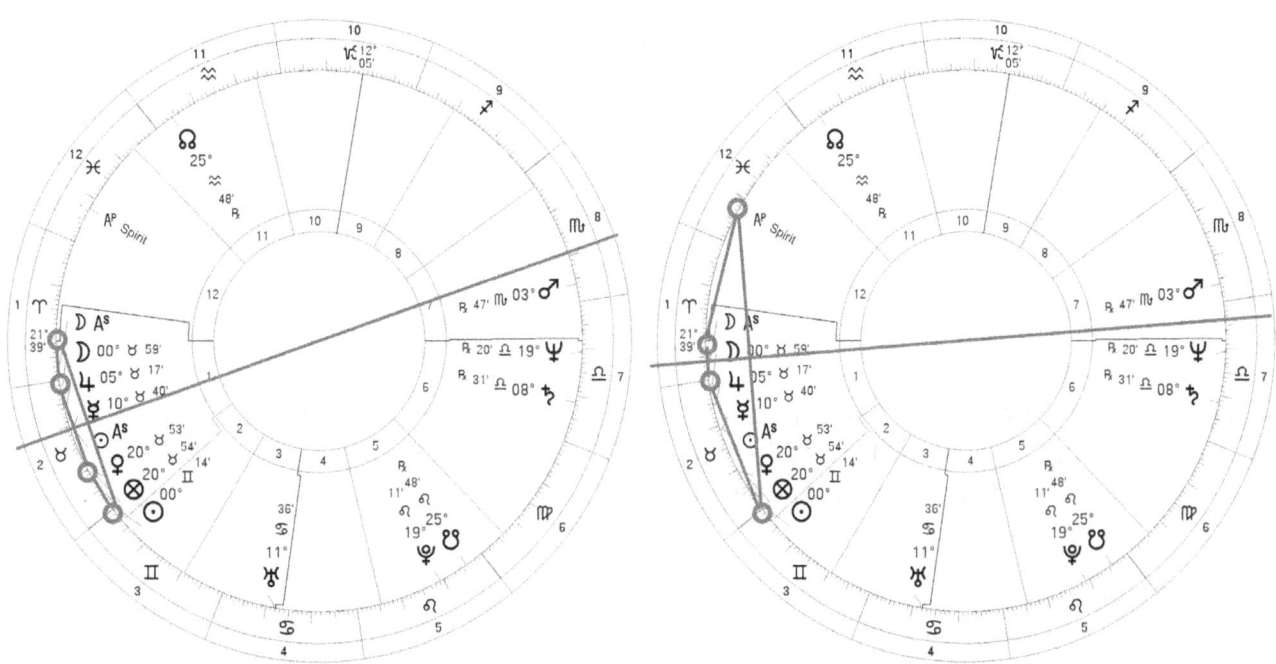

Cynthia Sue Kissee, May 21, 1952, 3:16 AM, Olathe, Kansas. Rodden Rating AA.

The Lot of Fortune is at the heart of the whole chart, the strong 4 planet stellium in Taurus, and 5 of the 7 traditional planets all fall between 0 Taurus and 0 Gemini. Fortune itself is at 20 Taurus tightly conjunct her Venus. Granted I'm biased, but she was fashion model beautiful, and her main interests were Venusian. She was a belly dancer, and spiritually she was immersed in goddess based religion.

Mars is over in Scorpio in her seventh house, opposite that Taurus stellium including the Lot. That Moon-Mars, Venus-Mars axis added energy to her Venusian charm.

That Venus Taurus stellium is further emphasized with the midpoint of that Lot being at 10 Taurus tightly conjunct her Mercury. The entire focus of this Lot is Taurus and fixed signs.

The other Lot, Spirit, is at 22 Pisces, in her 12th house, ruled by Jupiter and Venus, both in Taurus. The axis of that Lot is 26 Aries, not far from the Ascendant/Descendant axis.

Since Fortune is already activated by Venus, then any planet activating Spirit in this chart would play off of Venus and Fortune.

Charlie Lot of Fortune and Spirit

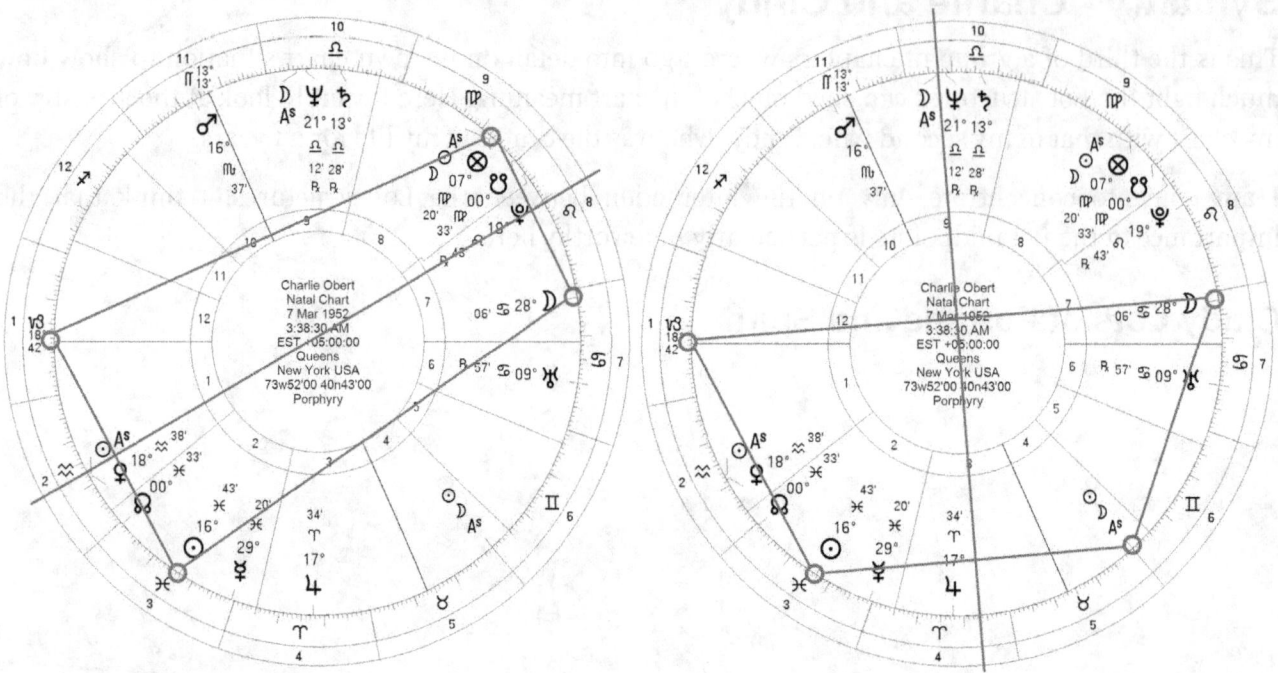

I discussed my Lot configurations in a previous chapter. Here I want to recall that the midpoint axis of Fortune at 18 Aquarius is on that strong Venus-Mars-Pluto configuration, with three of the fixed signs occupied, with the fourth sign Taurus vacant.

The other Lot, Spirit at 0 Gemini, has its midpoint 23 Aries in cardinal signs, not far from the Neptune-Saturn-Jupiter opposition axis.

Charlie and Cindy Synastry

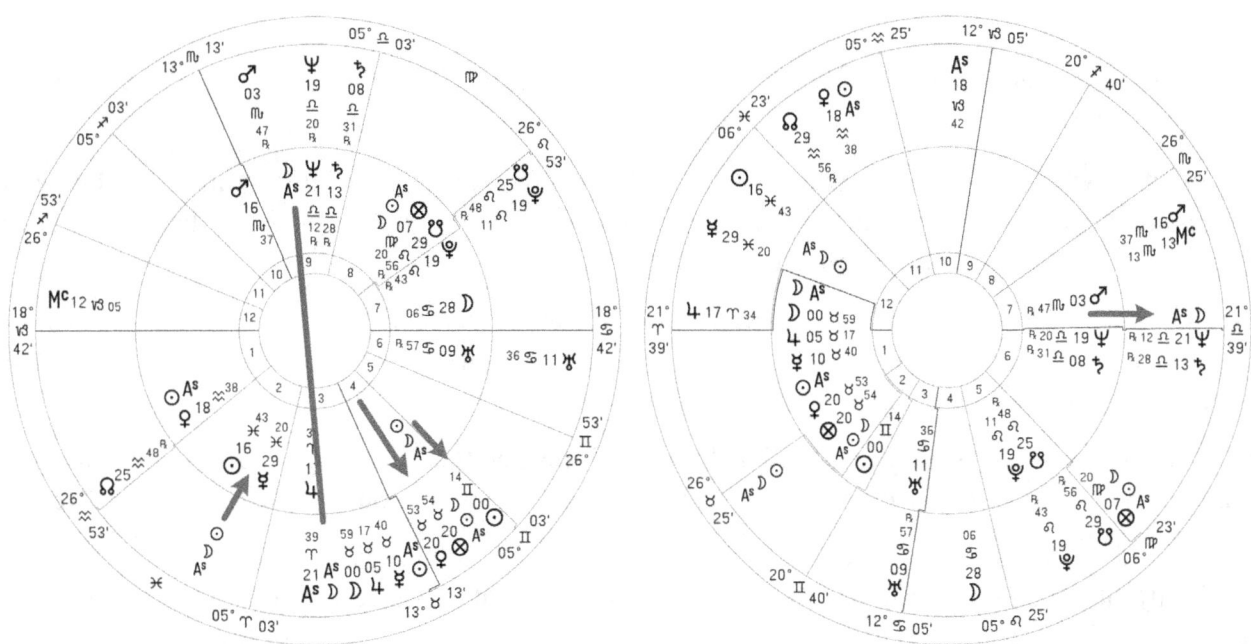

Left: Charlie Inner, Cindy Outer. Right: Cindy Inner, Charlie Outer.

The biwheel on the left has my natal in the middle with Cindy's around the outside, and the right has Cindy's in the middle.

I want to look just at Lot interaction here.

Cindy's Lot of Fortune, and Fortune midpoint, and her entire Taurus stellium, falls square to my Lot midpoint axis, opposite my Mars. That Taurus group fills in my fourth fixed sign and completes the cross.

That is important, but I think the strong connections with Spirit in the two charts is more noteworthy.

My Lot of Spirit is at 0 Gemini, and is exactly conjunct Cindy's Sun.

Cindy's Lot of Spirit at 22 Pisces is within 6 degrees of my Sun, and falls on the Sun/Mercury midpoint in my chart.

We share the same midpoint axis for the Lot of Spirit in each chart, mine at 23 Aries/Libra, hers at 26 Aries / Libra.

If you look at the chart on the right above, with Cindy's natal the frame of reference, you can see that my Spirit midpoint axis at 23 Aries is just a few degrees from her Descendant.

Our charts complete each other.

Lennon, McCartney & Company

In this final example I want to take a detailed look at a group of charts to see how the various Lot points interrelate.

We will start with John Lennon and Paul McCartney, songwriter team and members of the wildly successful rock group, The Beatles, which completely dominated pop music from their intro to the world scene in 1963 to the time they split up in 1970.

It seems much more natural for me to refer to these Beatles by their proper first names, as we did during their heyday. In the 60's, if you mentioned John and Paul everyone knew who you were talking about, and that it was not meant as a biblical reference.

Both John and Paul had significant relationships that impacted their professional lives, so we will look at the interaction of each of them with their main partners, John Lennon and Yoko Ono, and Paul and Linda McCartney.

And finally, at the end, we are going to look at another brief but very significant relationship in John's life - with Mark David Chapman, the man who murdered him. We will also check the chart for the time he was shot.

The interaction of this group of charts supports a couple of the main points of this study. This vividly demonstrates that the Lots are very important in synastry. The examples also show that the Lot midpoint axes can also be very important, and need to be taken into account.

Paul McCartney

Our study is complicated at the outset by the fact that there are two charts available for Paul out in the chart database at astro.com. There is an official chart for a birth time of 2 am, and an unofficial alternate birth time of 2 pm. They have the same birth hour, but there is a question whether the am or pm time is correct. After looking at both of charts, and how they play in with the synastry examples, I am persuaded that the 2 pm birth time is likely the correct one. This is largely because of some very striking synastry points with Paul and John, and also with Paul and his wife Linda.

Paul McCartney Lot of Fortune

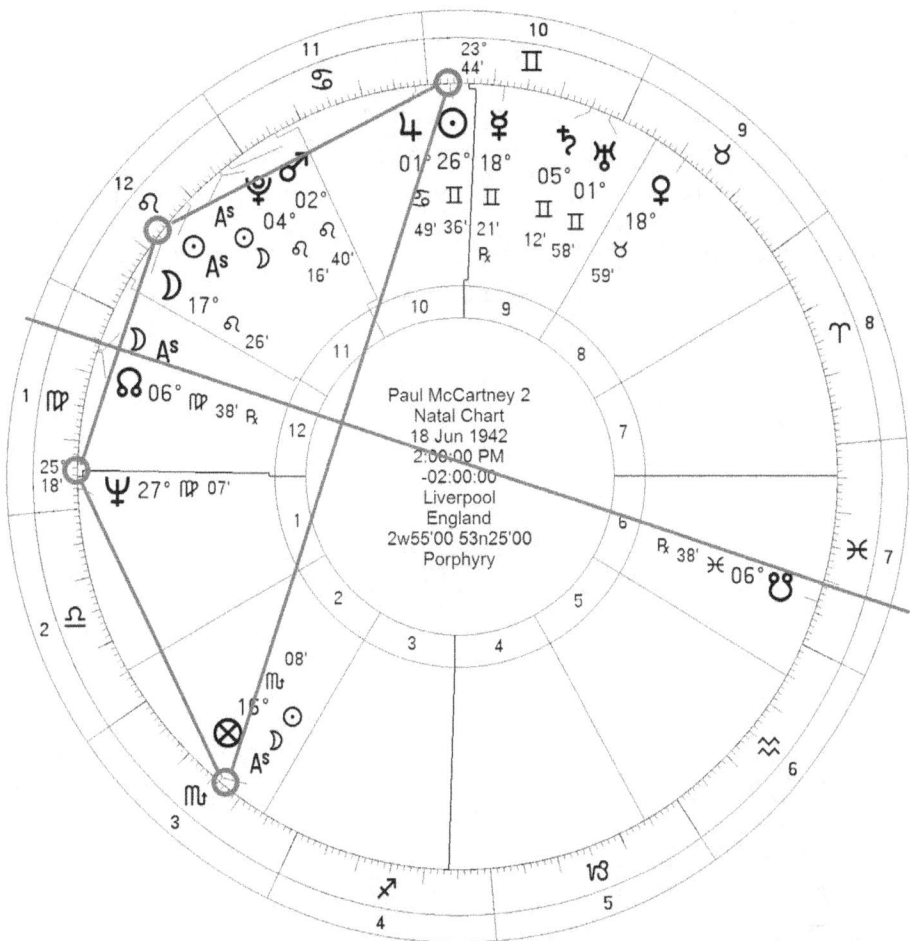

Paul McCartney, June 18, 1942, 2 PM, Liverpool, England. Alternate time from biography.

First note that the two Lots in Paul's chart here are both in fixed signs and so are square to each other. Fortune is at 16 Scorpio, and Spirit is at 4 Leo. Note that the Spirit midpoint of 10 Leo also is part of that configuration, and makes that group of planets in Leo very important. That square in fixed signs will end up being important when we look at synastry with both John and Linda.

Also note that one of the Lot points, the Sun, is at 26 Gemini, conjunct the Midheaven, and also conjunct its ruler Mercury on one side, and conjunct an exalted Jupiter in early Cancer on the other. We also have Neptune right on the Ascendant at 27 Virgo, ruled by that strong Mercury, and tightly square both the Midheaven and Paul's Sun. Mercury is the ruler of both angles in this chart, so Mercury is Paul. This strong group of points right on the angles is a very strong argument for the 2 pm chart for someone as famous, successful and charismatic as Paul.

I think that the Sun-Jupiter-Mercury conjunction defines Paul and his public image as a young man. He came across as outgoing, friendly, charismatic, cute, sexy, and lovable, with a sort of soft-faced perpetual youthfulness that a strong Mercury can give. Neptune adds a sort of fuzzy warm glow to the whole thing, an air of fantasy and illusion.

The Lot of Fortune at 15 Scorpio is ruled by Mars, and Mars is at 2 Leo conjunct Spirit, and also conjunct the Fortune midpoint. This means that Mars and Fortune together make a direct midpoint connection to the Ascendant/Neptune combination. Mix in Mars in Leo to the combination so far makes Paul seem more outgoing, dynamic, and even more sexy.

This is a case where, even though we have a planet conjunct a Lot, Mars conjunct Spirit, I don't think I would characterize Paul as primarily a Mars sort of person. That is a strong facet of his personality, but in this case I think that enormously strong Sun-Mercury-Jupiter complex dominates the chart.

The midpoint axis of Fortune is 6 Virgo, right on the North Node. I often see points on the nodes as connected with important relationships. The nodal axis here is in Virgo-Pisces, the 1st/7th house axis by whole sign.

Paul McCartney Lot of Spirit

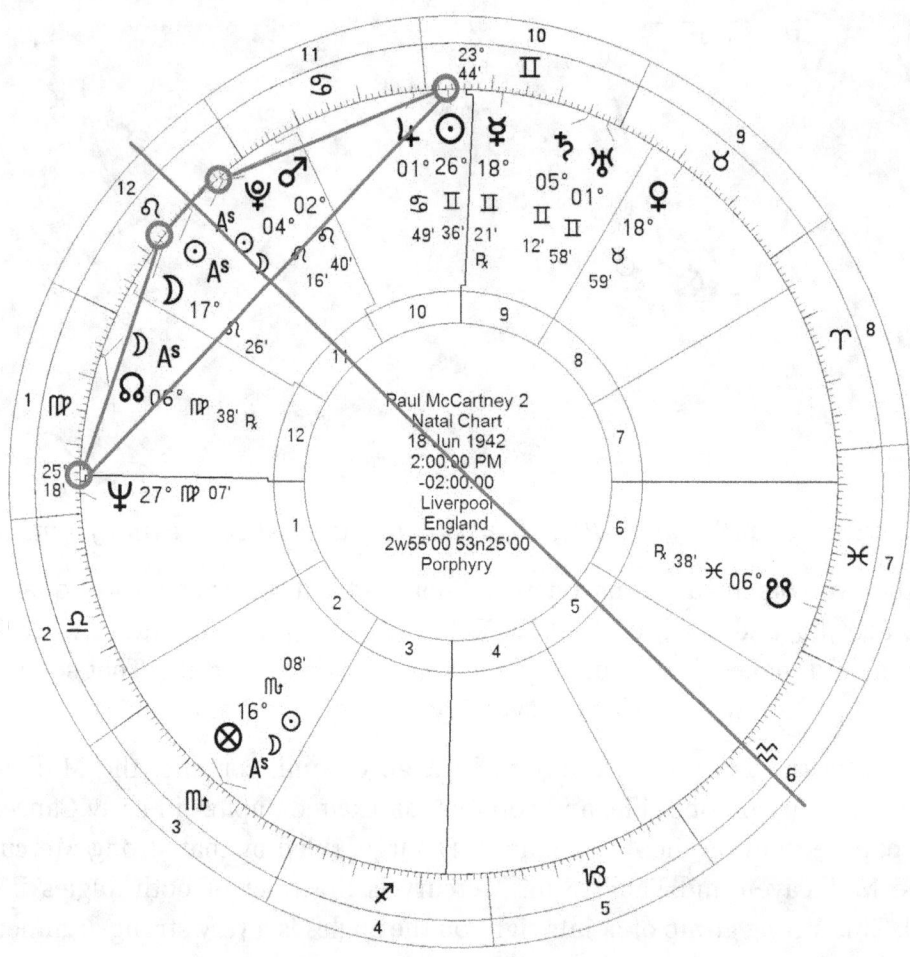

Spirit is at 4 Leo, tightly conjunct Pluto and Mars, and also conjunct the Lot midpoint at 10 Leo, which in turn is loosely conjunct the Moon at 17 Leo. The midpoint of the Moon to Mars and Pluto is also focused right on the Lot midpoint. This further emphasizes the strength of these planets in Leo, and we can expect to see this axis prominent in any major synastry we find.

John Lennon Lot of Fortune

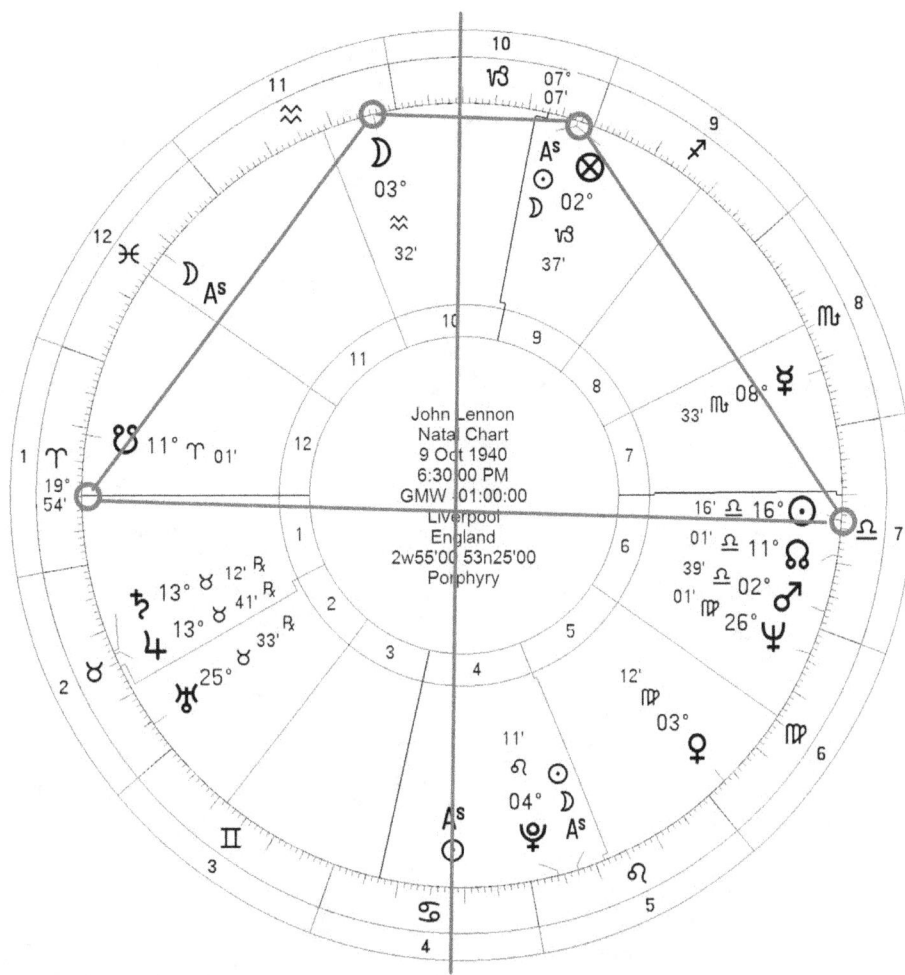

John Winston Lennon, October 9, 1940, 6:30 PM, Liverpool, England. Rating A.

The major configuration in John's chart is the very strong fixed cross. We have Mercury in Scorpio, the Lot of Spirit conjunct Pluto at 7 Leo, the Moon at 3 Aquarius, and Jupiter-Saturn conjunct at 13 Taurus. These planets all in early to mid fixed signs are definitive in this chart.

Lennon's Sun is very near his Descendant, and the midpoint axis of this Lot, 18 Cancer / Capricorn, is tightly square the Sun and that axis. Fortune is in early Capricorn around 5 degrees from his Midheaven, so the Lot itself is angular. The Lot's ruler Saturn is part of the fixed cross we mentioned.

John Lennon Lot of Spirit

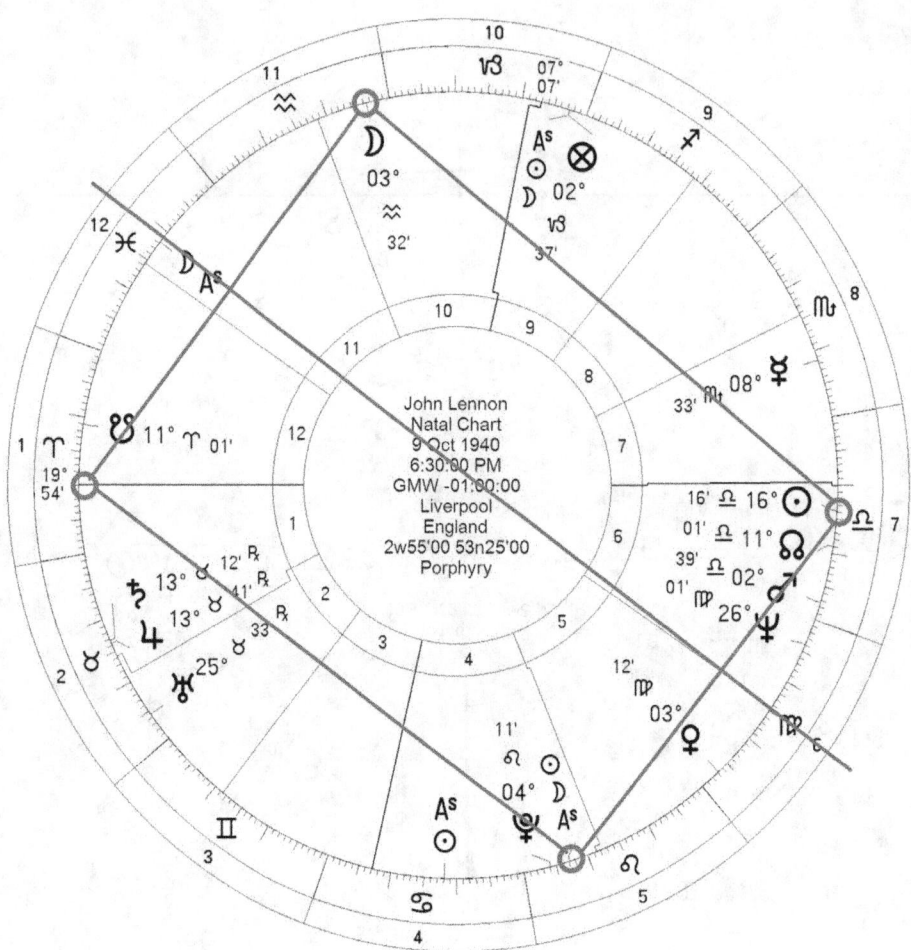

The Lot of Spirit is part of the fixed cross here, being opposite Lennon's Moon and square the Saturn-Jupiter and Mercury axis. The Lot ruler Sun is on the Descendant. The midpoint axis runs 11 Pisces/11 Virgo.

Now that we have seen the strong points of each chart individually we can combine them. Here is where things start to get interesting.

John Lennon and Paul McCartney

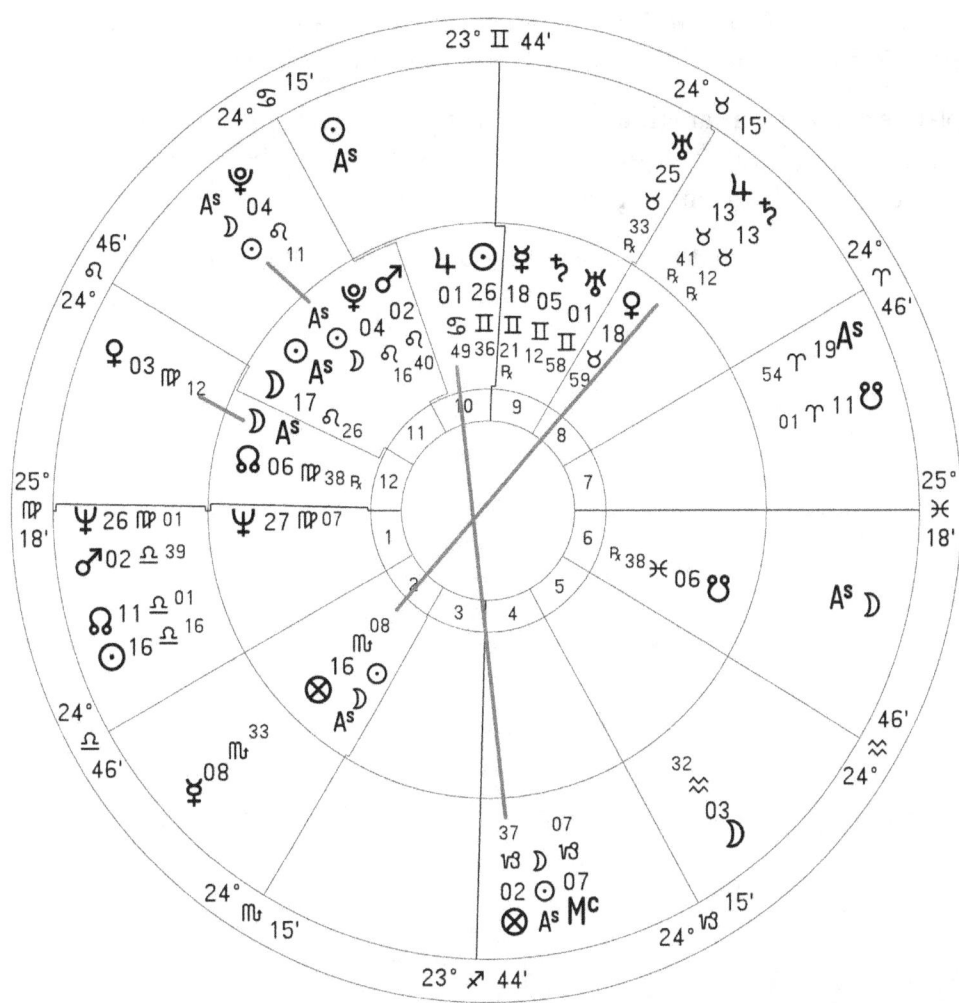

Inner: Paul McCartney. Outer: John Lennon.

Paul McCartney is on the inside wheel here, and John Lennon on the outside.

I am going to mention only configurations involving the Lot points, and focus only on hard aspects. There is much more going on between these two charts, but here I think these are the main points in their interaction.

First note that their Lots of Spirit are conjunct, at 4 and 7 Leo. This conjunction falls right at the midpoint axis of Paul's strong Spirit configuration, and right on the strong fixed cross in John's chart, including the LOS midpoint axis.

Paul's Lot of Fortune falls on John's fixed cross also, being at 8 Scorpio.

John's Lot of Fortune at 2 Capricorn is tightly opposite Paul's very strong Jupiter in Cancer, which also falls on Paul's MC/IC axis.

And finally, Paul's Moon/Ascendant midpoint is on the same axis as John's Moon/Ascendant midpoint. That is, Paul's Fortune and John's Spirit share the same midpoint axis.

So both of John's Lots, both of Paul's Lots, and both of Paul's Lot midpoints, have a strong conjunction or opposition aspect from the other chart.

The two complete each other. If anything, I think Paul's chart has more hooks from John's than the other way around. I recall that Paul did not want the Beatles to break up, and kept trying to re-establish the connection and reform the band.

It is John that left Paul. I think that looking at Yoko Ono's chart will help us understand why.

Yoko Ono Lot of Fortune

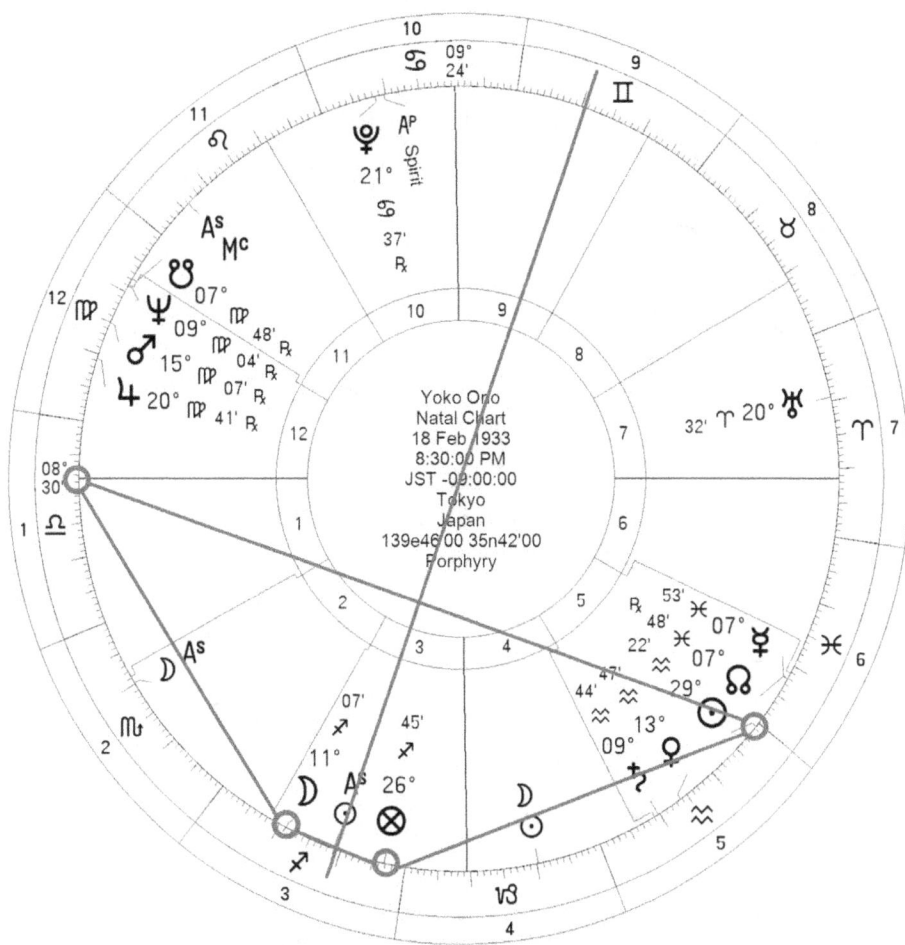

Yoko Ono, February 18, 1933, 8:30 PM, Tokyo, Japan. Rodden Rating A.

John did not leave the Beatles until after he started his relationship with Yoko Ono, and that relationship is part of what strained the band's work, leading to the breakup. We have competing relationships, so we should see some very strong connections between John's and Yoko's charts.

It unusual to see stelliums that do not involve the Sun or one of the other inner planets, and Yoko has one. Jupiter, Mars and Neptune and her south node are all conjunct in Virgo, and all four of those points are opposite her Mercury in Pisces. Jupiter and Mercury in this opposition have mutual reception by rulership, which greatly emphasizes their importance. Both ends of this opposition are square to her Moon at 15 Sagittarius. This mutable T configuration dominates the chart. The Moon and Fortune are close enough that both are conjunct the Lot midpoint at 11 Sagittarius, so the Lot and its midpoint axis tie into the most active configuration in her chart.

Yoko Ono Lot of Spirit

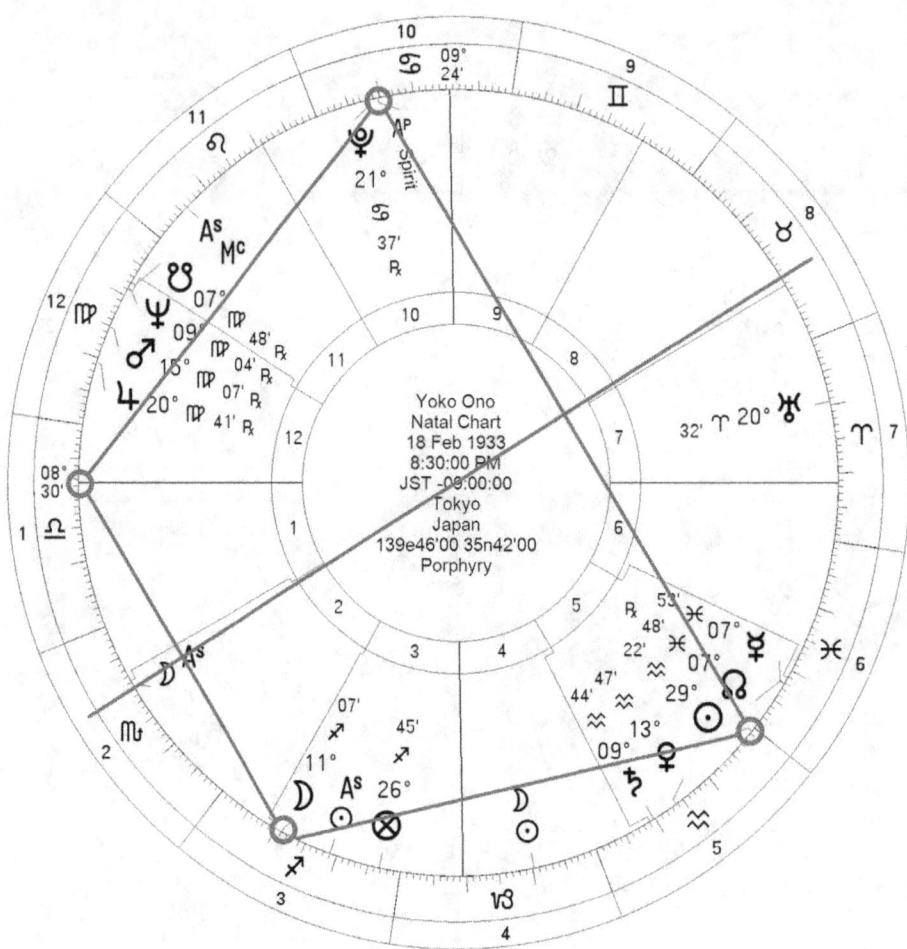

The Lot of Spirit is at 20 Cancer, conjunct Pluto, and is very nearly exactly opposite the chart's Sun/Moon midpoint. Typically the Sun/Moon midpoint is considered to be important to note for major relationships. The only planet in a cardinal sign with Spirit is Uranus, but that planet is tightly square to the Lot, exact by degree.

John and Yoko

In this chart I am going to focus on hard aspects. Again, the number of cross connections between the charts is quite remarkable.

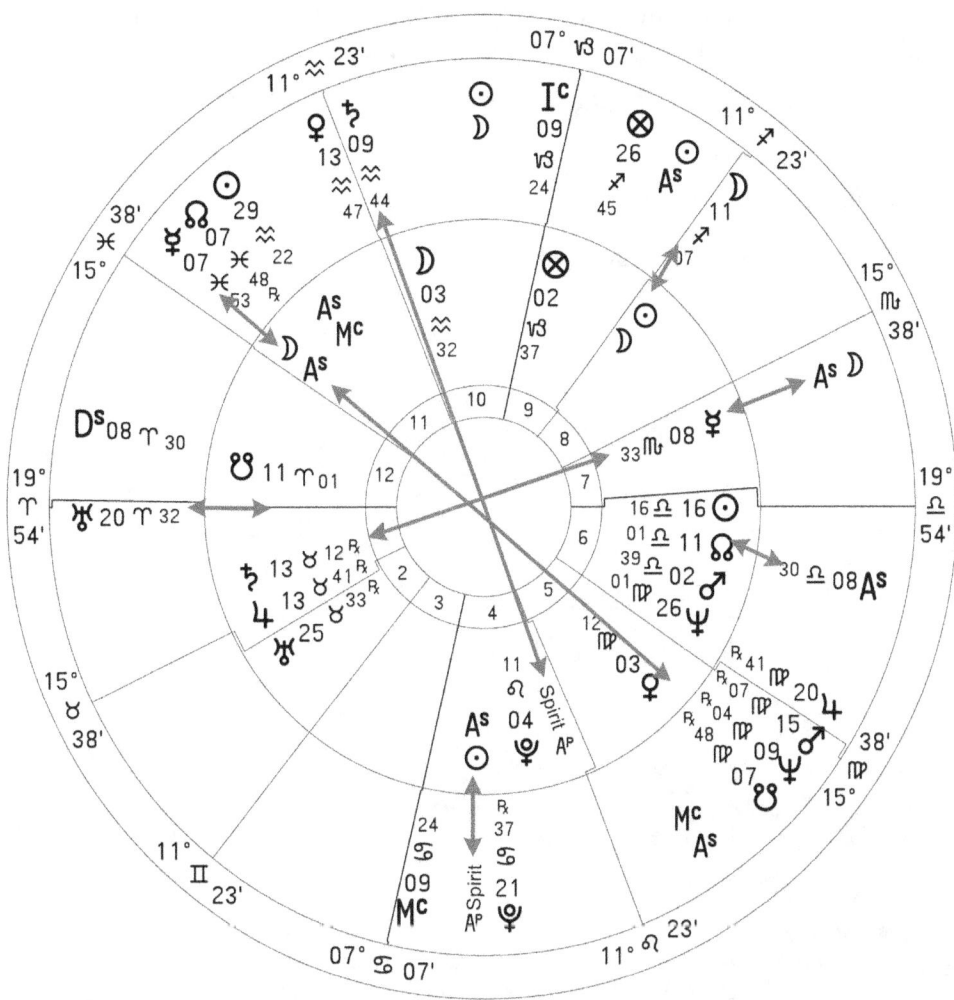

Inner: John Lennon. Outer: Yoko Ono.

Before we look at the Lot interactions, note that Yoko's Uranus sits very tightly conjunct John's Ascendant, and tightly square Yoko's Lot of Spirit. Yoko's Spirit is also conjunct John's Spirit midpoint at 18 Cancer. This combination is a good metaphor for an exciting, stimulating and very eccentric relationship.

John's Spirit at 7 Leo is pretty tightly opposite Yoko's Saturn and Venus at 9 and 14 Aquarius. The Spirit midpoint for Yoko at 9 Scorpio is on John's fixed cross, right on the Scorpio/Taurus axis. Saturn is very strong in Yoko's chart, in its rulership in fixed sign Aquarius, and ruling her Sun.

155

It has always felt to me like Yoko was the stronger and more controlling figure in this relationship, and I think that heavy strong Saturn on John's Mercury and cardinal cross is one of the main reasons why. Also, that Saturn sits heavily on the interaction with Paul and John's charts.

We mentioned that strong opposition in Yoko's chart, Mercury to South Node-Neptune-Mars-Jupiter, that sits on top of John's Spirit midpoint at 11 Pisces. John's Venus at 3 Virgo falls on that same axis, right on Yoko's nodal axis. So Yoko's chart ties into the strongest configuration in John's, and John's chart ties into the strongest configuration in Yoko's. They bring out each other's characteristic strengths, and what I am tempted to call their characteristic eccentricity. John's work after he left the Beatles is a Lot darker, weirder and stranger than anything he did while he was still in the group.

This Lot midpoint at 11 Pisces is square to Yoko's Fortune midpoint, exact to the degree, and in a square to Yoko's Moon, also exact to degree.

There are some other interactions, but those are the most significant.

Linda McCartney

Paul went on to have a very long and successful career after the Beatles's breakup, a career that involved his marriage and other work with Linda McCartney.

I will look at just at Linda's Lot of Fortune since is quite striking and is strongly involved in our synastry.

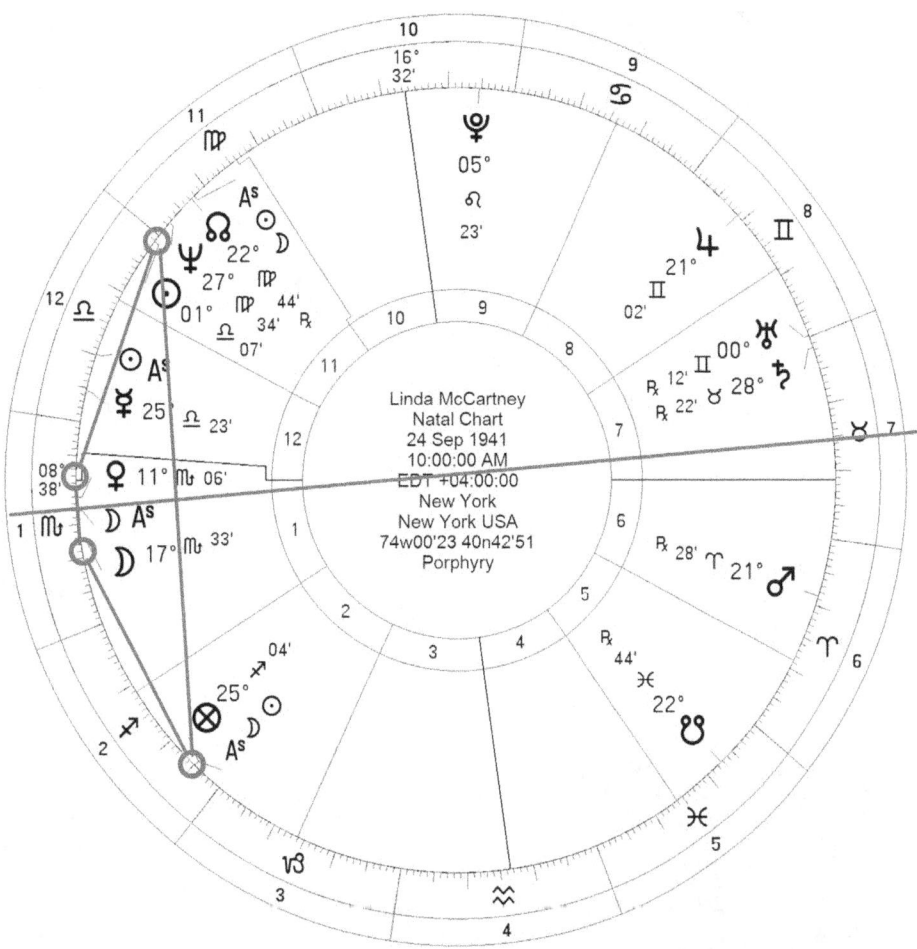

Linda Louise Eastman, September 24, 1941, 10 AM, New York, NY. Rating A.

In this chart we have, in close succession, the Ascendant at 8 Scorpio, followed by Venus and Lot midpoint tightly conjunct at 11 Scorpio, and then Moon at 17 Scorpio. Venus is at the Ascendant/Moon midpoint, which is the midpoint of Fortune.

Note that the focus of this Lot is early to middle in a fixed sign. We have seen that section of the zodiac as a common thread, a common strong point, in all of the charts we have looked at here.

Paul and Linda

From everything I have read about Paul and Linda McCartney, Paul was completely and deeply in love and stayed that way. I have seen the two described as being inseparable, spending only short periods of time apart, up to Linda's death from cancer.

Looking at the two charts together it is easy to see why.

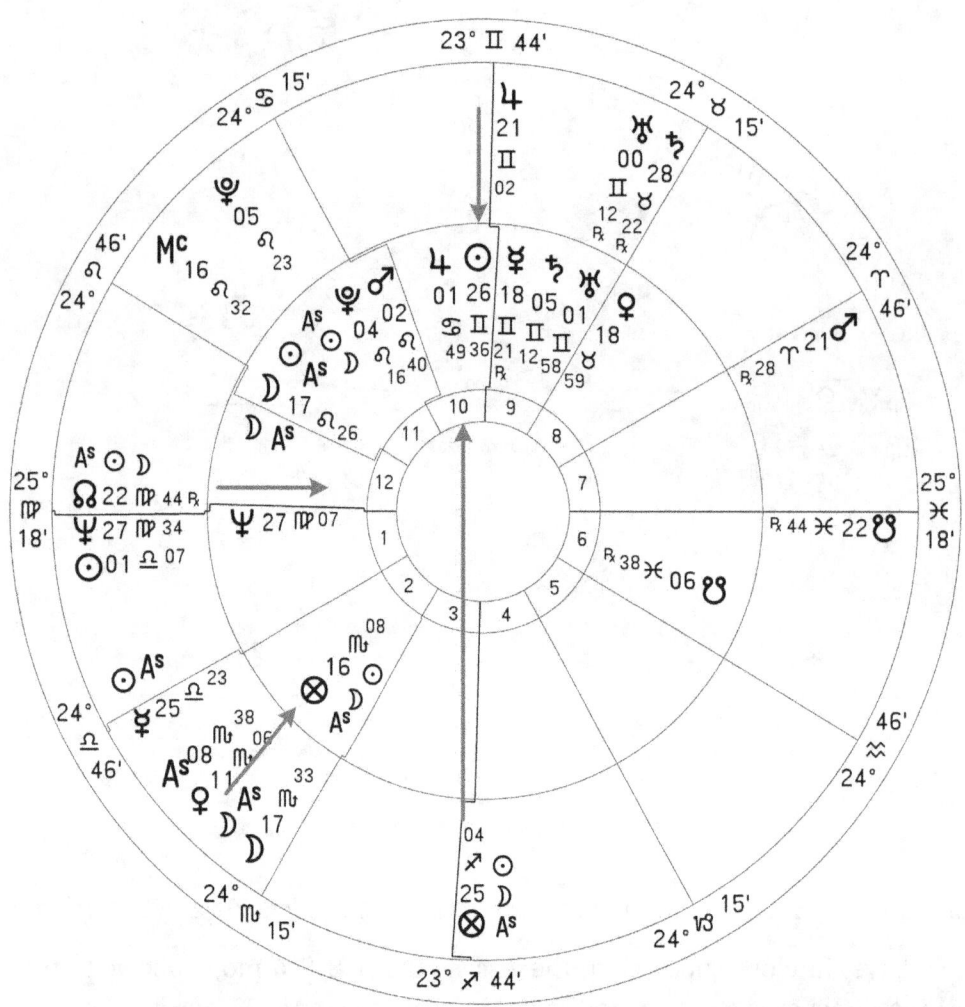

Inner: Paul McCartney. Outer: Linda McCartney.

Sitting right on Paul's Ascendant is Linda's Lot of Spirit, North Node, Neptune, and Sun.

The strong group of points in Scorpio in Linda's chart, the Ascendant, Venus, Fortune midpoint and Moon, all sit right on top of Paul's Lot of Fortune, opposite his Venus.

Paul's Lot of Spirit at 4 Leo, Lot midpoint at 10 Leo, and Moon at 17 Leo, are all angular in Linda's chart, sitting very close to her Midheaven at 16 Leo. These two groups of points in Scorpio and Leo are in a close square so they work together.

Linda's Lot of Fortune, at 25 Sagittarius, is tightly opposite Paul's Sun at 26 Gemini, near his Mercury, and near Linda's Jupiter at 21 Gemini, and this whole opposition is sitting right on Paul's MC/IC axis. With this much angularity involved in the interaction it is no wonder that the relationship was very public, and that they also toured and performed together.

Notice throughout this whole analysis how often we have found the Lot midpoints to be very important in the synastry. This emphasizes how important it is to consider the Lots as overall patterns, along with the importance of the Lot points themselves.

The Murder of John Lennon

Going into this project I was guessing that event charts were going to show Lots being triggered by faster moving planets. We have an example here, in the interaction of John Lennon's chart with the date and time of his murder at 10:50 pm on December 8, 1980.

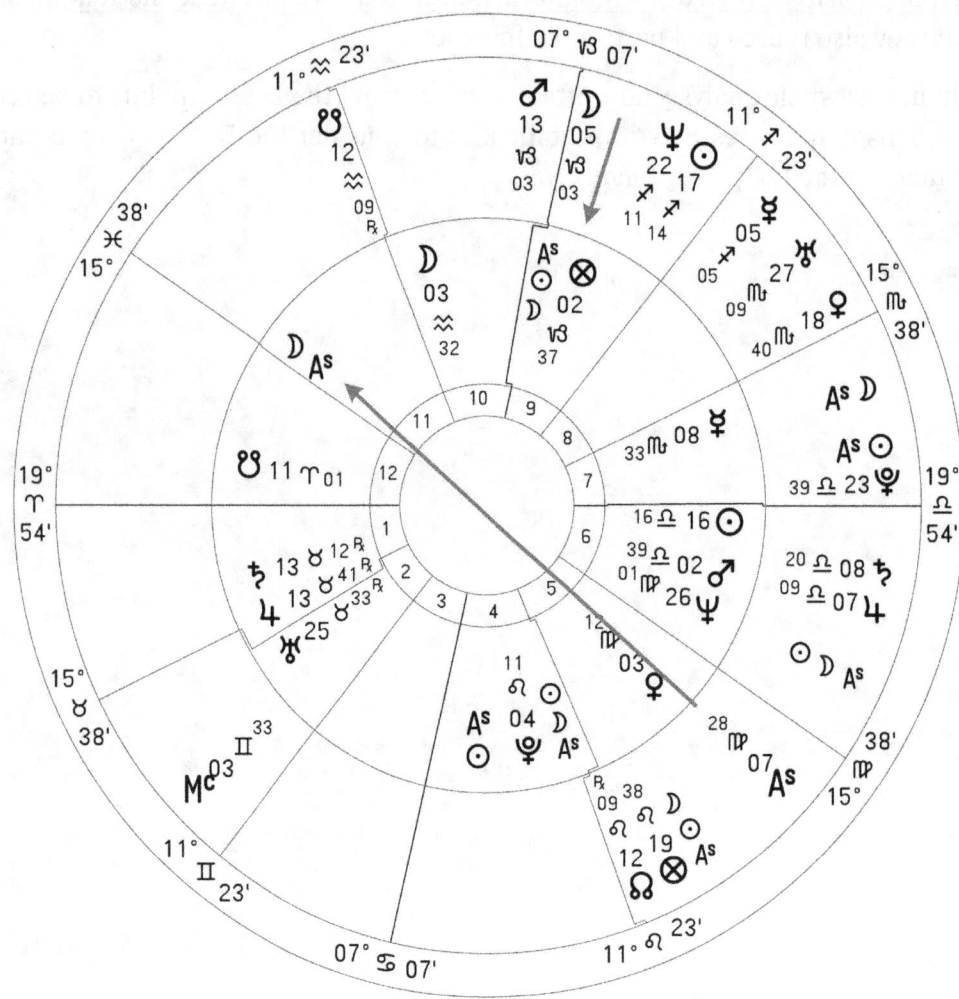

Inner: Lennon natal. Outer: Lennon murder, December 8, 1980, 10:50 pm, New York, NY.

The Ascendant right about the time of the murder is around 7 Virgo, right on one of John's Lot midpoint axes.

And, perhaps most significant, *transiting Moon is right around 5 Capricorn, on John's Lot of Fortune at 2 Capricorn 37.*

Mark Chapman, the man who shot John Lennon, has his natal moon at 4 Capricorn.

160

Final Notes

Using the Lots in Client Work

We have covered a great deal of material In this study. Along with going into the two main Lots in considerable detail, we also made the whole subject of Lots more complex by looking at the entire Lot structure. This one aspect of chart interpretation could take a great deal of time if you always addressed the Lots in detail.

Odds are you will not always be able to spend much time working with the Lots, or with any of a myriad of other important techniques. Assuming you don't have the luxury of spending the better part of a day preparing for a chart interpretation session, you have to pick and choose, and decide what areas are most important for you to concentrate your time.

Do I always spend time on the Lots in chart readings? No. Since completing this study, the Lots are now one among several factors that I scan for during initial chart analysis to determine if they need the focus. The purpose of my initial chart evaluation is to decide which points are worth going into greater detail.

Preliminary Evaluation

These are the points that I look for when first scanning a chart, before I decide if it is worth my going into either or both of the Lots in detail.

First and most important, check to see if a planet is conjunct a Lot. If there is, that means the Lot is already activated in the natal chart pattern, that in a sense the person makes their own fortune. There is also a very good chance that planet will characteristically define the person, what makes them unique. In the interviews I did with people I found that people with a planet conjunct a Lot always identified with that planet.

Planets conjunct the Ascendant, Sun or Moon are already considered important by most astrologers. I now note these three points as also being related to how the Lots express since those points are part of the Lot structure. After this study of the Lots I now place more importance on such planets than I did previously.

Note the mode the Lots are in, cardinal, fixed or mutable. If the two Lots are in the same mode that greatly increases the importance of other planets in that same mode.

Also note planets in stakes to the Lots by sign, conjunct, square or opposite. Those planets will be activated when the Lots are activated by hard aspect. If either of the Lots have a significant number of strong planets in the stakes with it, that increases the likelihood that a transit to that Lot will be significant and strong in effect, for good or for bad.

Note the ruler of each Lot, its location and condition, and if the Lot ruler aspects the Lot. A Lot with a strong ruler in good aspect is more likely to work out in a positive manner than a Lot with a debilitated ruler, or a ruler that is averse and out of touch.

Activation of the Lots by Transit and Direction

This first point stands out.

Note major hard transits to the Lots, especially Saturn transits, and most especially conjunctions when Saturn is in the same sign as a Lot. You can note the times the transit becomes exact, but it is very important to realize that the entire period that Saturn is in the same sign of the Lot is worth noting. Lind Weber also gave wide orbs to these transits, allowing up to 10 degrees either side for Saturn transits, and that matches my experience. When Saturn is anywhere in the same sign as a Lot it can set a tone for an entire period.

If there was a major Saturn transit to a Lot in the recent past, **ask what happened**.

If there is one coming up, or one currently active, ask what is going on. If there is one in the near future, it is worth checking the period of the most recent hard transit from Saturn, and ask what went on then. As always with working astrology, the past is your best guide to the future.

When your client comes to a session with a particular subject area of their lives that they wish to focus on, it is worth checking if the location and condition of either or both of the Lots is likely related to that topic. If so, check to see if there are significant transits to the Lots going on from any planets. In that situation I think it particularly worth checking to see if Mars is transiting in the sign of a Lot.

I also check to see if there was a recent Saturn transit to the sign of the Lot, within about the past 5 years. If so, it is worth taking time to ask the client what was going on in that period. The odds that it was both important and stressful is very high. The odds that it involves events regarding significant relationships is very high. It also gives a window into what is most characteristically important to the person.

Other Outer Planet Transits to the Lot

At this point in my experience I am not sure if I would pay much attention to transits of Pluto or Neptune to a Lot. Since both of those outer planets move so very slowly, and their influence can be both vague and diffuse over a long period of time, I would use only tight orbs, of 1 or 2 degrees at most, for the time frame.

The outer planet Uranus is different kind of animal, and I sit up and pay attention when I see a tight Uranus transit to any chart element. Again I use tight orbs, 3 degrees or less. It is worth checking for surprising, disruptive or catastrophic events related to the transit. The effect of Uranus can be harsh, abrupt and extreme.

The Lots and Other Predictive Systems

If you use another predictive system, it is worth noting when a Lot is activated by conjunction.

If you use Profections, where the chart is directed forward one zodiac sign per year, note when the sign of the Profection includes a Lot. In that case the Lot is very likely to be important that year and is worth spending time on.

For other predictive systems, like primary directions or secondary progressions, it is worth noting when a Lot is activated by conjunction by degree. Again, I suggest a very tight orb, one or two degrees at most.

Strokes of Fortune in Client Experience

Any time a Lot is activated it is very important to remember that we are dealing with strokes of Fortune in the common sense of the term. These are events that happen to people, often outside of their control, and often by surprise. This is a not a time to be talking about karmic responsibility, or creating your own life, or in any way blaming a person for what happens.

One of the good things about working with the Lots is learning that a goodly amount of the events of human life are outside of our direct control. The world is much, much bigger than we are. The astrology mirrors what is going on inside of us, but it also mirrors how we fit within a larger world.

As the Stoics remind us, we do not always control the events of our life. The one area we can control is our response. Taking responsibility for how you respond to an event is completely different from taking the blame for something bad happening. That is a crucial distinction.

Summing Up

Here I want to recap the main things that I learned from this study of the Lots.

Characteristic Themes

Yes, the Lots are very important as integrating points, connecting up the Ascendant, Sun and Moon into a single pattern. The geometry is the single most important key as to why that is so.

Given their importance as integrating points, this means that charts have their characteristic themes for the Lots. In any given chart, when the Lot is activated, there is a common thread or theme between the events and periods.

The theme of the events when the Lot is activated is a defining theme of the person's life, a main issue, or a defining life event. In that sense it really does show their Lot in life.

Times of Increased Activity

Working with the Lots shares common characteristics with other timing techniques. Talking of good or bad fortune is missing the point. Lot transits are times of increased activity, increased tension. The stress on the entire Lot pattern is turned up for the period.

Predicting Backwards to Predict Forwards

I use this as a consistently important and useful strategy in my client work. Before I can address interpreting a chart I need to get a past context in the person's life to see how the present and future will unfold. This isn't being psychic, this is data analysis. The best way to determine how the Lots will work in the future is to watch how they acted in the past.

Saturn and Jupiter Transits

The transits of Saturn and Jupiter to the two Lots are almost always significant.

Saturn transits are not always bad, nor are Jupiter transits always good. The effect of a transit depends on the state of Saturn or Jupiter in the natal. It also depends on the dignity of Saturn or Jupiter in the sign of the Lot and in the sign they currently occupy. Like any other factor in astrology, interpreting a Lot's meaning does not happen in isolation. Context is very important.

The Saturn conjunctions stand out as the most important and sustained transits to look for with the Lots. Those transits are not points in time, they are periods, and the orb of influence can be quite wide. Up to a 10 degree orb can be significant, and I think it worth considering the whole period that Saturn is in the sign of the Lot. I now always mention Saturn transits to a Lot sign whenever it arises in work with clients.

Squares and oppositions of Saturn to the Lots can be significant, but not as much as the conjunctions. In the studies I did the conjunctions were very consistently important, and the other hard aspects were more irregular.

Fortune and Spirit as a Pair

I came into this study with two related questions regarding the two main Lots of Fortune and Spirit.

First is the question as to which formula for calculating fortune is correct. Should the direction of casting the Lot be reversed for a night chart, or should the day and night formula be the same?

Second is the question of the difference in meaning between the two Lots. Does the Lot of Fortune consistently have one meaning, and the Lot of Spirit have a consistently different meaning?

I now think these are the wrong questions to be asking.

At this point I view the two Lots as a pair, equal in importance. I see differences in meaning between the Lots within individual charts, but no consistent pattern as to one or the other formulation being important, or as to there being a consistently different meaning between fortune and spirit.

I now look at both of them equally, and consider them, individually and together, in context.

Entire Lot Pattern Important

The entire Lot pattern is important, not just the Lot point itself. This pattern includes the midpoint axes of the two Lots.

Drawing up the Lot structure with midpoints in charts can shed some very important light on their interpretation. An example is the amazing series of converging midpoints that we saw in Albert Einstein's chart. I could only see that once I drew the Lot diagram, and then it was obvious.

Looking at the overall pattern also emphasizes the increased importance of any other planet on one of the Lot points, most importantly the Lot point itself, but the other three points also.

In terms of using the Lots, both these two primary ones, and any of the other Lots, I think it important and useful to learn to pick out the Lot patterns by eye. Drawing up the pattern on multiple charts helped me learn how to pick out the patterns looking at charts without needing to draw in the lines. That helped me see patterns I would not have otherwise noticed.

Related Midpoints

This next point is a logical consequence of viewing the Lot pattern as an overall structure. There are two important pairs of midpoints related to each Lot, and they need to be taken into account. This means that the Sun/Ascendant and Moon/Ascendant midpoints are sensitive points worth considering.

Given a Lot midpoint axis it is worth seeing if any other pairs of planets line up their midpoints on that same axis, and if there are other midpoints that converge on a Lot or on a Lot midpoint axis.

In Natal Charts

In natal charts I consider it conclusively proven that having a planet conjunct a Lot does make that planet a defining force or characteristic of the person.

It is also worth considering any other planets that are part of the natal Lot configuration, meaning planets conjunct the Sun, Moon or Ascendant, and also any planets on the Lot midpoint axis.

Aspects to Lots can be very important, since those aspects are triggered at the same time the Lot is triggered. An aspect to a Lot by itself is an empty space that comes alive and becomes a real aspect when that space is occupied.

Synastry

Synastry with Lots is VERY important, and is very characteristic of important relationships.

That makes good sense. Given that the Lots are points of relation, activation and integration, we should expect Lot connections to tie charts together and integrate them. Lot synastry shows places where people complete each other, or turn each other on for better or for worse.

Lot midpoints are especially important in synastry.

I also found that Lot synastry to the nodes shows up very often in relationships.

Other Lots or Proliferations

These two basic Lots, Fortune and Spirit, are the primary Lots. They most likely were the first ones discovered, and they are the most frequently used. They are also the most consistently important. Hopefully this study will encourage astrologers to regularly consider both of the Lots, their overall pattern, and how they interact as a pair.

All the other Lots, involving other combinations of points, are derivative or secondary, and they can be used to address specific issues or needs or questions.

To really understand the use of ANY of the Lots I think will be very helpful to have a firm understanding of the basic material that we covered in this study.

Final Notes

This study is not meant to be either exhaustive nor conclusive. I think it is a good solid starting point for working with the Lots in a systematic and meaningful way.

Are the Lots important in chart interpretation? Yes. Are they absolutely necessary? I don't think I'd go that far.

The Lots can be very helpful to zero in on important configurations and issues in charts. They are important patterns of integration that are worth considering. They are also worth noting for periods of increased significance and likely important events.

I hope that this brief study will provide a useful framework for further research on the meaning and use of the Lots.

Sources

On the Lots or Arabic Parts

By Benjamin N. Dykes, Ph. D.

- Audio recording - A Traditional Approach to Lots

    https://www.bendykes.com/product/a-traditional-approach-to-lots/

By Lind Weber

- Book - The Arabian Parts Decoded. American Federation of Astrologers, 1997.

By David Cochrane

- Video - Arabic Parts - A Marriage of Hellenistic Astrology and Harmonic Astrology

    https://www.youtube.com/watch?v=n26S-NgH0CA

- Essay - The Mathematical Basis of Arabic Parts and a Paradigm Shift in Astrology

    http://astrosoftware.com/ArabicParts.htm

On Midpoints

By Alfred Witte

- Book - Rules for Planetary Pictures: The Astrology of Tomorrow, 6th edition. Penelope Publications, 1990.

By Reinhold Ebertin

- Book - The Combination of Stellar Influences. Ebertin-Verlag, 1940.

- Book - Man in the Universe: An Introduction to Cosmobiology. Ebertin-Verlag, 1973.

On House Systems

- Blog Post - Using 2 House Systems

    https://studentofastrology.com/2018/09/using-two-house-systems/